THE SUN GOES DOWN

Thin Lizzy's Final Years

Martin Popoff

THE SUN GOES DOWN

Thin Lizzy's Final Years

Martin Popoff

WP
WYMER
PUBLISHING
Bedford, England

First published in Canada in 2012
This edition published 2018 by Wymer Publishing
Bedford, England
www.wymerpublishing.co.uk
Tel: 01234 326691
Wymer Publishing is a trading name of Wymer (UK) Ltd

ISBN 978-1-908724-90-8

Edited by Jerry Bloom.

Every effort has been made to trace the copyright holders of the
photographs in this book but some were unreachable. We would
be grateful if the photographers concerned would contact us.

Front cover © Alan Perry.
Back cover © Kelvin Fagan

A catalogue record for this book is available from the British Library.

Cover design by The Andys.

CONTENTS

CONTENTS

PROLOGUE

I am quite sure that whatever your plotted level of diggin' *From Dublin to Jailbreak: Thin Lizzy 69-76*, you'll be finding this one the more enjoyable read. Part of that is the tacit eye-winked understanding among most of us Phil fanatics that our fave Lizzy albums are almost exclusively from the back half of the catalogue, which this book addresses lovingly, track by track by Downey drum whack.

Guilty as charged, and really, for me specifically, how could it be otherwise, given the overpowering allure of nostalgia as I age toward not power and possibility and hope, but decline and death at the door!

Ha ha, okay, what I'm getting at is that I know personally, really, very few folks whose first handful of records at that magic age of 14 and 15 and 16 included *Vagabonds* or *Shades* or *Nightlife*. But it seems I have a veritable army of friends, acquaintances, and otherwise sodden-eyed saps who will cry over a beer with me about Phil and his works circa *Bad Reputation* through *Black Rose*, arguing like old ladies o'er production points and writing credits, making comparisons with the careers of Rush and UFO and Rainbow. And even as these filmy-eyed friends of mine were of the specific age to have been there for those, buying them as new releases (a pre-requisite to the top level of furtive, pathetic nostalgic attachment), in his wise old age, any given old headbanger amongst them may lean to *Renegade* as his favourite Lizzy spin (as it is mine!), and also revel in the NWOBHM excitement of *Thunder And Lightning* as a fun record chucked into an exciting second wave dimension to a music fandom already established and jaded. Yeah, that pretty much sums up my relationship with Lizzy, even though I generalized it as that of my buddies, 'cos damn it, I think me an' my gang see much of this band's career exactly the same way.

So to recap, you'll see more passion from my end in second installment of our two-part Lizzy saga than found within the more academic first one, because yeah, that's me. First Lizzy album as a new release was *Johnny The Fox*. I was 13, had my subscription to Circus, saw the ads, knew the band a bit, was waiting for its arrival and bought it immediately, of course loving the heavy songs and hating the ballads. One record previous, *Jailbreak*, that was just an album without a year on it sitting within the mountain of albums from sorta '70 to '76 that might warm my cockles for $4.99 or $5.99 as I embarked on the baby steps of what has been a vast hard rock fandom (visit me at my office— man cave doesn't begin to describe it).

From there it was bang, bang, bang, every Lizzy album as a new release, and yeah, if I had to pick a favourite now (certainly not then, as an angry headbanger), it would be *Renegade*. Plus, as alluded to, being a teen in the lead-up to 1980, my intense adoption of music as a hobby grew at a regular up-pointing line through the second half of the '70s, but got a fire lit under 'er come the New Wave Of British Heavy Metal. It was the first new and definable exciting time for any hard rocker since, I suppose, the E.T. landing of Hendrix or the rain and the bell of the first Black Sabbath song. However, Lizzy was pretty inconsequential within that metal mayhem movement, actively not identifying with it, demonstrating as much by making a light album and then staying away until...

...Thunder And Lighting, the controversial harsh last record of Lizzy's life, and frankly, one of my least favourite, although good enough for me to love it a lot. Nice asterisk to my personal relationship to it, I was a drummer in a bar band around this time called Torque (blocked out in Iron Maiden letters, of course!) and we played both 'Bad Habits' and 'Cold Sweat' from this album and... yeah, I don't think any other Lizzy songs. Which... you can see why we never had much of a career, nail in the coffin coming with our refusal to play anything from ZZ Top's Eliminator but the two heaviest songs, namely 'Bad Girl' and 'I Got The Six' (and from Blue Öyster Cult, why, the obvious choice would have to be 'The Vigil,' now, wouldn't it?).

Anyway, again, scratch many, many a blue-blooded Lizzy fan, and they sorta line up around the melancholic, wistful experience of your author: the biggest nostalgic bulge coming around Johnny or *Bad Reputation*, lively diametrically opposed opinions around *Thunder And Lightning*, and a top fave from the catalogue that might seem surprising.

Anyhow, thanks to y'all (and of course to Peter Nielsen–geez!) for making the first Lizzy book successful enough to make this one worth doing. Believe me, *From Dublin to Jailbreak* seemed to grind on for months and months and months, and even though I'm sure a hard look would result in a realization I worked for well below minimum wage on it, you tend to forget all that in the spirit of documenting rock 'n' roll history, putting down on paper words of what you love. And like I say, with The Sun Goes Down, there's all that plus the beauty of reliving the memories of records I've played remarkably and geekingly regularly since 1976 to this day, friggin' 42 years of Lizzy later.

Martin Popoff
martinp@inforamp.net
www.martinpopoff.com

1

BAD REPUTATION

"This is how we're going to go out, right?"

Potentially robust touring for *Johnny The Fox*, having first been thwarted by Robbo's hand injury, was further hobbled by rumours that Robbo had been kicked out of the band. More than rumours actually, announcements, but announcements that didn't stick, that seemed in flux, were possessive of wobble. Wild Horses with Jimmy Bain was mentioned for the first time but again, as Robbo sneers, "I was kicked out of the band every second week."

From '76 into late '77, members of Lizzy past and present surfaced from time to time, some of these tiny events featuring Lizzy-themed reunions. There was Eric's gig with the boys at Morans Hotel in Dublin, Eric also showing up as guitarist of choice on the Noel Redding Band album Blowin', just as he did on the '75 debut Clonakilty Cowboys. On January 3rd of '77, the guys got together with Rat Scabies, The Troggs and Larry Wallis from the Pink Fairies and Motörhead as The Dire Ear Band for a "closing down" show for London's legendary Hope And Anchor. Phil produced a single called 'Look At Love Bleed' by Ron McGuinn which also featured a rendition of 'Banshee' as the b-side, guitarist for the session being Eric Bell, with Brian Downey drumming.

In May '77, Phil added further to his production resume by twiddling knobs on a single for his old friend and mentor Brush Shiels, who issued a full-length LP called *The Green Album*, which included Eric on guitar.

Furthermore, talk surfaced again about a Phil Lynott solo album, with Brian May touted as a possible guitarist on it. Robbo, not to be outdone, mused over a record of his own, with talk about town having him joining Graham Parker & The Rumour. The following month featured two events that were somewhat tied together if you think about it — it was announced that Thin Lizzy was once again a three-piece, and Gary Moore had put out a new album with his jazz-fusion band Colosseum II, effectively shelving negotiations that Phil had in mind to re-acquire Gary long before Robbo had cut up his moneymaker.

But as alluded to, the main Lizzy milestone through the early months of '77 (January 18th through March 18th) was the band's high profile tour as opener/special guest for Queen, white hot with their No.1 *A Day At The Races* album, on what was called the Tour Of The Americas. "There were about a dozen bands who wanted to do the tour," hyped Queen drummer Roger Taylor, talking to Harry Doherty. "But we thought that Lizzy suited our audience better than any of the others, and they were probably better than any of those bands anyway. I mean there's no point in making it easier for yourself: 'Come on, let's get a folk singer,' because he would have a bad time and the audience would be bored, so why not make it a good all-round show?"

Added Gorham, upon finding himself playing with Gary Moore because of Robbo's hand injury and "nervous exhaustion," "I thought it was going to be a really tough one. It took Brian and me two years to get to where we were as dual lead guitarists, and when we found that Brian was out, I was a bit more freaked than anybody else. But after just 11 days rehearsal with Gary, it worked. We worked on the harmonies a lot and I'm taking more leads now than before. It's hard to say why there's more harmony work."

"Brian, I think, was more into playing lead guitar, and after a while he lost some interest in the harmony things, so we were starting to do less and less of it. But Gary likes it as much as I do, so that we reintroduced the harmony guitar work into Thin Lizzy. I've always liked Gary. He's easily one of the best new guitar players around. He's a technical wizard, and he's got great feel, a really inventive player."

"Playing with Gary is the happiest I've been in a long, long time," continued Scott. "It's like breathing fresh air again. I guess it was kinda getting stale there for a while. I know that on the last English tour, I was getting pretty depressed with a lot of those gigs. I would go back to the dressing room and I wouldn't talk to anybody, and just go back to the hotel and lock myself in there. There was really a lot of heavy raving going on. People were losing control of themselves, and it wasn't making for good music. It seems sometimes that just a lifetime of noise was coming out, although we did have our nights when we came off and felt great. Brian was drinking pretty heavily, and I was going a bit crazy too, and Phil, of course, still had hepatitis and he would get depressed. So this whole thing is just a breath of fresh air where everybody has perked themselves out of the staleness."

"Brian's hand wasn't fully healed," explained Phil to Record Mirror.

"We didn't want to take chances, so we played it safe and took a substitute. Gary used to be with Thin Lizzy before. He's been playing with Jon Hiseman's Colosseum — they just finished their tour and Gary was free. With having to cancel two tours before, we were getting a bad reputation over here."

"Mainly I take care about having time off, so we can both enjoy ourselves," continues Phil, concerning the surprise decision to bring his mother, Philomena, out to America for a few days (highlight being a visit to see Scott's wealthy parents in the Hollywood hills). "We see each other in the daytime, then I tell her I'm going out in the evening — make up some excuse. I think I watch her more than she watches me. She's great. I've told her if the singles get to No.1, she can come out for a week."

Tour manager Frank Murray recalls the Queen dates with fondness, except that, "The first prop I suppose we ever got, and I mean the only prop we ever had, the Thin Lizzy logo, when we toured with Queen, we were never allowed to hang that up. Queen had issues of that coming down, because it was over Roger Taylor's drum kit, saying there was a chance we might hit... I mean, there was a slim chance it might have hit something like Roger's cymbals, which would've wrecked the mic setting that they had done in the sound check. So there would be troubles (laughs) and Phil, not to be outdone, would insist that we would put the logo to the side of the stage, in front of the PA stack. Because by hook or by crook, people are going to see that thing, you know? (laughs). It just became one of those stubborn things with Phil, which was to make sure the logo was up and let Queen see that we were going to fight them, you know what I mean? Not only on the stage, but in every way."

"The Queen thing was good; that was healthy," continues Frank. "They were good. It was competitive, like with the sound check. Always trying to get sound checks. Again, it was five minutes before the doors would open, Phil would want us to go out and do a line check, even if we had to hold the doors for a few minutes. But often they would come along and they would be taking an hour, hour-and-a-half sound check, and we would be sitting around going crazy backstage, because we wanted to do our own sound check, and they would say, 'Well, you can't have a sound check now, because it's too late.' We would fight over that. That's all normal stuff, in the life of a band. Or it was in those days. That would often cause tension, but other than that, ourselves and their crew got on really well with them all. I mean, they kept to themselves a lot, but we would speak at airports and stuff like that."

"That was a great package," muses Scott on this seminal stand, "a great vehicle for Thin Lizzy, because basically, Queen were going out selling out all these arenas, all the way across America, and so we ended up playing in front of a shit-load of people every night, for about two months or something. So yeah, they were great. I'm friends with the guys to this day. That was the tour that really helped out Thin Lizzy a lot in terms of getting us out in front of a lot of people, in introducing us to a lot of potential new fans."

Further on the personal dynamic, it was said that Roger Taylor and Brian May were affable enough drinking buddies to the band, but that John Deacon, who had brought his wife and child along, kept to himself, as did Freddie Mercury, who seemed to be on some sort of a star trip, not to mention in a constant boil over how well Lizzy were going down with both the fans and the critics doing their write-ups for next morning's papers.

Before hitting the road, however, the band had rehearsed for the tour in New York City, where they made extensive use of a limousine that they thought was complimentary, only to be stuck with a bill for thousands of dollars weeks down the line. Phil managed to indulge his leading edge taste in music, by catching Talking Heads at CBGB's and at Max's Kansas City, Mink Deville, an idiosyncratic act that one might take for a distorted version of Phil as a lounge lizard.

In fact, cue what is essentially a reconstitution of the irritating Springsteen comparisons Phil had been getting in the press ever since 'The Boys Are Back In Town' had hit. "I was very aware of the Bruce Springsteen thing," Phil told High Roller magazine. "I got this amazing telegram the other day saying Mink Deville was getting a hard time 'cause of me. A lot of people were saying to them, 'Hey man, are you copying Phil Lynott?' I was really laughing to myself. Because when I went over, seemingly two people, one in New York and one in LA, wrote, 'This guy's ripping off Bruce Springsteen,' and all of a sudden I was defending myself. I swear to God it was the hardest thing in the world because I was actually getting into Bruce Springsteen around about that time, so I couldn't turn around and say I dislike the guy, I hate what he's doing. I actually did like what he was doing. But at the same time, there was no way I could see that I was drawing anything off Bruce Springsteen at all. Same way as I don't think the Bay City Rollers influenced me. Then in the end it must've been down to Van Morrison. 'Cause Van Morrison, I'll openly say, I learned a lot off."

On the American tour, Frank could sense that the excitement around the band wasn't as intense as it was through the *Jailbreak* cycle. "Yeah, I felt that Mercury were not the best record company in the world, at that time. They got 'The Boys Are Back In Town' up and away, but then I don't know if they went cold on the band? What happened was; we then had to cancel the tour, because of Brian Robertson's accident; as you know, he had his fingers cut in the Speakeasy club. But then the next tour we went out on was of course this Queen tour. So I don't know — nobody can complain about that. But then I personally think — and I've said this on a number of occasions — we should've gone out there pretty soon afterwards. Toured and worked America then, while there was still a good vibe on the band, and on the shows, irrespective of the record company or anything like that. I wasn't privy to what they thought. I remember around Texas and stuff like that, there were good people. In Los Angeles there were good people. But then again, when we went back later on with Graham Parker. The standards of the record company seemed to have dropped then. The actual guys didn't have the quality of the men that worked with us the first time around. There was no… we weren't the record company darlings or anything like that."

"They were probably not interested, at that point," seconds Robbo. "I think Phonogram at that time were basically a money-laundering business for you know who. So they weren't putting anything into promotion or whatever. I think we had to do a lot of it ourselves. I mean, when you get three bands leaving the label at the same time, right? It was us, Graham Parker and the Boomtown Rats. We had a little chat and said, 'Well, this isn't working.' So we all decided to leave. That was the reason. There was nothing getting put into promotions or whatever, and like I say, it was basically an offshore bank for the lads (laughs)."

"Oh, I couldn't use the language that was used," laughs Frank when asked what the reaction was to Brian slicing up his hand on the eve of an American tour. "Brian was brash, maybe a bit overconfident, and drank more than he should have. But he was a great guitar player. But he could be hard to be around at times. I think he also did a bit too much drinking before he went on stage. He could've waited until he got off stage. Loading up on whiskey is normally not a good thing to do before you go on stage."

And Scott? "Everybody got on great with Scott," says Frank. "Scott was one of those guys… he would just blow with the wind, you know what I mean? Scott was like a sheaf of corn. If the wind blows, he goes that way, he's fine. He was always likable, always fairly neutral. He wouldn't lose his temper that much. Now and again myself and Robbo would have some run-ins, but I'm sure that happened with everybody."

Gorham fully admits to the competitive nature of Thin Lizzy, remembering various admonishments from Queen, including one time Gary had used a sort of catwalk part of the stage for one of his blazing solos, then being told to never do that again.

"Oh yeah, I mean, that was always part of the game plan," chuckles Scott. "You don't want to follow us. That was the whole deal. We wanted to make sure that anybody that was headlining was going to be really fucking uncomfortable after we left the stage. We did everything in our power to kick the shit out of any headliner. That was the attitude that you took, there was no way that we were going to be the nice little support band and all that. That wasn't on our menu at all. Our whole game plan was we were going to get the stage, we're going to own that fucker, and really, by the time we leave, we're still going to own it. So you're going to have to fucking buy that back when you get on there. But I thought that was a really healthy attitude. It might sound like we were a bunch of pricks and all that, but you've got to remember, the era that we were in was a super-competitive era, and a lot of people had that attitude. We might've had it a little more than most, but that's the attitude that we took with us. All the time.

Any dirty tricks?

"No, no. Absolutely not. There was no need for that. We pretty much played by the rules because we figured we were good enough. We didn't have to do anything underhanded. 'Oh, you're only gonna give us 30 minutes tonight? Okay, we're going to give you a kick-ass 30 minutes.' 'You're only giving us half the lights? Fuck it, that's fine with us, man, because it's the music everybody is here to listen to.' And so on and so forth. We just adapted."

Mike Slamer from City Boy could attest to the power of Lizzy live that Scott describes, having backed the band up in the UK the previous year. "I loved Thin Lizzy — I just wanted to watch them every night. I mean, they were hardcore into a lot of stuff I wasn't (laughs), the hanging out and socialising after the gig, but I liked to watch them. Phil left a huge impression on me. I've never seen anybody control an audience the way he used to. It was absolutely marvellous to watch him, nearly every night. When I'm working with new bands, I bring his name up a lot, and what a master of audience control he was. He could get everybody totally wound up, and then he could just calm them all down while he talked to them about something, in that beautiful soft voice he could have. You could hear a bloody pin drop in the theatre. It was really unique, his audience control."

Once the Queen tour was over (and with Phil the proud owner of a new home in West Hampstead), Thin Lizzy were on their way to recording the follow-up to *Johnny The Fox*, six months after that record's launch, and in Toronto, Canada no less, with controversial producer Tony Visconti presiding. Jetting off to Toronto was, like the Munich trip, a tax dodge seen as necessary during the legendary "tax exile" era in Britain. Manager Chris O'Donnell had been all set to send Lizzy on the road again, but had read an article in which Visconti had singled out Lizzy as a band that had never been produced to their potential. O'Donnell then decided to call him on it and an agreement was struck, plans to work with Queen genius Roy Thomas Baker once again falling through. Meanwhile, unsurprisingly, Phil had asked Gary Moore to join the band permanently. Gary thought about it, but his loyalty to Hiseman and Colosseum II had him reasoning that he would stick it out and see how their new album did, re-assessing the decision after a year.

"It was Chris O'Donnell's idea," explained Phil to Pete Makowski, on the acquisition of Visconti as a co-worker. "John Alcock couldn't make it to Canada and neither could Will Reid Dick, the engineer, who also worked on the last two albums, so we obviously had to find somebody else. Plus the scene that we've gone through with Brian and Gary: We said, look, me and Brian are used to working as a three-piece, I've written a lot of songs, Scott was capable of handling most of the guitars himself, and we knew that we weren't enemies with Gary and we weren't enemies with Brian and people were saying they'd play on my solo album and stuff like that. We knew we could get people to jam on the album. So basically we said let's see if we can co-produce this one, because I never want to produce Thin Lizzy again. It's just too much along with writing songs and playing. Tony Visconti really likes to work on a co-production basis, where he engineers it and half produces it and lets the band have a good say in it. So we said yeah, why not? That's what we're really after. So the initial idea was to go to and see how far we could go as a three-piece and then pull people in. Tony Visconti was dynamite; he was really good to work with."

"Great vibe; it was nice and sunny. It was nice being in a different environment. The only thing was the air-conditioning got to me after a while. Of course you missed everybody; you missed what was going on. That was the worst part."

"We had some great times in Toronto recording *Bad Reputation*," recalls Brian Downey. "We had, obviously, a really nice hotel and we had lots of friends and people coming up to see us. Phil wasn't really into abusing drugs too badly at that stage. It was later, that happened. Maybe Phil was coming into the studio an hour or two late because he went out raving the night before, in a club in Toronto or something. But we tried to make it as comfortable as we could for the few weeks that we were there. Just the fact that it's a great town to go out and party, and clubbing and all the rest of it, and there are some great bands there as well. So we went to see lots of things. We went to see the Space Needle obviously, and it was just a great experience to be in Toronto. You know, Canada generally was good to Thin Lizzy. We used to sort of enjoy getting to Canada after playing in America. It had had a nice sort of laid-back atmosphere to it, so yeah, when we got to Toronto, we really enjoyed it, the studio was great and we had Tony Visconti doing the producing, so we were very comfortable when we got there. Everything seemed to click into place nicely."

Everything except the fact that Brian Robertson was only quasi part of the band at that point, and unsurprisingly not there in Toronto for much of the recording, although to be fair, he wound up staying longer than planned, helping with the mix and advising Scott on some of his parts, particularly 'Soldier Of Fortune', on which he also provided keyboards, and would continue to do so live.

"I don't think there was a butting of heads as such," reflects Downey. "I think maybe Scott, at some stages during those songs, obviously left gaps and stuff and wanted him to fill them in with Brian Robertson's guitar. But I remember everything gelling nicely when these two guys played. I don't remember too many conversations coming up where you should play this and I should play that. They seemed to have a natural... maybe there were a couple times where Scott mentioned a couple of things. But there were no real problems musically within the band. The problems became problems outside the band (laughs). People partying too hard, getting into strange fights and squabbles and all that kind of thing, in pubs. That really was the basic problem with the band. It was more problems outside the band, than musically inside the band. There was conflict, oddly, because Brian Robertson is a very headstrong guy; he was a very independent kind of a person, and he really didn't like people telling him exactly what to do. But I can't remember it as being too much of a problem."

As regards Tony Visconti, Downey says, "I had no problem with him at all. I found him really creative in the studio and full of enthusiasm and ideas and all the rest of it. For *Bad Reputation*, we got a fantastic drum sound in the studio, because he suggested we use these Perspex screens around the kit. I remember that was the first time I ever used Perspex screens in the studio, and we got a really, really good live drum sound there in Canada. The only problem with *Bad Reputation*, we went through a period of falling out with Brian Robertson, and unfortunately, he only played on one or two tracks on that album. So there was a bit of discontent because of that."

"We spent three months in Toronto, recording at Toronto Sound, and we had a fucking blast!" recalls Gorham. "Are you kidding, man? There was like a whole school of women we met up with there, man, which was great — we had a really good time, going to all the clubs there. I really have a lot of fond memories of Toronto. It was probably the first time that Thin Lizzy actually went out of our comfort zone, if you will, of the UK or Ireland or whatever, and went to a completely different country to do an album. You've got to remember, so we're going into a new country, and Tony Visconti said he had worked in this place called Toronto Sound. He really liked it and he really wanted to work there, so we went with that. But we were nervous about what are we going to find there? What are the people going to be like? What is the atmosphere going to be like? But after about a week there we settled in and had a great time and it all worked out really great for us. So yeah, we all have a lot of really fond memories of Toronto. Didn't see Rush, but Pat Travers came by; he was recording some stuff there. The guys from Supertramp came by on tour. So we met a few friends when we were over there."

Phil, always one to keep abreast of new music, frequented the likes of Larry's Hideaway and the El Mocambo and regularly brought punkers back to the hotel to party. He also showed up regularly at Toronto's infamous and violent Crash 'n' Burn club, typically, one night getting into a scrap over a bird. Crash 'n' Burn is also where Phil met Cheetah Chrome of the Dead Boys, one of many non-Canadian acts to play the place. The swank part of town, Yorkville, was also a favourite Phil haunt, if only for the opportunity to indulge his newly expensive tastes and to watch the rich girls walk by. As well, at Larry's Hideaway, Scott and Brian got up on stage to jam with an act called Wireless, who eventually came to record three records for Rush's homegrown label Anthem.

"You know, again, Lizzy was probably one of the only bands from that era that the punks seemed to recognise as being slightly different than your run-of-the-mill heavy rock band," laughs Downey, on punk's reciprocal appreciation of Lizzy. "They appreciated that, and I think they took to us in some ways because of the ways we approached it. I don't think it was ever contrived. But we went on stage, we just wanted to play the best show to the best of our abilities, and I think that came across to the punks as well. Don't forget, we were also a fairly hard rock band."

"When it came to playing live on stage... I remember reading somewhere that we were untouched as a live band. Nobody could touch us, and also, the image we had seemed to appeal to punks as well. We seriously were into just getting out there and playing the hard rock as best as we could. When we met some of the Sex Pistols. I remember meeting Paul Cook; he loved our band and said that we were one of the only bands from that hard rock era that he could listen to without cringing. So that was a nice compliment. Phil used to meet them in the clubs in London, and have a few drinks with them and go to the gigs as well. So that whole period was weird. Because they were slagging off some of the bands like Led Zeppelin and Deep Purple and all the rest of them, and we were getting praise from the punks (laughs). An unusual sort of situation to be in."

"Phil was pretty astute," recalls Rat Scabies of The Damned. "He kind of saw what we were doing and what was going on. I think if he would have been five years younger, Lizzy would've been a punk band. I used to quite like hanging out with them. To me, with a lot of groups back then, you only liked one of their songs. Because there was one that kind of fit the bill that you liked; King Crimson, '21st Century Schizoid Man' was a cool track to listen to, but you didn't bother with the rest of the album. Lizzy had 'The Rocker', which was good for me, because that had a lot of balls. I was pretty impressed with that. They were doing very good business and they had the double guitar thing happening, and Phil wanted to find out how it works. I think he eventually realised there was a lot of common ground with punk. It didn't take him very long to realise that there was a lot of common ground in the way we looked at the world and the way we wanted to do things and what was acceptable and what wasn't. That's where the common ground came, more so than musically."

Phil even had plans to record something with Stiff Records, home of Scabies and The Damned. "Yeah, I was gonna, and my managers found out about it and went berserk and the record company heard about it, so it was shelved. But I was going to get together with Nick (Lowe) and do something with him at the time. It's terrible the way the business can bind you down sometimes when you want to work with somebody. The thing I like about Stiff Records is that they sell records in an unconventional way and therefore break the market down and make it more accessible for people, rather than go through a system. I'm just into that. I'm into letting the artists have control over what he wants to do. '77 is the year, man; it's happened this year. Everybody was saying, 'When are the '70s gonna happen?' It's fookin' happened."

"I didn't go out much in Toronto at all," recalls Robbo, asked about Phil and the punks. "Phil might have done it. I went to a blues bar off of Yonge and Bloor Street, with sort of live blues bands. We got up and have a jam and whatnot. That's the sort of place I like going to. I didn't go to any punk bars there, no. What punk did was take away quite a bit of the complexity. Because the kids that should have been listening in the audience were sticking needles and safety pins through their lips, and going out and listening to noise basically. But then again you had bands coming out like The Clash, who had something different from that. I liked the Pistols as well simply because of their sound — not the songwriting but the sound. Phil got into it quite a lot actually; he embraced it. I didn't see any of those bands live. I mean you don't want to be there when all the people are jumping about spitting at you. Not with the temper that I've got. But Phil was hanging out with Sid Vicious and them, and was always into stuff that was new because he wanted to keep up with the Joneses — the Steve Joneses (laughs). Phil was ambitious, 'course he was, yeah. He wanted to be a star and he lived that way. Unfortunately he died that way as well."

"The last time I saw Phil was down at Blitz, with all the Blitz kids," recalls journalist John Ingham, who had interviewed Phil a number of times. "He came in and he was just hanging out, and treated as an equal. When you go back to the Pistols and the Clash and that and who their influences and heroes were, he was one of them, but he wasn't a big rock star yet. So Jones was into Zeppelin and the Stones and all that, they were already gods, where Phil was still on that ground level, and the same with the Pistols. Not Lydon but definitely the other guys. You ran into somebody like Phil and he takes them at face value. He didn't put any judgment on them. The same with Lemmy. I can remember the first time Lemmy and the Pistols came together, it was a meeting of like minds without any doubt. Again, these guys just saw characters that they could relate to."

"There was a fabulous review about Thin Lizzy that said they're the most ordinary band in the world," continues Ingham with a laugh, "which is what it was. I mean, their impact was massive and it was a slow build. I did an interview with Phil once, and I went around to his house, in Earls Court, an area of London that was famous for Australians living there because it was really transient and you could get flats there very easily. Phil was living in this really dingy, transient flat, and there was nothing personal that you could tell it was his place. You know, there's a kind of rock star that's very nervous and they don't want to be alone? So we're doing the interview and he's really polite, really soft-spoken, and we got to the end of the interview and he said, 'Do you have to go?' I said no. He said, 'Do you want to hang out and smoke a joint and hear some music?' At that point I knew that was the signal that he was one of these nervous guys. In the course of talking, he said, 'Can I play you this new guy called Bruce Springsteen?' Yeah, okay, because I heard him and I didn't really like it. He said, 'One track, I've got to play you this one track.' It was 'Sandy'; that's on the second album. It's like a ballad, and he said, 'What I do is when I'm about to go on the road, I get a bunch of new records, and I just skip through them, and if I find something that I think sounds good, I stick it on a cassette. Then when I go on the road I've got a cassette of all these songs. I find out the ones I like and the ones that are good,' and that's how he'd come across this Bruce Springsteen one. For all his being that macho hero guy onstage, he was really the opposite off stage. Very quiet, quite nervous in a way."

"It was Pearl and Dean Street," relates Paul Robinson of The Diodes, explaining Toronto's infamous Crash 'n' Burn club along with his connection to Phil, "and it was the basement of a building that was owned by the Center For Experimental Art & Communication, but it also housed on the first two floors, the headquarters for the Liberal Party Of Ontario. It's law firms now. I was there when Phil visited but Phil became a friend of mine in England as well, which is really funny. Because I had all these associations with him over here, when I moved over there a few years later. What basically happened was, Thin Lizzy was recording in the studio that we ended up using as a recording studio. It was called Manta Sound, and Tony Visconti was over here recording them. I guess they'd heard about the Crash 'n' Burn, and they came down to it, came into the club, got to meet them then, and then we were friends, him and I, up until the time he died."

"Sadly, he was a heroin addict that died," sighs Paul, asked for his key impression of the man. "But I think everybody probably knows about that. They probably don't know that my girlfriend ran off with him. Which was a bit of a bone of contention. Well, she wasn't really my girlfriend. She was my ex-girlfriend, but we were together, and she was one of the Toronto seminal punks, really. She moved to England; she did our first album jacket as well. She ended up teaming up and marrying Chalkie Davis, who is a really famous rock photographer. She's the one who did a lot of the Phil Lynott stuff, and she's still with Chalkie to this day and she lives in New York. Anyway, with the club, I don't know if he was a big punk fan. He was just there to have a good time, and he just watched all the bands. I don't know what he thought of it, but I don't think that it was really his type of music. I always thought that he thought that what he was doing was much more musical. That whole, sort of London, pub music scene, which his band was sort of associated with. But he was incredibly talented. He was a great performer. He was also an extremely nice guy. I didn't see him again until I moved to England in '81. He was already married to another woman and he was also on the slide with drugs; I used to see him and he was out of it. You knew that he was doing drugs. You'd see him in the clubs and in the street. I would've loved to work with him. You know, incredibly talented person. I wish he was still alive. It's a shame that he died."

Recalls another Diode, John Catto, "One night, in walk all members of Thin Lizzy going, 'We're rock stars, let us in.' Ha ha ha and we were like, 'No, we won't let you in. Who the fuck are you?' Basically, they eventually paid, or someone broke down or whatever and they ended up hanging out there for the entire duration. I would guess that there was some member of Thin Lizzy at almost every night the Crash 'n' Burn was open. There's loads of stories about Phil Lynott getting into fights with people."

"Phil Lynott took a swing at me because he was after Cynthia Ross of the B-Girls," said Paul Eknes, of The Wads. "And I said, 'She's with me.' He goes, 'What are you, some little Toronto punk?' and I went, 'Kinda' and he goes, 'Do you know who am?' I go, 'Yeah, fucking Thin Lizzy, Phil

Lynott. I love you. Boys Are Back In Town!' He goes, 'Yeah? She's with me.' He was drunk and took a swing. I ducked and gutted him — not gutted him, I didn't actually take his intestines out, but I gave him a shot in the gut and we were pulled apart. Cynthia said, 'What are you doing? You are a stupid little Toronto punk! This is Phil Lynott from Thin Lizzy!' I think Mike Nightmare might have stood up for me. Back in the day I was less buff. All I remember is somebody pulled Phil off me and me off him."

Adds punk fan Nora Currie, "Mike got into this big fight with the guy from Thin Lizzy. It was brutal. Here's this guy in our country, checking out the scene, and Mike made racist comments to him along the lines of being black Irish, which is ironic. Phil was a black man who was Irish. Mike was Irish and he made really racist remarks to him. It was just such a vicious fucking beating."

Final word on the matter goes to Steve Leckie of the Viletones: "It was a stack deal because Mike Nightmare was a beautiful street fighter, really good boxer, and what he didn't reckon on was that Thin Lizzy had around half a dozen bodyguards that weren't gonna let anything happen to Phil. Mike got his nose all busted, but what a brave boy; what a beautiful, brave boy."

Back to *Bad Reputation*, Scott explains that the band vowed not to repeat the mistakes that they had that caused *Johnny The Fox* to sort of wither on the vine. "We did a lot more rehearsing; we demoed a lot more songs for it. You've got to remember, with *Johnny The Fox*, it almost came straight off the heels of *Jailbreak*. Because the *Jailbreak* album caught everybody by surprise. All of a sudden, out of nowhere, 'The Boys Are Back In Town' became a huge worldwide hit, as did the *Jailbreak* album. So now it's all fucking chaos. It took us by surprise, it took the management by surprise, and within really about six months, we were doing the *Johnny The Fox* album. To tell you the truth, I don't think we were ready for it. In fact, I know we weren't. We didn't have the songs. So with *Bad Reputation*, we weren't going to let that one happen to us. We, for once, took a little time off. We rented this little farmhouse thing, where we brought our own little studio with us, and the three of us at that point — it was just me, Phil and Brian Downey — we just sat there for three or four weeks and just went through a lot of different riffs, a lot of different arrangements, and gave Phil a lot of time to work on his lyrics and all that. So we felt a lot more ready with *Bad Reputation* than we ever did with *Johnny The Fox*."

So, keeping score, there were three of them at the farmhouse, but four of them in *Bad Reputation's* back cover photo (which was shot on July 20th in New York). Robertson was also listed as a band member, but then again, he received zero songwriting credits. Finally, there's that horrendous front cover, a grainy black and white shot with ill-placed text (is this an attempt to look punk?), and in that shot, it's only Phil, Scott and Brian.

"Well, that was a message to everybody," says Gorham. "The front cover shows you how it went down, but the back cover shows the four of us, but this is how we're going to go out, right? So yeah, the three of us did it, but on the back you see that the four of us are still a band, a four-piece band. It was as simple as that." One nice touch to an otherwise botch-job of a sleeve was the playing card suits assigned to each member of the band by Phil, who of course gave himself spades.

But after three classic, iconic Jim Fitzpatrick cover images, what the heck happened? Why did the band end up with a sleeve that… well, it would be hard to argue that by some measures, it's one of the crappiest album covers of all time.

"It's a long story there," says Jim, "but I'd moved to America because I got a publishing deal over there, and I wanted to live there for a while anyway. Took my whole family, kids, the whole works, set up in Connecticut in a beautiful house, and really enjoyed the lifestyle over there. It got boring after awhile though — I like a bit of action — very suburban, very Stepford Wives kind of country. There were doilies everywhere. Bloody doilies, they wore them, and had them on the tables. Philip was in America, and we were supposed to catch up and get a proper briefing on the album cover. I did a couple of roughs, but he wasn't even very clear himself, even on the title of the album. The story is — it's a very well-known story — but I was living in Madison, Connecticut, and I got a phone call from Philip saying, 'Listen, we're on East Wharf Road and we can't find you anywhere.' I said, 'Put me on to Frank.' Frank Murray was the driver, and Philip's best friend. 'Frank, look, just go down to the end of East Wharf Road, take a left, you'll see a house there, and it's made of red wood, different from all the others, can't miss it. It's contemporary, and there's a tyre swing on the tree.' He couldn't find it at all. Long story short, he went up to a cop and said, 'We're looking for East Wharf Road,' and the cop directed him, and, 'There's a huge wharf, right?' I said, 'What are you looking at? Because there's no huge wharf down at East Wharf Road; it's a tiny wharf.' He says, 'There's a gigantic wharf, big ships and everything.' I said, 'Where the fuck are you?' 'I'm in Madison.' I said, 'Which Madison?' He was in Madison, Wisconsin and I was in Madison, Connecticut. So we never got together on that. They needed something very quick, and the record company wanted to do something different, so they came up with that. It's a pity, because that broke the link. We had a nice run of really superb artwork that got into all the polls and the NME and all these things, and I think we had two of the Top 10 for, whatever year that was, 1981, I think, and

I was very pleased with the work I was doing for them. So it came as a bit of a shock when I saw that thing. I was living in America so it didn't bother me much, but I felt, that's the end of that, they're going to start using photographic covers, because that was the way the industry was going. Because illustration is too expensive."

"The three of us were getting along famously," continues Scott, back at the fragile band dynamic. "Me, Phil and Brian Downey. Brian Robertson was the sticky point, obviously to the point where there's really only three of us on the album. I really had to lay back on two of the tracks, one of them being 'Opium Trail', to try to talk Phil into getting Brian back into the band, flying him over to Toronto. I said, 'Look, I purposely left two tracks for Brian to do — it's a two guitar band.' I kept going on, over and over again with Phil. And he finally relented. So after the record, it was really a tour where Brian had to buck up. He had to pull his socks up, and have him toe the line, which he was doing. So at that point it was all going fine. It was only afterwards when we got together again after the *Bad Reputation* tour that things started to go tits up. Drug-wise, there wasn't a problem really, at this point."

"But, yeah, that's how it went down," continues Scott. "I remember arguing the whole time with Phil. It's a two guitar band, I mean, it's what we based our whole sound on, was the twin guitar attack. But here I am, you know, writing a lot of this stuff, with Phil, and I'm playing almost all of the guitars, all the harmonies, the whole deal, and arguing with Phil the whole time saying, you know, 'What are we going to do when this thing is finished? We have to go out and sell it, we have to play it.' I kept arguing that we really should get Brian back into the band, keep the Fab Four up and running, and back together, and he would argue back with me, 'You can't trust this fucking guy.' I mean, he had a great argument, right? But in the end I finally convinced him, we should get Brian over, let's fly him over. I've saved two guitar spots for him. He can come over and play them, and we can lay the law down to him, and see if he is okay, if he's going to fit in, still.' So we did, and you know, Phil put it squarely on my shoulders. He said, 'Right, if this doesn't work out, it's your fucking fault.' 'Yeah, yeah, yeah.' So we get Brian over, I sit him right down and I say, 'Brian, for fuck's sake, this is the last chance saloon, here. Just keep your fucking head down and shut the fuck up, and play the guitar, man.' He was a pain in the ass, even for those two songs. I don't know what he was trying to prove. He wasn't very communicative to anybody. Urgh, I could see this was the starting of a big mistake. But he did a great job with the songs that he was given. I think he was disappointed that the bulk of the album had really been done. But this was really just a way back for him, to get back into Thin Lizzy. Of course it didn't take him long to actually blow that whole thing and the next mistake he made, unfortunately, he was just out of there. I couldn't defend him any longer."

"I guess he had something to do with that, yeah," says Robbo, about Scott getting him involved with *Bad Reputation*. "As far as I know he did, yeah. But it was never discussed with me. You know, I just did what I had to do, really. I wasn't on the backing tracks. We were recording in Toronto, and I was flown over to do the overdubs." So was there indeed a butting of heads with Phil? "Yeah, but I always say it was more of a constructive thing in a lot of ways. I was a bit of a hothead anyway. I think most kids are at that age, especially if they're put into that situation. Whereas these days, I'm a lot different from that."

An added wrinkle to the situation was that Robbo had been trying to parlay a management deal for his Wild Horses mate Jimmy Bain in exchange for his doing the Lizzy cameo, or re-joining Lizzy — it wasn't all that clear.

So the twin leads on the album, as Gorham admits, in most cases that's Scott doubling up on his own tracks... "Yes, Brian was disappointed that I had done it all, not that he didn't like what I did, but it just meant that there was less for him to do, and to be part of. I told him, I said, 'Brian, you're just going to have to shut the fuck up and go with this here. Just get in the studio and play these two bits, and just shut the fuck up.' Because I'm trying to get this thing coordinated and back online and he did — he shut the fuck up and he did his two bits and it ended up being okay. I was always the one who tried to keep this thing together. I was always a big believer in the magic circle. Don't fuck with the magic circle. If it ain't broke, for God's sake, don't fix it. All the other clichés you could come up with. So I was always the one trying to bring Phil back into line, get Brian to shut the fuck up, trying to be the mediator, just to try to glue this thing together. But those two guys, man, they were always butting heads. Finally in the end, Robertson fucked up that one time too many, and I went to Phil and threw my hands up and said, 'Okay man, you were right, we're done'."

"But like I say, we had a lot of fun in that studio putting that record together. It enabled me and Phil and Brian and Tony to gel a lot better. I think if we had done it in London, each day everybody would've gone home to their respective houses and not really hung out. But because we were in Toronto and we were staying in the same hotel, it allowed us to say, 'Let's go out to dinner;' or 'Let's go and have a drink.' It made it so everybody could get a lot closer. So that was a really cool aspect of doing it in Toronto. I'm really happy with the production — Tony did a great job on it."

"It has proved to me that the band is now basically Scott, Downey and me," said Phil to journalist Harry Doherty, who had made the trip to

Toronto. "Before we did the tour of America and got Gary in, we were always suffering a guitarists crisis. Our whole career seemed to be that we were constantly finding guitarists who would always give us headaches."

"When Brian left the band, we just said: 'We'll just ride this out and see what type of guitarist we need.' I always considered that Scott was being vastly underrated in what he was contributing. I knew that he could handle what was going down. Me and Brian had been used to working in the three-piece idiom anyway, so I figured that we should go out to Canada, lay down the backing tracks and get maybe Brian Robertson, Gary Moore and maybe Brian May to put on some solos. As it turned out, Gary had his Colosseum II commitments, and it was going so well that we only used Brian on a couple of tracks. Scott's done great."

"With this album," continued Phil, "Brian has really been interested in what's been going on. On the *Johnny The Fox* album, he didn't even want to hear his solos. He'd take a solo and say, 'Don't play it when I'm here' but this time he's checking everything. It pleases me a lot that whereas he doesn't have to be into what we're doing, he's very keen about it and is helping to build it. It's a complete opposite to when we worked together last time. I think he's come of age in the period of transition, as the man says."

Bad Reputation would be recorded in the summer of '77 and issued September 2nd of that year, rising to a No.4 placement in the UK charts and No.39 in the US, appetite for the record whetted by the advance UK release of the explosive title track as a single on July 29th, as a "double a-side" with 'Dancing In The Moonlight', a fully Springsteen-esque number that, once the dust settled, would serve as the album's defacto hit song.

The record opens with 'Soldier Of Fortune' (original title: 'Ireland'), a moderately involved epic framed on a simple old rock 'n' roll chord pattern (think Kiss, BTO) but passionately sung and steeped in dramatic, sublimely melodic twin leads.

"I was trying to write a story that was anti-mercenary," commented Phil on the 'Soldier Of Fortune' lyric. "But as I wrote it, I began to find that it was very hard to put mercenaries down. If the cause is right, mercenaries are fairly cool — like those guys that zoom into Mexico and pull out them guys that are in jail for dope and take them back to the states — they're fairly cool."

Elaborating on the story with Pete Makowski, Phil explains, "That came about through mercenaries. This really freaked me. I only found out after I had written the song, but about two years ago, I got into a fight down Dingwalls... nearly got battered. We got drunk, me and Frank Murray and Ted Carroll, who was our manager at the time, and we'd drunk a bottle and a half of Southern Comfort, and I got into a fight. Now, one of the bouncers there was Callan. Now Callan was also in the British Army in Ireland and the reason he got thrown out of the British Army was that he was caught robbing a bank in Ireland and burying the money, which goes on over there but you don't read too much about it obviously because the English papers don't write about it."

"Then he goes and becomes a mercenary and gets himself killed. I didn't know at the time, but Frank told me and it really freaked me. So anyway, I started off writing the song to put down mercenaries, saying how disgusting it was going off and becoming a trained killer, then as I started to write the lyrics, I began to realise that everybody has a little bit of mercenary blood in them. You know, like sometimes I'm real brutal with chicks, just go after them, get what I want and 'See you later.' Everything I do and say is to get what I want. So at the end of the song, I had to say, 'I am a soldier of fortune,' so it wasn't as heavy as it was initially intended to be, because as I look more into it, it wasn't a simple question of black and white. Because you get the guys going over the American border busting people out of the jails in Mexico — them guys are cool. But if it's some guy shooting every black dude he likes because he likes the feel of a gun in his hand, then that makes the guy a little berserk."

Immediately, with the first track's relative simplicity and pregnant pauses, one notices that the production Visconti achieves is less powerful than that of *Johnny The Fox*, a little more radio-tilted toward *Jailbreak*, given the lack of bass and indeed highs, which leaves, well, mids. Not that Visconti had been known for fully hi-fidelity work in the past, his directly previous credits with Sparks, Argent, Caravan, David Bowie and T. Rex were characterised as various forms of boxy and crude.

Any shortcomings concerning the tonal range of Visconti's production job, however, become minimized come the prog-metal monster that is the record's title track. Indeed, an "everything up front" palette makes perfect sense for this symphony of riff and dastardly drumming, drumming so prominent that Downey receives a co-credit on the track.

"They were really nice to play, those sorts of songs that Phil was writing then," says Brian, asked about the song. "He left lots of spaces for me to play, and that was a great bonus as well. Nowadays, I don't hear many drummers doing much on the records; it's very straightforward. Obviously Phil was a friend of mine, but there was never a conscious effort of me saying, 'Okay Phil, leave a gap here.' It was none of that. It was just a case of Phil arranging the songs and me filling in as best I could, where it needed to be filled in."

"We had the chord structure already done, with that," adds Scott. "But I think it was Brian who came up with the odd time signature in there, which inspired both me and Phil to go, 'Oh yeah, well, Brian, if you're going to do that, that means we can go... there and we can do... that.' So Brian really got the credit on that for inspiration value more than anything else. With him putting on those drums, it enabled me and Phil to go over there, if you will. So that's why it worked out with him for the song credit."

"A bad reputation does have a certain fascination attached to it," quipped Philip to *Circus* magazine. "Sometimes it's even a very handy thing to have. In the long run, though, it's really not good for you." Commenting on the song's equal footing single status with the diametrically opposed 'Dancing In The Moonlight', Phil told Pete Makowski, "I'd much prefer everybody playing 'Bad Reputation', because in a way, like, 'Dancing In The Moonlight' is a nice song, but 'Bad Reputation' is much more representative about what we're about live. I don't want people expecting us to be one thing and seeing another. That's why I was very keen for the company to make the single a double A."

"I just like the idea of 'Bad Reputation'," continued Phil. "Lizzy were definitely getting a bad reputation around. The interviews before we went away were like Brian Robertson was drunk and getting into fights. Scott was always talking about his hippie days when he was a drug addict. My interviews always seemed to be about my sex life and Brian Downey just didn't speak at all. There seemed to be very little talking about the music."

'Opium Trail' is the second of three very heavy metal rockers on the record, and a second in a row, right there on the first side, slash 'n' burners that rival the likes of 'Emerald', 'Massacre' and 'Boogie Woogie Dance' for axe-mad intellect. But unlike 'Bad Reputation', it's not rhythmic intensity that distinguishes it but rather an almost inscrutable weave of guitars that create not so much a riff, but a blanket on top of the bass line, which in fact represents the riff. Lyrically, one could almost view it as a short sketch that fleshed out, becomes the *Chinatown* concept of three years hence.

"We really loved playing that song," reflects Scott. "Phil really loved the subject matter, the whole triad thing, and like you say, the musical complexity of it all. There was a really nice drive to it. Brian Robertson did a really cool solo on it, live. So that was one that actually stayed in the set for quite a while."

Commented Phil, "Scott came up with what I considered to be this real Eastern guitar hook, so that gave me the idea. I'd seen, yet again, from the great media of television two really fine documentaries on the

Hong Kong triads in the Golden States of Shan. You know, there's a triangle where about 50% of the world's opium comes from. It's on the border of North Vietnam, Burma and China. It's a really weird area because it has all the ex-warlords from China. They have all the deserters from the North Vietnamese Army. There was this great program where this French chick went right to the source where they make this opium and she had to hire an army just to go into the area. It was that heavy, everybody had guns, young kids had guns. Then I saw another documentary in Canada about the triads, and they've got this whole sort of trip where they have to say a mantra or somethin' like that. There's different triads and there's these gang wars where they're blowing one another away."

"It's an anti-drug song," continued Phil. "I remember years ago even when I first came to England, where it was very cool to take acid and smoke, but to actually have any powders was very, very uncool, even among musicians. Within a period of about two years, it became very hip to be into cocaine. I remember when I was a kid, I'd say, 'Man, if I met any dealers, I'd kill them.' Now I know a lot of dealers and I don't kill them, though I might dislike what goes down. So it was to make me aware that you can flirt around with these sorts of things but eventually they'll trap you. There's no two ways that it won't trap you."

The pace relents for 'Southbound', an unshowy yet charming desperado song of hard rock light, somewhere between 'Soldier Of Fortune', 'Fools Gold' and 'Old Flame'. "Me and Phil loved that song," reflects Scott, who neglects to mention that Gary swears up and down the writing of the song originated with him and that he even extracted some money out of Phil for it years later. "Phil had sort of the basic chord structure to it. I remember I was sitting in his living room, and he said, 'I have this thing; what do you think?' He starts to play it, and to sing verses to it. I really liked the whole flow to it. That's when I picked up the guitar and went, 'How about if we go to here?' and 'Let's do this line here' (sings it), putting in the harmony thing, and he loved all of that. Pretty simple song, but it had a really good feel to it, and both he and I fell in love with it as soon as we started working on it. You know, I'd like to go in there and sort of re-mix that or do something with that song production-wise, bring it up to date. Because I think it still has a lot of potential to get to more people. I mean, me and Sykes even tried it out onstage and we love playing it to this day, right? John used to put in this really cool Police-y guitar bit to it, and soon as he did that, I went, 'Oh shit, that is so cool.' Maybe one day we'll get to it and add things to it."

'Dancing In The Moonlight' caused some consternation among the Lizzy faithful, given its light swing and funk, not to mention the finger snaps and sax, the latter courtesy of John Helliwell of Supertramp, the band Scott had flown over to join three years earlier. If Phil was getting fed up with comparisons with Springsteen, this wasn't the way to go about quashing those mutterings. The lyric picks up some inspiration from Phil's wayward youth, his staying out past the curfew imposed by his grandmother who loathed his hippie lifestyle. Plus there's the famed "chocolate stains on my pants" line, inspired by some messy snacking with Frank Murray at a showing of the movie Mean Streets back in 1973. More so than the Springsteen comparative was the song's obvious nod to Van Morrison, with whom Phil found himself striking up a friendship around this time, after a nervous introduction from Frank Murray.

Pendulum swinging hard, 'Killer Without A Cause' was the record's third uncompromising metal construct, this one containing both tricks at the time signature and rhythm end of things as well as mensa-metal riffing, the track being the second of three Robertson is credited on as axeman. Come chorus time, the band injects an incongruous spread of melody, guitars switching to acoustic with soft power chords in the backdrop.

"Killer was a single," says Scott. "In fact, we got in trouble with that one. I think we were in Liverpool, and it was on the Bad Reputation tour, there was a big story that came out that while we were on stage, and... this is so much bullshit, right? But while we were playing 'Killer Without A Cause', and this did happen, a girl was being raped in the back of the arena we were playing in. You know, whether we were actually playing that song or not is really up for debate. But over here it became a huge thing. People wrote in and called in and said, 'How dare this band play a song like that while this poor girl is being raped?' It kept going on and on to the point where we had to relent, and tell everybody, 'Okay, we dropped the song, we're very sorry, we won't play it again.' That was the last time we ever played it live. It's a shame, because it's a really cool song to play live."

From this point on, *Bad Reputation* unwinds down-wound, with 'Downtown Sundown' revelling in the band's tradition of periodic blues pop in a mournful mode — John Helliwell notches his second brass cameo on this one.

Commented Phil, "Downtown Sundown is a funny story, because I wrote 'Don't Believe A Word', and every chick I went out with after that used to throw it back in my face every time... 'I don't believe a word you're saying.' I used to get it all the time, and it was really sort of sarcastic all the time, so I figured I'd write a song that was actually a statement of love, so this would be an answer to it."

'That Woman's Gonna Break Your Heart' (another track where Robbo plays) is an urgent, more creatively successful example of the form, Phil always writing up to and past the potential of anything of a desperado country & western disposition, given his doleful vocal delivery, his conversational phrasing and the crack band of tasteful writers around him versatile enough to fulfil his visions. Later a co-producer with Robbo on his solo album, Sören Lindberg picks this track as receptacle of Brian's greatest guitar solo with Lizzy. "A bit of a weird one, I would say, where Scott starts the solo, and you can hear that he's not going anywhere, really. Robbo takes over with his absolutely fluent, lovely melodies. Not so much the technique, but it's just a very fluid melody. Ever since I heard that song for the first time, it's always been, 'Wow, what a great guitar solo'."

Offering his take on what Robbo contributed to the *Bad Reputation* album as a whole, Sören figures that "Studio-wise, what I've heard is that they recorded six or eight weeks in Toronto, and Robbo was flown in for the last two weeks. That's actually the official story. Any band member you ask will probably have a different timeline on that. But what I've heard is that Robbo was there for the last two weeks. I would say that all keyboards on *Bad Reputation*, which obviously is mainly 'Soldier Of Fortune', but all keyboards you hear on *Bad Reputation* is actually Robbo playing. Of course Robbo was brought in to sort of do the lead guitar, but he's also a musician, so he spent a lot of time in the studio. He plays a lot more on that album that those three tracks he's credited for. He's basically just credited for the guitar solos, but you know, there are several tracks where he plays rhythm guitar, keyboards, and also some of the melody lines. But I suppose they sort of wanted to slap him on the wrist a little bit there. You have behaved badly, so you can't come in here and be credited for everything you've done on this album."

Completing what feels like a three-song psychological spiral, 'Dear Lord' opens with a soundtrack to a peaceful and fulfilling death, 16 tracks of angelic backing vocals provided by the producer's wife, Mary-Hopkin Visconti, a renowned folk singer and one of the first Apple signings. The track is essentially a recalcitrant prayer set to a delicate countrified boogie. But despite the Fighting album vibe of both this track and its predecessor, the desperation is as palpable as that from *Black Rose's* 'I've Got To Give It Up'.

Notes Scott on this baleful album death knell, "I just had this chord pattern that I'd been working on for a while, and just whipped it out one day. Phil was really good with that. You know, almost absentmindedly, you can throw out chord patterns or whatever, and he was really good at going, 'What's that? What are you playing there? How are you doing that?' You would go, shit, okay, boom boom, and he would immediately slap on his bass, and then take it a little further into the next bit, and he would go, 'How about if we put on a melody line like this over it?' Then you played and sang it, and he would go, 'That's really cool — how are you doing that?' 'Dear Lord' was sort of one of those developing songs, if you will. It wasn't a whole song that somebody just brought in and it was there. We developed it on the spot."

All told, *Bad Reputation* was generally well-received, most fans figuring the album tough and heavy, blinded by the uncompromising heft and mastery of its three pure metal rockers. 'Soldier Of Fortune' was also a respected track, and 'Dancing In The Moonlight' was a minor single hit in most major markets, even winning over most grumbling angry headbangers who were, in the end, always a sucker for Phil's charms. In general, there was a sense of high quality craft to the album that served as proof that Lizzy was still moving forward.

But not too forcefully or impressively, figured Rolling Stone's Stephen Demorest. "Like the good-bad characters in its songs, Thin Lizzy is no better than it should be," wrote Demorest, in an issue with a massive punk rock cover story. "Catering to the moderate-hard-rock mainstream, the band's music has changed remarkably little over the last five albums: a scrappy, and often insouciant blend of cantering melodies, crunching chords and colourful arrangements. If the members of Lizzy are not particularly innovative, they do explore their chosen territory with uncommon flair, polishing their reliable style a little more each year."

"As a result, *Bad Reputation* is a fine, solid album. Songwriter Phil Lynott's lyrics portray a roguish, though God-fearing Irish soul that is full of heat-lightning dreams that stir his blood at sundown. His ballads are laced with tender and often charming blarney, and his more feisty songs are dashing mini-epics of urban romance. Only when he yields to the temptation of martial swaggering does he begin to resemble the archetypal rock thug. *Bad Reputation* may not be the stuff of legend and may not hold many surprises, but it does satisfy as a first-rate rock 'n' roll consumer good."

The NME's Charles Shaar Murray takes another tack, recognising the craft and the detail to the record, but surmising that the band had gone overboard. "Visconti's taste for the grandiose and the fact that the whole band wasn't working together for the entire period of recording have resulted in a drastic loss of the crackling immediacy that has always been one of Thin Lizzy's calling cards on record. *Bad Reputation* sounds studio-ish in the worst sense of the word: technological cuteness substituted for straight-shooting rock power, a fussed-over staleness muffling direct communication and the reek of overdubs oozing from the grooves. The arrangements and production are similarly snared; the intro to 'Dear Lord' is a de Milleian extravaganza more suited to one of our more absurd techno-grandiose outfits, and the intro to 'Soldier Of

Fortune' with Lynott declaiming over phased gongs and synthesized goulash is similarly over-the-top. *Bad Reputation* is something of a holding operation. It presents a smoother, more obviously 'produced' variation on various Lizzy staples with a corresponding lessening of impact. It's a dilution — in the final analysis — and while I have too much respect for Lynott and his colleagues to suspect that they'd ever go in for bland-out, this is far too damn close to it for comfort. The relegation of Brian Robertson — a far tougher and meaner guitarist than Gorham — to a supporting role may not be of Lizzy's choosing, but it certainly results in an diminution of their impact."

"I hope their next album represents a return to basics," continues Murray, in his long and perceptive piece, "one step back to go two steps forward. Thin Lizzy have an honourable and prominent position in the rock landscape and hip MOR should have absolutely nothing to do with it. *Bad Reputation* isn't even a step in that direction — more like a nod — but the sound and approach on the album doesn't do the band even halfway justice. The power and frenzy of their live appearances demonstrates beyond a shadow of a doubt that they haven't lost one whit of their strength and commitment. Therefore it is both puzzling and disheartening that they should have made an album which sounds as if they have."

After living with the album for a few months, Thin Lizzy's own drummer seemed to agree with the critics, telling Niall Stokes from Hot Press, "I thought there were a couple of numbers that were really duff on it. The sound was very good but we just didn't have enough time to get the numbers together. I found that after a while, when a few of the numbers weren't happening, you couldn't say, 'Stop! Let's forget it and go back home and start again. Everyone said that *Johnny The Fox* was a flop, which is totally untrue; I've got a gold record there for it — it went gold in the States but over a period of time. But it didn't get into the charts so people automatically say it was a bum album. So we were going over saying we'd have to do something better than *Johnny The Fox*, but we just weren't ready for the short space of time we had which was three to four weeks recording. We needed more. *Jailbreak* was the culmination of a lot of work over a long stretch of time. It wasn't an album that was written over a period of a few weeks or months; it took nine months to a year for the whole thing to fit into place, whereas *Johnny The Fox* was written over a period of three to four months. We've seemed to have less and less times for the albums since *Jailbreak* because we were more successful with that album."

Following the crafting of the *Bad Reputation* album, Lizzy-related events through the summer of '77 included a bit of hoopla in the press about Queen and Thin Lizzy staging a concert on June 11th for the

Queen's Silver Jubilee. It was eventually scotched, "due to lack of interest," but one can really attach oneself to the symbolism of it. Queen were as far away from punk as you could envisage, punk was all the rage, and the circus around the Sex Pistols and their 'God Save The Queen' song, lyrics, 45 sleeve, and daffy boat trip down the Thames... score one for the punks. In tandem, Lizzy were finding themselves playing second publicity and buzz fiddle to a band they had been so kind to offer a leg up: The Boomtown Rats. Suddenly the audacious Geldof was in the press and the charts, being showered with attention from Nigel Grainge, the guy who had signed Lizzy, and from Lizzy's management and Lizzy's record label. Score two for the punks.

Noted Phil, "The thing I really noticed in the last year is that Lizzy have become popular and that third generation that I was talking about last year has really come to the front with this punk rock thing. The paradox is that Lizzy have almost become old-fashioned within a year. We're a young enough and fresh enough band for all these punk rockers to dig, but we haven't got the punk rock identity. I was saying a long time ago that these kids were going to come out of the walls, and at that time we were saying it was for those kids. We've been away for a year, and not only has this punk rock thing started speaking for these kids, but they've also given it image, so much so that our image seems to counteract it in a way. So Lizzy are in a funny state at the moment, although the music and live shows pull us out of it. We were out playing places like Manchester and Newcastle, and seeing the build-up to this and talking to kids after the gigs. All I'm saying is that due to Lizzy's success, we've almost become Establishment, but this whole thing has just started. It's far from over. The point is that the kids are making statements that they want and are listened to. They're demanding the right to retain freedom and the more people backlash against it, the stronger it will get. Image had never bugged me. The music is the thing that grabs you in the end. That's what'll grab everybody in the end. The style of presenting it might change. I don't worry about it. I never have."

Back to America in July (for no good reason), the same day Robbo was announced as part of Thin Lizzy again, the guys took the shot on the steps of a New York brownstone that would be used for the back cover. Catching Pink Floyd on their *Animals* tour at Madison Square Garden earlier in the month, Scott and Phil meet future Lizzy axeman Snowy White for the first time. With Robbo now back in the band, the guys spent six weeks through August and September playing mostly festival dates throughout Europe, including Reading Rock '77, at which they headlined the second of three nights, August 27th, going on right after Aerosmith, who Lizzy had already backed up in America. Down the bill from Aerosmith was Graham Parker, John Miles and Ultravox, all who sported or would sport Lizzy ties (Brian's chum Frankie Miller played on the Sunday). At Reading, Phil found himself in a much publicised brawl with a journalist, his patience notably and periodically shortening at sentiments arising from the British press that well-crafted rock was obsolete in the face of punk's incendiary relevance and vitality.

On August 16th, rock's past suffers another blow when Phil's hero Elvis Presley dies. This doesn't stop Phil, however, from throwing a massive 28th birthday party for himself four days later (Bob Geldof and Graham Parker in attendance), with the bash ending in a drug raid. Held in a "stately Georgian mansion" in Celbridge Co., Kildaire, the party was apparently gate-crashed, resulting in a crowd of "several hundred." The next night, says Raymond Wright, "Phil was in Dublin for the big Dalymount gig in August '77, and he got fixed up in the Skylon Hotel with rooms etc. We were having a drink, could have been Neary's pub. My mate Dave was going out with this girl Annette, and he said that to Phil. Phil just gave him the keys to his room and said it was on him, breakfast and all. He already had a place to stay."

Also in '77, Robbo showed up on a rendition of 'Statesboro Blues' for Makin' Magic, Pat Travers' second record (with Gorham guesting on Pat's third record!), as well playing all over an album's worth of tracks with Steve Ellis, a collection provisionally titled The Last Angry Man. The Ellis album was subsequently shelved (issued as an archival release in '01), but a single did emerge, on which Robbo is featured on the b-side, 'Save All The Encores'. "That was just another one of those silly things I used to do," says Brian. "They were all friends of mine, and I didn't even charge them (laughs). It was just, 'Oh yeah, I'll play. Yeah, that's no problem. Just give me a crate of champagne and some cocaine, and I'll be by.' Which they did, and you know, all the boys came into the studio, and Henry McCulloch and Jimmy Hinkley were there, all the usual suspects, and it was fun, but that's about it, really. Looking back on it, it was never going to be a serious thing anyway."

Fuelling the rumours concerning Brian joining Graham Parker's band was the fact that Robbo did indeed do some recording with the pub rocking bard… "Yeah, I ended up recording a single with him, the Pink EP. I played guitar. The b-side was supposed to be called 'Brian's Boogie'. I did it for no money. I just flew out, with no clothes or anything, and I walked straight on stage, about half hour into the set, started playing, did the whole tour, and we ended up somewhere in Germany — Stuttgart or Frankfurt or somewhere — in a studio with Mutt Lange, producing it. I was playing a hired Stratocaster on the stuff, right? Just to sort of blend in with the band. I put a sort of melody guitar on, and he hadn't actually written any lyrics at that point, and he said to me, 'okay, look, we haven't paid you, so we're going to give you a song. We're going to call it 'Brian's Boogie'.' I went, 'Yeah, cool, no problem.' This is after I nearly killed Mutt Lange with a guitar. He tried to fuck about with the amplifier, right? I didn't even know who the guy was at the time, so I'm playing away, and he came walking into the booth and started farting around with the knobs on my guitar amp, and I just went, 'Oi, get the fuck out of here,' right? I was about to break the guitar over his head, and he ran off back into the control room. So there you go (laughs)."

All the while Phil was remaining patient with Gary Moore, as well as very complimentary in the press. "I can't say to him, 'Hey man, this is going to be far more successful than Colosseum.' I gotta respect him for wanting to play what he wants. I mean, I think Gary Moore is the best living rock 'n' roll guitarist in the world today, but he is in what I consider to be a jazz-rock field. In that field, there's a lot of great guitarists. Like the competition is heavy! That's basically the paradox that Gary is in, but all the great guitarists go after that. You either do what Clapton has done and go simpler and become a songwriter, or you do what Beck is doing and chase it into the realms of where it becomes musicianship. That's what Gary is doing. He is just ahead of his audience. When Gary Moore was playing rock, the audiences should have been there to hear him. But it might dawn on Gary, 'I've got this down; I want to play rock again.' He has these two sides to him all the time: the musician side and this basic energy side where he just wants to go out and boogie, and he gets that chance occasionally to blow out as a rock guitarist with Lizzy. But with Colosseum, he satisfies a much more demanding need, playing with excellent musicians such as Jon Hiseman."

Meanwhile, Robbo found himself in the thick of it again when a huge brawl ensued in Turku, Finland on August 5th, day before a festival which drew 7,700 to see Lizzy, Gasolin and Wigwam.

Brian wound up taking five shots to the face even if the road crew had gotten the worst of it, specifically driver John Rivet who was the first to react to the local lumberjacks brewing for a brawl. Along more civilised lines, August also saw the release of Phil's second poetry book, *Philip*, followed quickly by the release of *Bad Reputation* at the beginning of September. Of note, adding to the subtext/fable rivulet of Phil as Johnny, working title for the second poetry book was *J Is For Johnny*.

Proving his mettle through these isolated dates with often incongruous, quixotic bills, Brian Robertson was once again guitarist of choice for an extensive assault on North America, the band kicking off in San Diego on September 21st 1977 and closing out in Chicago on November 5th.

Before the tour was out, Frank Murray would announce that once this leg was over, he was leaving the band, after being Phil's sidekick since the boys were teenagers back in Dublin. "I had gone before it got unmanageable. Phil was my friend, you know what I mean? I'd been with Philip together since we were 16, so we were always doing Thin Lizzy. Even if I wasn't working, he would always check stuff out with me, but yeah, from 'Whisky In The Jar'... I was there through all of that period, and then *Jailbreak, Johnny The Fox, Bad Reputation,* and *Live And Dangerous.* So I could see different changes in him. I remember having a chat with him, actually a row with him at the launch of the *Chinatown* album. He was in denial. There wasn't much you could do; he was so much in denial."

Frank has also explained over the years that his main reason for leaving was seeing Phil's ego blow up to Freddie Mercury proportions, complaining about travel arrangements, hotels, and treating the back up band of this swing of US dates, Graham Parker & The Rumour, like second class citizens.

"I think you'll find he probably got fired, actually," figures Robertson, with regard to Frank. "I don't think he'll ever admit to that, because Frank is that sort of guy. I think he probably did get pissed off with Phil, because of the drug thing. Not that Frank is innocent in this respect; he's not. Because everybody was at it, you know? So he's not entirely innocent, but I think possibly he might have seen the light before Phil; well, Phil never did see the light, did he? But he might've thought, right, I'm out of here. On the other hand, I think he might've been pushed out by the management, for making too much of a stink, and maybe trying to help Phil too much. I don't think the management — i.e., Chris Morrison — didn't like anybody rocking the boat, as far as Phil Lynott was concerned. Because Phil Lynott was his meal ticket. Frank might've been involved in all the drugs and all the rest of it, but as I say, he probably saw the light and thought, 'Oh, for God's sake, we need to stop this nonsense; it's going nowhere.' Management didn't want him screwing it up for them. In other words, talking to Phil about, you know, 'Come on, we should screw the knot here and stop being so silly with these drugs and stuff.' I reckon he got elbowed out, to be honest. I don't think it was a conscious decision on his part. Maybe it was. It wouldn't surprise me if it was because Frank is a good man. But maybe he did decide enough is enough, I'm out of here. But I think he might've gotten a shot from the management — because anybody else did. Anybody who threatened Phil's sort of dominance of the situation, especially road crew- wise, were given short shrift, shall we say."

There was definitely cause for concern. Robbo was a constant handful, but it was both Brian Downey and Scott that talked openly about quitting the band. Furthermore, Phil was often in an irascible mood having started to take downers in order to sleep after drinking and doing coke all night. The crew was no better, emerging at the end of every tour without a penny to their names because of all the money spent buying drugs and drink on the road.

Illustrating the trials and tribulations of Thin Lizzy on the road in America is this story from band insider Sören Lindberg. "I remember talking to Chris Morrison and Chris O'Donnell, 'round about 1983, when the band was sort of breaking up, and they were both saying, actually that it was a total nightmare to keep the finances running for Thin Lizzy. Because at that point, they were sort of spending more than they were earning. I think, what happened was that after the success of *Jailbreak* and the albums in the mid-'70s, the band, and very much Phil Lynott, wasn't interested in touring with a bus. He wanted to fly; he wanted to have first-class hotels. The American tours they did, they could have made a lot of money. A lot of other bands went around in a bus and sort of saved money, didn't have to pay for hotels, whereas Thin Lizzy was always flying and always staying in hotels and spending money. The boys were having a good time, obviously, but they didn't really think about the money situation."

"Robbo told me a story about when they were in Las Vegas, and they had a night off in Las Vegas, which was obviously the wrong place to be when you have a night off. So Robbo went to the casino and ended up with Rick Wakeman from Yes, Rick was playing roulette or something, and Robbo didn't have any money, so he went up to the hotel room to talk to the accountant they had with them on the tour. He said, 'Can I get my wages? Because I want to play in the casino.' He went downstairs and again found Rick Wakeman and ended up playing. You get a lot of free drinks when you're sort of the heavy roller and play a lot, and obviously Robbo was just drinking the zombies, and he got severely pissed, and basically he lost all his wages for the whole tour, in one night in Las Vegas."

"Phil wouldn't do it," affirms Robbo, on the band's lack of tour buses and why? "Because he likes fuckin' women too much (laughs). I mean, don't tell me there's any other reason for it, because it made no financial sense, for us as a support act, to fly everywhere, right? I mean that basically took all the money out of the tour. But he refused to go on a bus, simply because, I mean, how are you going to pull a bird when you've got to get on the bus and bugger off? But if you fly, you've got a hotel room; there you go (laughs). He was a Romeo you know (laughs). Romeo and the lonely bus."

Robbo wasn't the only one prone to cause trouble, says Scott, putting himself at the centre of this one. "In Chicago, one time... because the mafia owned all the limousines and all that, after the show, you know, there were a lot of fans around and people wanting to get autographs. I'd had a fair bit to drink, and the rest of the guys were in the car and I'm still signing autographs, and the car starts to take off, right? All I could see was a couple hundred fans around me, and the car's leaving. So I started pounding on this car, he's still not stopping, and I ended up kicking the fucking door four or five times, and the guy stopped. I guess I put a few welts in the door. The driver was well pissed off, and I basically told him to go fuck himself because he was leaving me. So the next day we get out, it's the same guy, we're driving to the airport, and the guy all of a sudden makes a left turn off the freeway and down to this really seedy area of the docks. He parks up in front of these huge wooden doors, and two of the biggest fucking guys you ever saw in your life come out, walking shoulder to shoulder, right to our car, and the window gets rolled down, and this big-ass fuckin' head that was blocking the sun, sticks his head in and says, 'Right, which one of you guys is Scott?' (laughs). I'm thinking, holy crap, man, this guy's going to kick the shit out of me. Chris O'Donnell said, 'Oh, oh, come on, let's sort this out.' These two guys took Chris behind these wooden doors, and I didn't think we were ever going to see the fuckin' dude again. He just walked out, and I think he just paid them a fair few bucks to get their door fixed and that was the end of that. But you could see that these mafia-type guys, if they wanted to do you harm, they could easily do it and feel no remorse whatsoever. Don't fuck with our shit, because we will kick the shit out of you."

"Fights were happening all the time," continues Gorham. "Once, in Wyoming, where we had just got done with the show, and the promoter just loved us to death, right? He said, 'Do you guys want to go anywhere?' 'Yeah, yeah.' 'Well here, take my pink convertible Cadillac, and drive it anywhere you want.' So we took one of the local guys, and we went to this fucking cowboy bar, man. It was like a real shit-kicker cowboy bar. Where there was a sea of cowboy ass and shit-kicker cowboy boots, and as soon as we walked in, I knew we were in trouble, man. Because there were about a thousand people in there and it seemed like everybody went silent at once. Phil was the only black guy in the whole place. But you know, it seemed like it settled down, and that it was going to be okay. I walked to one side of the bar and Phil is in the middle, and all of a sudden I heard a smashing glass. I thought... the red flags were up for me now. I'm ready for anything. I see Phil over there leaning against the bar, and a circle has formed around him and this guy is in the karate stance (laughs). Phil's looking at him and he's laughing. This guy's going, 'Come on motherfucker, come on, I'll fuckin' take you.' Phil says, 'Now come on, man, you don't want to'... Pow and just laid him out!

(laughs). It was the end of the fight. So the old karate Jet Li thing didn't quite fly. But things like that would be happening all the time. I can remember saying in several interviews, I think before Thin Lizzy, I had been in maybe one or two fights, now it seemed like there was a fight every other week."

After Frank's departure, Thin Lizzy were back in the UK for a full-on blanketing in November and December to close out the year, with Robbo, incredibly, screwing up his hand for the third time in not much more than a year.

"Well, yeah, that was an accident," cringes Robbo. "It wasn't a fight or anything. I was... I'm actually not going to go into that story because it's just so stupid (laughs). It was a thing with a flick knife and a girl, and farting around, just being silly, and she wanted me to show her some particular moves, as far as taking it off of somebody. When you think about it, it's absolutely ridiculous (laughs). So I thought, 'Okay, wait, you've got the knife, and you try to stab me, and I take the knife off you, okay?' So I was just doing some of my Taekwondo on her. Swedish girl, a lovely girl called Lena who I was very much in love with. I didn't think, grabbed her wrist, but I didn't do it as hard as I would have done it if it would have been real. So she was holding the knife upside down, so the blade was facing upwards, right, (laughs), and she pulled the blade back and it just sliced my right thumb open. She was gutted. I went, 'Oh, it's okay'."

"I thought I'd better put a plaster on it," continues Brian. "Of course it needed about six or seven stitches, so I went to the doctor and got it stitched up, at the hospital and of course we had a gig the next night. I think it was in Southend, actually, here in Essex, where I am now (note: last gig ever at The Kursaal Ballroom, Southend, December 17th, 1977). On "Johnny", I think it was, at the gig the next night, I couldn't do all the pickup switching, which I do like a hundred times, to go from the heavy guitar to clean guitar, you know what I mean? Because I had turned up at the gig with a Band-Aid; it was more like a plaster cast thing, and the boys are, 'Oh, for God's sake, Robbo, what have ya done?' I'm like, 'I'm not telling.' Because it was just so stupid. It was just dumb. But it wasn't Lena's fault. It was my fault. So you hold your hands up and say, Jesus. A really stupid thing to do (laughs)."

2

LIVE AND DANGEROUS

"This is not Kiss"

Lizzy entered 1978 well and truly spent. Morale was low, but this was papered over by evolving plans to issue a live album. Visconti and the boys in the band were right chuffed with the mounds of live tape they had been amassing through '76 and '77. Looking around, they could see that live albums were saving and reviving careers everywhere, evidenced by the happy receptions afforded Blue Öyster Cult's *On Your Feet Or On Your Knees*, *Kiss' Alive!*, Rush's *All The World's A Stage*, Uriah Heep's *Live*, *Frampton Comes Alive!* and Ted Nugent's *Double Live Gonzo!*. It was just the thing to do, particularly if you were a hard rock act.

Meanwhile Phil worked more deliberately than ever on plans for a solo album, recording (basically with Lizzy members) on January 21st and 22nd at Ramport, and on February 21st at Good Earth — demo and sometimes better than demo takes of tracks such as 'A Night In The Life Of A Blues Singer' (issued as a b-side in '85), 'Rock Your Love' a.k.a. 'Rockula', 'Ode To A Black Man', 'Spanish Guitar', 'Parisienne Walkways', 'Are You Ready', 'Blackmail', 'Waiting For An Alibi', 'Fanatical Fascists', 'Hate', 'With Love, Black Rose', 'Got To Give It Up', 'Toughest Street In Town' and the slow blues version of 'Don't Believe A Word'.

These sessions morphed into both Philip and Brian helping out Gary on his *Back In The Streets* solo album, which would eventually be issued in December of that year. Phil's 'Fanatical Fascists' would make the cut, as would 'Don't Believe A Word' and 'Parisienne Walkways', which would become a Top 10 hit.

"Every hit single Gary had, Philip was involved in it," chuckles Frank Murray, "especially 'Parisienne Walkways'. That was a very calculated move by Phil, to do that. What I mean is, the instrumental of that had been hanging around for a long time. I remember I was in his flat, and Philip was playing it and one day, Philip decided to put lyrics to this. So he made it his song as well. Then Gary had a hit. But it was like, you couldn't have that a hit without me doing that, you know what I mean? You had the melody all right, but I had to put the lyrics to it to make it a hit."

As a bit of trivia about these sessions, first off, beginning with the future *Black Rose* material, 'With Love' sounds very much like the version recorded a year later for *Black Rose*, except for the fact that the lyrics are almost entirely different. 'Got To Give It Up' was laid-back, languid, a bit conventional with respect to guitar sound, but there's a prominent bongo drum track turning it decidedly Santana. As well, there are some amusing lyric differences, particularly the part about the easy chair. Also with a raft of different lyrics is 'Waiting For An Alibi', which also is distinguished in this version by a double time or "snare on one and three" beat from Brian Downey come chorus time; otherwise, it's pretty similar to the eventual definitive take. Finally there's *Black Rose*, which is shown here to have started much shorter, with less parts, and also slower. Also quite shocking is the harmonica added by Huey Lewis. One can also hear Phil trying out different chunks of lyrics.

On the rarities front, there was the unremarkable twee pop metal of 'Rockula' or 'Rock Your Love', which apparently was a Jimmy Bain composition. 'Cold Black Night' was a bit of a swinging funkster, but toughened with a biting accompanying riff. 'Blackmail', a bit of a punky rocker with a tough guy/film noir theme actually shows up officially later on the first Wild Horses album, credited to Jimmy Bain and Brian Robertson. Finally, Hate gets a pretty well-arranged, full-bodied workout — one could see this track not making the final cut for the *Black Rose* album perhaps due to its slight inferiority to two loosely similar songs on that record, namely 'Toughest Street In Town' and 'Get Out Of Here'.

"We've been in the studio putting down some new material," Downey had been telling Hot Press. "Originally, it was for Phil's solo album. We've done about five or six tracks, one or two of which he wants to use as a solo single. The rest of the stuff may be on Thin Lizzy's album. If Phil wants to use some stuff on his own with Gary, it's up to him, but it's easy to take Gary off and put Brian on. It's a new direction for Thin Lizzy, maybe. One or two of them are more laid-back — they're not out and out rockers. A lot of people describe us as heavy metal, which surprises me. I wouldn't like to see the band get into a position where it had to depend on hard rock material to sell. Maybe if we slowed down a bit on stage, interspersed the hard rock material with other material, the way we used to... when it started, Lizzy wasn't a hard rock band."

On the personal side, Phil had started a relationship with one Caroline Crowther, who had been working with famous British publicist Tony Brainsby. Phil found himself moving house yet again, helping her (almost) convert to Catholicism and by April, making her with child.

In the press, Phil was beginning to assert a sense of separation between what his solo material was going to sound like versus the evolving canon of Lizzy. As well, he started to take a dismissive stance against *Johnny The Fox*. "*Jailbreak* is a more complete album than *Johnny The Fox*," Philip told Niall Stokes of Hot Press. "When I was writing the material for *Johnny The Fox*, I was in hospital so I couldn't work out the other parts — I just had an acoustic guitar and voice so that was all I could use to show them to the other members of the band. When I was writing the songs, it was just after I'd had hepatitis and I was really weak. But then I'm glad that it worked out like that 'cos I couldn't have a song like 'Massacre'. That was when I got really mad at religion, the priest coming around the hospital, 'Can I offer you a little solace?' I'm no longer trying to make a Sgt. Pepper, which was the great fallacy. When I'm doing an album, I'm not necessarily thinking, 'This is something that's going down forever.' People forget albums very fast. I'm on my ninth album now; I no longer think that people remember if you make a mistake on the fourth bar of the third track of the second side or whatever! When I make an album now, it's more a reflection of how I feel at the time."

"I'd say that the band stuff, especially now that we've done *Bad Reputation*, will get harder and heavier — a lot harder and heavier, 'cos we've done a lot of mid-tempo songs recently. But my solo album, which I'm definitely going to do, will take in the soft melodic stuff. I think Lizzy are particularly good at playing the heavier numbers. Also I think I haven't interpreted the soft stuff as I'd like to. Working solo, I have complete control over the stuff, so it's if it suited the mood, I could use strings or use other people. Like I was talking to Terry Woods and I'd like to use Terry's voice and my voice together. And maybe his banjo playing."

In another interview from that same year, Phil indeed picked up on this curious but valid feeling that there was something light or laid-back about *Johnny The Fox*, even if mathematically, riff for riff, it really wasn't any less heavy metal than *Jailbreak* or *Bad Reputation*, in fact, arguably a shade heftier than either of them!

"We did *Johnny The Fox*, which I consider to be a mellow album — it's much mellower than *Jailbreak* or Fighting. We'd done these two heavy albums, and I thought, well, if we bring out another heavy album, people are just gonna say, these guys are heavy metal and nothing else.

Plus I was ill, and I think that contributed to me slowing down. So we came up with *Johnny The Fox*, which had songs like 'Borderline' and 'Sweet Marie', which were nice mellow songs, which totally freaked all the heavy metal kids that were really wanting us to keep rocking. Bad Rep is up again, but it's still not as up as *Jailbreak*. It's more complete, a total album. Now that we've got Bad Rep out of the way, the next one will either be live or a heavy one."

"I didn't want to do a live one right away," continued Phil, "because after Peter Frampton doing it, I thought everybody would be jumping on the bandwagon and I thought it was a bit much to precondition the American audience where — let's have it right — the biggest record sales are, to our act, when we actually hadn't headlined in America. It would have been a bit much to say, 'Here's what we're like live on record and when you come to our gigs, this is how you must respond.' I'd much prefer it to be a natural development. We're gonna record some of the gigs in America and up in Canada, and we've got some recordings we've done in England on the last tour, and everybody will know the response we get worldwide."

Music aside however, in interview after interview, Phil usually gets around to some sort of treatise that let's slip or otherwise implies the importance of the ladies. "The biggest paradox that the press have is trying to explain what we're like or give us an angle," mused Phil. "'Cause Scott appeals to the guys on the level he's a great guitarist and they all like his style. The chicks all like him 'cause of his hair. I went down to the Vortex the other night, a very punky club, and a lot of the punks are going, 'Hey, what are you doing down here?' And I go, 'Get off, 'cause I don't give a fuck — don't mess me around.' So after a while... they're young kids and they're really nice, really; I get on great with a lot of them. So they're saying, 'We really dig that guy, Scott, 'cause he won't get his haircut and spike it out.' They really respect him for it. And these punk rock chicks, one of them from The Slits was saying, 'Yeah, I think he's really cute.' He has this amazing sex appeal to all the girls and it goes right across the board. Brian is the baby of the band. A lot of the chicks go for him because he's the baby and he has the dog with him, and yet he's one of the tearaways in the band — he's forever getting into fights. It's just totally bizarre: two Irishmen, a Scotsman and an American. Brian Downey's the quietest of the lot, but put him on a drum kit and he kicks like mad and then there's myself."

What's this about a dog?!

"That was a stuffed dog," remembers Scott with chuckle. "Derek the dog. Geez, everybody wanted to take that dog and stuff a firecracker up its ass. Blow it to smithereens. But Brian would use that dog so he could pick up women. He would walk over to them and say, 'Here, can you guard my dog for a while?' And the chick would be stuck with this fucking dirty dog. He never washed the damn thing. Then he would go over and get a few drinks, and this chick would still be with this stuffed dog. So that was his pickup line. Derek the dog."

Fun and games aside, Lizzy had a live album to get on with, so there's Phil on the cover, captured full splendour, on his knees to please like Hendrix, on the seminal double live album that was to become *Live And Dangerous*. The full-band live shot on the back cover was supposed to be used for the front, and the guys were right miffed when the Phil-alone pose was chosen by the label instead. Making up for it somewhat is the presence of fully 72 additional shots, through the gate and the inner sleeves. The expense was taken however, 'cos management was convinced that the album would be a smash, Chris and Chris chuffed by the muscular rhythm guitar chug of the tapes, particularly the Hammersmith masters. Additional slant to the Chalkie Davis photo spread was the idea that all those photos in succession almost acted as a visual representation of a full Thin Lizzy show. The title derives from a conversation that Chris O'Donnell had had with Clash manager Bernie Rhodes, who had been raving about how dangerous, meaning incendiary pretty much, Clash were live in concert.

Contrary to the credits, none of the record's sizzling and electric selections hail from the Seneca College Fieldhouse gig in Toronto from October 28, '77 — that was stuck there as a tax dodge, again the idea being that the band had to spend a certain amount of time away from England for portions of their income not to be taxed there. Rather, the album consists of songs from three sources, one being two shows conducted a week earlier than Toronto, at the Tower Theater in Upper Darby, a burb on the west side of Philadelphia. Attendance at these gigs hovered around 3,000, and the event was mainly documented for a King Biscuit Flower Hour broadcast. In addition to these two outlets for the recordings, 2008 saw the release of *Still Dangerous: Live At The Tower Theatre Philadelphia 1977*, erroneous spelling of "theater" included. A second source was the band's sold-out three-date Hammersmith Odeon stand back on November 14 — 16th, 1976, Clover supporting.

The final source was a special gig set up at the Rainbow in London, recorded for TV and also released as the *Live And Dangerous* video, a 60-minute affair most notable for the inclusion of naff non-LP cut 'Me And The Boys'. This was the only show for the band in '78 until scatter dates in May followed by a brief UK leg in June, which corresponded with the release of the live album, June 2, 1978. Highlight of this swing would be two nights at Empire Pool, Wembley, supported by Horslips — on the first night, U2 bassist Adam Clayton and the band's manager Paul McGuinness were spotted backstage. Fond memories for Phil playing Manchester as well, that northern city being a second home for the band, given that Phil's mom Philomena ran the notorious Showbiz hotel there, and that Phil always made sure members of his beloved Manchester United were well represented at the gigs.

"*Live And Dangerous* was the first album that actually showed what we were all about, in actual fact," figures Scott Gorham, on a record that is widely cited as one of the great live records of all time. "I don't think that any of the studio albums up to that point were actually able to capture what we really did, what we really sounded like and how we really played on stage."

"I think basically the band was on top form," agrees Brian Robertson, "although I don't necessarily agree with the choice of tracks. I think there were better takes of certain tracks. But most of those decisions are out of your hands, really. However much Phil would like to paint it as a democracy, it was not a democracy (laughs), by any stretch of the imagination. So whatever you said, 'All right, we'll take that on board,' and then you could just kiss it goodbye."

Asked whether the guys, while touring, were pretty sure that the follow-up to *Bad Reputation* was going to be a live spread, Brian answers in the affirmative, explaining that, "We wouldn't have been carrying around trucks for all that time if we weren't sure about it (laughs). Because I mean, listen, we recorded everything, for about a year, so you're talking about all around the states, Toronto, up in your country, all in the States, Europe, Britain. You know, you don't hire 24-track trucks unless you're actually serious about releasing a live album. So yeah, it was obviously a predetermined idea. In any case, it was the right thing to do. We all knew that."

"The mood was very buoyant," explains Downey. "Because we were on the road for quite a few years, Scott Gorham, Brian Robertson, Phil and me.

We obviously had problems before that with guitar players leaving, so when we got Brian and Scott in, it stabilised the band. We were playing a lot of gigs in the UK and Ireland and all of Europe, and we had a lot of really good gigs under our belt, but yeah, we felt very confident playing *Live And Dangerous*, because it was a culmination of a couple of albums. Because we wanted to get in there and make it a double album, because there are lots of bands around like The Who, who had live albums, and we were very, very confident we could do it and do better, and we were honestly proven, because it turned out really well. It's one of those albums that sounds really good even now."

What drives Robbo nuts, as we shall see, is producer Tony Visconti's recollection of the album, concerning to what extent the tapes were augmented by studio fixes. "He comes out and says 75% of the album is re-recorded," fumes Robbo. "But I'm sorry, I don't know what drugs he's on. It's bollocks! Right? Not only is it bollocks. I mean, I love Tony, right? He was at my fucking wedding, for Christ sake, right? I love the guy, I think he's a brilliant, brilliant producer, but where he comes off with this, I just don't understand it."

"Let's just put the record straight here, because I think I should, really. I'm a very loud guitar player. I've always had sound engineers bitching at me for being too loud on stage, right? The band itself was bloody loud, okay?

You've got two bass stacks next to the drum kit, right? You've got three open mics at the front, for backing vocals and lead vocals. So put all that together, and you tell me, how does he re-record 75% of the live tracks? It's totally impossible. It's physically impossible. My guitar is bleeding all over the vocal mics, all over the bass mics right next to my stacks, all over the drum mics. It's not physically possible to start segregating all the instruments. There is Tony Visconti saying, 'Yeah, the only thing they didn't do was replace any drums' (laughs). How could he? When I heard him say that, I just thought... well I felt sorry for him, to be honest. Because I just felt, there's something going on in his head, right?"

"Now I remember, in Good Earth studios, his studio, replacing a couple of bits of backing vocals on 'Southbound', which we recorded at sound checks, so there's no audience there, right? We could replace a couple of bits and pieces. I remember doing that, and a couple of bum notes on backing vocals, just to boost them up, but you couldn't get rid of the entire backing vocal, because it's already in there, right? But he's saying that all these guitar solos and guitar parts and blah blah blah — no. It's total fiction."

"The reason, as you asked in the first place, why the album was a hit, was because it was live," continues Brian. "This is not Kiss. This isn't going in and re-recording and sticking an audience on it. Right, we stuck an audience on 'Southbound', to use it as an extra track; we took the audience from one of the other things and stuck it on there, so that's a bit of a cheat. But it's an extra track for the punters, so... it was great live, albeit, in a sound check situation, right? But what Visconti has to say on... I'm sorry, but I guess me and him will never speak again. Because I've said this on television, that you're completely off your tits, mate. If you ask any of the other boys, they'll tell you exactly the same thing. The majority of that... I mean, Scott replaced a couple of guitars, like three notes or something, something that could be hidden in the original recording, but you cannot replace whole parts of guitars! Whole vocals, in a live situation like that. It's physically impossible. It might be physically possible now, if you've got like Perspex screens up against the drum so there's no bleeding from the bass — that's entirely possible."

"But I can tell you that the best version of 'Still In Love With You', we couldn't use, because Phil had an MXR phaser, an MXR 90 phaser, and he had accidentally left it on fast. Now, the guitar solo in that was totally, in my opinion, brilliant. But we couldn't use the damn bass, because it was going 'bbbrrr' and it was so loud it was going over his vocal. Now, the only other way around that would be to take the DI, the direct injection bass, right and all the rest of it. But that 'bbbrrr' would still be going through my mics in my amps and the drum amps and everything else. So, much to my disgust, we had to let that one go, and I was really pissed off, because that was one of the best solos I probably ever played, and I was so proud of it, but I couldn't use it because of the bass."

Sören Lindberg is in full agreement. "A highlight of Brian's recorded work, any time, is 'Still In Love With You', from the live recording. Being such a fanatic that I am, I've got so many live tapes from those days. I would agree, actually, with Robbo, that maybe what's on *Live And Dangerous*, that's a classic guitar solo, but there were nights when he was actually better. Because he tended to change certain things from night to night, depending on emotion. I know that it's basically Gary Moore's guitar solo that he copied, more or less. But he made it his own, and it's played with so much emotion, and again it's within a very emotional song."

"But yeah, I think Scott probably overdubbed maybe one or two guitar licks, and that's about it," continues Robertson. "But according to Visconti, Phil came in wanting to overdub all his basses, and he did, and according to him, me and Scott came in and said, 'Well, if he could fix his stuff, we can fix ours.' That's absolute bollocks. I don't know, it's fantasy to me. Brian Downey has said as well that it's absolute nonsense. I don't know why Tony says that, because it makes him look a bit daft, really."

"So you tell me who's telling the truth. Visconti? I don't think so. None of it adds up or makes any sense whatsoever, and in fact logistically and technically and in every other sense. I don't know where his brain is at. I know he got into existentialism. Maybe that's got something to do with it, I don't know. I'm not quite sure what it actually means. As far as I'm actually concerned is that it just means people go mental. And turn into an idiot."

"I think you'll find that most of the ex-Lizzy members are a bit surprised and shocked about what Tony had to say about *Live And Dangerous*, today, with all the overdubs and whatnot," sums up

Lindberg. "I've heard the original recording of all 17 songs, and yes, there are edits, and yes there are overdubs, but not as much as he seems to think there were. Again, I think Robbo was very happy working with Tony Visconti. He's a very professional producer. Tony, as well, being a musician, it was easy to connect with him. Tony Visconti used to be a bass player so he knew what he was talking about when he was talking to Robbo and Scott about guitars and stuff like that."

"I certainly can't remember any problems with Tony Visconti on *Live And Dangerous*, when he mixed and recorded that album," adds Brian Downey, who nonetheless agrees with Robertson's view on the matter. "Maybe the periods when I wasn't in the studio, on *Black Rose*, with Kit and Phil and Tony, there could've been an argument or two. But my recollection was no, we didn't have any problems with Tony Visconti whatsoever. I found Tony excellent in the studio, in all aspects of recording, no problem at all. It was only later when he started coming up with some of these fantasies where he said we were overdubbing *Live And Dangerous*. This was years later, this happened. His memory might have played tricks on him, saying there were all sorts of overdubs and the album was 75% recorded in the studio, which is total fallacy. That wasn't the case at all. But apart from that, I had no problems with Tony, and I don't remember anybody else having any problems with him either (laughs)."

Highlights to the *Live And Dangerous* album are many. Fans have always celebrated how 'Cowboy Song' explodes into 'The Boys Are Back In Town', as well as the taste we get of 'Cowboy Song' within 'Rosalie', therein billed as 'Cowgirl's Song'. 'Rosalie' would constitute the album's chief single, issued a month in advance of the album, reaching No.20 in the UK and No.14 in Ireland, and prompting a trip to Top Of The Pops for the lads. "I went on and on at him to do it," says Phil, recalling his tour dates with Bob Seger, penner of 'Rosalie'. "But do you know, in six weeks, he didn't play it once.

So we started doing it ourselves, and somehow it's been the only number by someone else to make it through our rehearsals and sound checks and into the show."

"The most challenging would've been 'Sha La La', the drum solo, because I tried to vary it most nights," recalls Downey concerning another of his personal favourites. "It was a challenge just to find new ideas to put into that solo to make it more interesting every night." Indeed 'Sha La La' represents one of the great positive features of *Live And Dangerous*, namely the power boost given to the very oldest material, songs like 'Suicide' and 'The Rocker' — of note, the latter is the only selection from the three albums that comprise the Eric Bell era of the band.

Strangely, the *Bad Reputation* record is given short shrift. Only 'Dancing In The Moonlight' and 'Southbound' hail from the band's then freshest record, conspicuous absence being any of the three heaviest numbers. The Still Dangerous set (from 30 years later!) somewhat makes up for this curio, offering 'Soldier Of Fortune' with some novel lead bits, and 'Opium Trail', rendered in a radically altered "chug" arrangement, eschewing the studio version's sinewy, Egypto lead weaves.

Perhaps the album's chief highlight however is the inclusion of a brisk, non-LP rocker called 'Are You Ready'. Far be it for Lizzy fans to ever complain about fresh metal from the boys, but this one indeed lacked full-on finish or craft or the band's usual level of the remarkable, its simplicity and brevity evoking similarities with Cheap Trick's 'Hello There', also heavy, also a bit tossed-off.

"I think that was just one of those songs that worked live," agrees Scott, dismissively. "I don't know if it would work in the studio. You never know, I might try it on the next album. It would be changed a lot, believe me. It was one of those kinds of songs that was basically written for the road, period, full stop. But somehow it became a really known song. Everybody knows, 'are you ready?' It's a phrase that everybody uses all the time. You know, are you ready? A lot of rock bands even still use that to this day. So they probably got that from us (laughs). But yeah, it was one of those songs that we used to play at sound checks; it evolved during sound checks and rehearsals, and like I say, it never made it to the studio, on any studio album. But it's one of those songs that's got a punch to it, and that's why we like to start out the set with it, because it lets everybody know that Thin Lizzy is in the building."

Live And Dangerous included, as well, a worse example of this idea of songs not really good enough to cut it on a studio album, namely 'Baby Drives Me Crazy', while *Still Dangerous* included that one as well as the sub-par 'Me And The Boys'.

"Those two songs were written flat-out just for live," says Scott. "We just figured that we had a lot more songs in us than those two kinds of songs. They were just two songs that came out of consecutive jam sessions and all that; it was like an end-of-set kind of song where everybody could have a blow-out. Phil could fuck around with the audience, make them sing and just have a good time with it. There was never any talk of getting serious and getting them into the studio. But good question. No one's ever asked me that before."

Did I neglect to mention 'Still In Love With You'? Surely I'd be remiss to do so, as of course Brian calls it out in the quotes back a bit, as do most fans and pundits when talking about *Live And Dangerous*, lauding this rendition in hushed tones. Personally, I consider it one of the lamest songs of the Thin Lizzy catalogue and no "inspired performance" thereof can paper over that personal sentiment. Next.

All told, *Live And Dangerous* captured the attention of the record-buying public, who had proven time and time again, much to the surprise of those in the industry, an appetite for this sort of thing. The album hit an astounding No.2 in the UK (kept from number one for weeks by the smash *Saturday Night Fever* soundtrack), going double platinum there, the album's eventual sales of over 600,000 copies no doubt helped by a blitz of TV ads rumoured to have cost a half million pounds. American audiences, conversely, pushed it to a mere No.84 placement.

After leading with the significant business fact that in the US, *Live And Dangerous* was the band's first album with Warner Bros., John Millward from Rolling Stone wrote that, "While it effectively documents the boys-with-blazing-guitars style of the five previous Mercury discs from which most of these songs were taken, it's also clearly meant to be the breakout, double-LP sampler from a group that failed to consolidate the front-line success of their 1976 single, 'The Boys Are Back In Town'. Though such a package is ideal for those who passed on the earlier records, it's still a baby step by band that needs a giant leap. *Live And Dangerous* works as a cogent commercial vehicle by avoiding filler, not because anything significant has been added. But the holding pattern that Thin Lizzy established with *Jailbreak* is indicative of the stylistic problems inherent in many solid but unarguably derivative rock groups. These guys have their roots down cold, and have embroidered them with a neat, guitar-toting street-gang image. But so far, they've yet to give us an album upon which future rockers will build."

Eight gigs after the release of *Live And Dangerous*, Brian Robertson would fall out of the band, this time for good, first clue being that he was not along for the band's May '78 Bahamas trip, where Phil did some work on his solo tracks. "You know, did some drugs," corrects Robbo, who nonetheless admits his own aggressive tendencies were caused by near continuous swilling of Johnnie Walker Black Label punctuated by snorts of speed. "There wasn't an awful a lot of work done in the Bahamas, I can tell you that. I know that for a fact." Scott and Huey Lewis both concur, the trip turning out to be a big mess of drinking, drugging, sun-tanning and clubbing and little else, the supposedly earnest and hard-working Phil as remiss and missing in action as the next guy. One piece of workmanship achieved, however, would be the song 'Tattoo (Giving It All Up For Love)' which would show up on both Huey Lewis And The News's second album, Picture This as well as on Phil's first solo album, *Solo In Soho*, in both places credited to Phil alone.

So was Robertson no longer a member of Thin Lizzy at this point? "I'm really not sure, and I probably wasn't sure in May '78 either," laughs Brian. "Because I was a bit volatile, they kept me under tenterhooks, really. Didn't tell me an awful lot of what was going on. Not that I gave a shit at the time, to be honest. I probably do more now than I did then, because it was not the way I would treat my band. But then again, we all grew. I think they thought I was a loose cannon, which I guess is entirely correct. But maybe you should use things like that to create other things, you know? Instead of going, 'Sorry, loose cannon, keep him in the dark, don't tell him shit,' right? Maybe if they hadn't done that I would've taken a little more responsibility and not been such a loose cannon. Then the only loose cannon side of it was when I was supposed to play a solo, which is exactly the way I play now. When I'm in a studio playing a solo, you can guarantee I'm a loose cannon."

Of course, Robbo was driving the band around the bend on the road as well. "Yes, well, we'd sit around a backstage, just shooting the breeze," recalls tour manager Frank Murray. "Then there would come a time, people would just say, I suppose, get ready, you're on in half an hour or something. Everybody would just start dressing up in whatever clothing they were going to get into, and then tuning could be tough, sitting there. It could be a tough thing. I remember Brian taking an awful lot of time to tune up. It would just seem to take forever. Half an hour, isn't that thing in tune yet? You'd be going past your stage time. Maybe you should've been on stage ten minutes ago…"

What's certain however is that come July 6th 1978, Robbo was playing a gig with Thin Lizzy that would be his last.

"It was in Ibiza in a bullring," recalls Robertson. "It fits maybe eight to ten thousand, I'd say? Anyway, we took the whole band and road crew out there, for a holiday, and we thought we would do the gig to pay for the holiday. I think we spent about a week over there, ten days, and hired a villa. I got severely burned, because I fell asleep by the side of the pool, for about six hours in the blazing sun, so by the time I got on stage, my entire back… I remember crazy pain, breaking out, pus everywhere, and I'm taking painkillers. I couldn't put the guitar strap on, so I had a water-soaked towel over where the guitar strap went — it wasn't the best of situations (laughs), no."

"We threw this gig in because we needed some time off," laughs Gorham, "We rented this big old villa down there, and it had a beautiful swimming pool; the beach was just down the road.

You've got four guys who've been on the road for six months, their backs are the same colour as their ass, as far as the tan line goes. So nobody has seen any sun for quite a while, so of course we go out there, sit beside the pool, and Robertson, man, he just sat up there for hours and got fuckin' cooked! I don't think he'd ever actually had sunburn before (laughs). But he got burned really bad, and all he could wear were these Japanese kimonos, and to put the guitar on with the strap and all that would just kill. So he learned a big lesson that day, like when to get out of the fucking sun. But we all got pretty wrecked there, in Ibiza. It was time off. Like I say, we'd been on the road for two months and we were hammered, tired-wise. So once the chains came off, we just went crazy."

"There was a lot of other stuff going on there too," continues Robbo. "Suzi Quatro, who was backing up, was a complete pain in the butt. Charlie, who is the guy who got me into Thin Lizzy in the first place, who I went to school with... they were supposed to be off stage because there was a curfew, so Charlie basically pulled the main plug on Suzi Quatro (laughs). Then we found our trucks had all their tyres slashed the next morning. Interesting times."

"Although I did meet the actor Terry Thomas, on that trip," laughs Brian. "He was a very English actor with a sort of handlebar moustache who always played the cad in all the movies. I'd got completely stoned and went off on this little Bultaco 250 trails bike, and basically jumped through a hedge, which then led about 20 foot down onto his patio, where he was sitting with three beautiful busty young girls in bikinis. Keeping in mind that the guy is probably about 75 at this point, right? They're sitting there, and I just landed with this Bultaco on the side of the pool, trashed the bike, and he invited me for a drink. So I had a drink with him, got back on the Bultaco, went straight through the hole I made in his hedge, drove up to my villa. Phil wasn't staying there because he decided he was going to move into town because all the women were there, right? Typical Phil, that. So anyway, there were a few birds up on the side of the pool at the villa, so I drove up there, tripping on acid, which was given to me by the record company guy, Dave Houseman. He said, 'Try this,' and I'd never tried it before, so I was totally out of my mind for days. So I decided I was going to ride this Bultaco up the steps, onto the side of the pool, skid it to a halt and get off and say, 'Hey, hi girls.' Real cool, like, you know? Anyway, I drove up, I got up the steps and skidded to a halt, but the back wheel went in the pool. The bike ended up at the bottom of the pool and so did I, and the girls left, so that was that and this is all before the gig (laughs)."

"Of course I didn't, no," replies Brian, asked if he knew that Ibiza was to be his last gig with the band. "I never knew when it was going to be my last gig. I had so many last gigs with Lizzy, right? (laughs). It was a weekly occurrence. You get used to it. 'Oh, you're fired again.' 'Okay then. Cool'."

3

BLACK ROSE

"I can't work with this sort of hypocrisy"

Phil celebrated the departure of Brian Robertson from Thin Lizzy by joining a punk rock band. Or maybe he joined a punk band to celebrate the reinstatement of Gary Moore within the ranks of Lizzy. In any event, that particular announcement was made on July 30th 1978, the day after a casual roustabout show by The Greedy Bastards, also known as The Greedies, when a kinder moniker was required.

The Electric Ballroom in Camden, London was ground zero for the first Greedies gig, the band consisting of Phil, Gary, Scott and Brian, as well as Chris Spedding, Jimmy Bain, and a couple of Sex Pistols, Steve Jones and Paul Cook. The line-up would, unsurprisingly, pare down for the handful of scattered dates to come, and one would have to say that the most official would be the gathering of rogues — Phil, Scott, Brian, Paul and Steve — that produced the band's lone spot of output, a festive single called 'A Merry Jingle', backed with 'A Merry Jangle', out just in time for Santa '79.

Recalls Downey, "Phil suggested to me one day... he came up with the idea of recording some stuff with Sid Vicious, Paul Cook, and Steve Jones, and when that was suggested, someone said, 'Well, let's forget about Sid Vicious. Why don't we just get you, Phil, to play the bass, and have a couple of drummers? Get Brian Downey in to play and Scott Gorham on guitar.' We got a couple of gigs under our belts before we got in the studio, and that became The Greedy Bastards. That sort of morphed into The Greedies, because obviously they didn't like Greedy Bastards (laughs). So we went on a mini tour, did some dates in London, some dates in Ireland, and the whole thing went down really well. Then we went into the studio and recorded 'A Merry Jingle', which came out as a single, and it was fun. As well as just doing something apart from Thin Lizzy. That whole period was a lot of fun. The guys became really good friends as well, so it was an interesting period."

"That was a case of just getting a bunch of people together, whoever was around at that time, and all getting together having a blast," remembers the band's other drummer, Paul Cook. "Because when you're in bands, you get stuck in your way and your sound a little bit, and this was just another... not an extension of that, but an area where people could turn up and just have some fun, just let go a little bit. Because as I said, you do get a bit restricted in the sound of your band, and people like to go off and do different stuff and that became The Greedies. It was really just an amalgam of different people who came in and we played live shows and jammed."

"I wouldn't say they were a part of it, but they definitely would empathise with you," continues Paul, summing up Lizzy's place within the punk scene. "There was this attitude that went around, realistic, I suppose, that there were the punk bands and that all the old bands hated them, and didn't like it. But there were a lot of other musicians around, like older musicians, shall we say, that would empathise with the punks, like Phil Lynott and Lemmy from Motörhead, as well as Pete Townsend. They were all into it and they weren't scared of it. It's not that they wanted to get involved in it, but that they'd empathise; it wasn't them and us, as much as people think."

"Yeah, we used to hang around with Steve and Paul," confirms Gary, part of the Greedies later on. "And Sid Vicious used to come around to Phil's house all the time. We knew a lot of those guys, including the Boomtown Rats, who weren't really, really punk but they were from that same era. Phil knew a lot of people from that whole scene."

"Phil had a certain contempt for that overblown, over-hyped rock," notes cover artist Jim Fitzpatrick, recognising the young punk in Phil. "That's why he identified with the Sex Pistols.

You have to remember, rock had gone from Pink Floyd, who I love, down the path of prog rock, Emerson, Lake & Palmer. It was turning into complete pretentious nonsense, for lack of a better word. Some of the bands were doing it brilliantly like Pink Floyd. But some of them were dreadful. All great players, and they were certainly try to make rock more orchestral, but they were moving so far away from their own audiences, and I think pretentious is the only word to describe it. I remember when that big rebellion of the Sex Pistols and the punk rock movement happened, Philip was on their side, and I think they were quite amazed. He felt the way they did, that the whole thing had just turned up its own ass. That's why he got on with them so well. He was the only one of that period, with the only band of that period, that identified with the Sex Pistols. All the others kept going their overblown, hyped way. But I loved him when he joined up with Sex Pistols. That was my perfect band. I would've spent my life listening to them. I loved the vibe as well. I love that rebelliousness. I remember Philip saying to me, after they had played a couple of gigs, 'Geez, I can't play with them anymore.' I said, 'Why not? They're brilliant! They're amazing.' He said, 'Yeah, Jim, but do you have any idea what it's like to be standing there in your fucking leather jeans and people are gobbing at ya? Then look down on my leg and it was green.' Phil was like me — he was clean. That sort of stuff wouldn't appeal to me at all. That was the downside of it."

"Well, it was the whole energy that punk rock brought back into the rock scene," affirms Scott, on the magic of those times. "These were guys that were just irreverent with everything. They didn't give a shit what anybody thought about them. The playing, a lot of times, just wasn't up to scratch, but you know something? Most of the time you didn't care, because you looked at the characters on the stage and they were pretty outrageous guys. They may not have been able to play all that great, but they just gave it hell for leather. It was just so much fun watching a lot of these guys doing what they were doing, and I know both Phil and myself got into the whole character side of the punk machine or genre. We just thought it was great, and that's why the idea of The Greedy Bastards came out. It was Thin Lizzy and the Sex Pistols, and I think we did three or four shows as The Greedy Bastards. It was funny back then, because a lot of the rock bands, when they saw punk coming in, it scared them to death! I think they could almost see the writing on the wall for them. The whole music scene had changed, and now their band is going to die, because of these new guys coming in, these guys called punks. But we embraced the whole thing, just because, like I was saying, the sheer energy these guys were showing, the characters that they came up with, it was showbiz, you know? We just thought it was really fun."

"It did go away," says Downey, referring to the behemoth establishment bands of England, "mainly because most of them just ended up touring America for months on end (laughs). Lots of people were actually leaving the country because of the tax situation as well. See, all these major bands... that's where you had this punk revolution against all these bands. The punks obviously reckoned they were on their high horses, on their big thrones up there, too big for their boots, more or less. That obviously affected the music scene, especially in the UK. These guys had left the country; there was a huge big open gaping chasm there for bands to fill, and that seemed to be the case. Lots of bands started to form around there that weren't necessarily talented, but obviously with that huge gap there, they filled it, yeah. But there again, don't forget, the punks brought in this huge change of attitude to rock music anyway. It was a case of anybody could play these instruments, and they tried. They weren't great musicians by any means, but they were just chancers, they were chancing around, and they knew a few chords, but that's what rock 'n' roll always was. These guys seemed to know this; some of punk was absolute rubbish and some of it was great as well. There were great bands from the punk era. But other bands were absolutely crap. So yeah, there was that gap and it was certainly filled. The sign of the times was there as well. It was a big changing of the guard, don't forget. People were seriously sick of what was happening from the old school, and wanted something completely new, and that was the result. The punk scene seemed to take over."

"Me and Steve got on with Phil really well," continues Paul "Cookie" Cook. "He was a really cool guy. We hung out quite a lot around that time, before he went off the rails a bit later. As I say, he was really supportive of what we were doing, and he was great back then, because we were hated by everyone, including all the musicians, and that was a really good feeling to know that there were people who were into what you're doing, especially respected musicians as well."

What were the circumstances surrounding this Christmas single? "I don't know, really; it was strange, just a bit of fun. I guess we were all playing together around Christmas time, and we had only done a handful of shows, with different people involved. We got together, and we were in the studio one day and we just said, 'Hey, let's put a Christmas song together, just for the crack, and see what happens.' Not to be taken too seriously, but the live shows were good, because people like Chris Spedding would turn up and Bob Geldof would jump up there, and people doing different songs and stuff like that."

"Phil, bless him, absolutely embraced the punk movement," reflects Chris Tsangarides, producer of this single, as well as Lizzy projects to come, "to the extent that we did this Christmas song with the Pistols guys (laughs), and it was hysterical. They actually played one gig at the Electric Ballroom in Camden, and there was no guest list because they were The Greedy Bastards, so, you had to pay (laughs). But I mean, he was very friendly with Paul Cook and Steve Jones and Sid Vicious even, who used to go around his house, hang out quite a lot together."

And no sort of hang-ups from Paul and Steve about long-haired hard rock? "Not a bit! Not a bit of it, no, no, no. Very up for it, very respectful of who they were working with, absolutely. They turned up in very nice clothes. It wasn't like they'd been dragged up off the street."

"We were around at the end of Thin Lizzy really," adds Paul, "and it's a shame what happened to Phil, you know? I didn't realise he was going to go so far over the edge with that stuff. But he was a real party guy. It would always be back to his place after a gig, or after we'd been out. He liked to enjoy himself and have a party and we were always going back there until late, until early into the morning. Those were fun days. All sorts of characters were turning up. He used to like to have a party, shall we say (laughs)."

Demonstrating further scope, Phil would also show up on an indulgent, expensive concept album behemoth called The War Of The Worlds, a Jeff Wayne-commandeered musical rendition of that classic, Phil singing on 'The Spirit Of Man'. Considerably down-market, Phil also guested on notorious junkie Johnny Thunders' So Alone solo album, singing on one track and playing bass on three. In a parallel universe, Brian and Jimmy Bain got serious about Wild Horses, at this early stage the line-up including Kenney Jones and Jimmy McCulloch (Stone The Crows, Wings), both recently with a reformed Small Faces. Brian Robertson also guests on an album by Pete French called Ducks In Flight, issued on Polydor in Germany.

On August 8th 1978, Lizzy set sail for an American tour; the opening dates as special guests to Kansas. Brian Downey, who had "personal matters" to attend to in Dublin, was replaced by Mark Nauseef for the tour. Word was that Brian was returning to Dublin to look after his sick son but he admits it was just pure exhaustion on his part, especially in the face of proposed Australian dates.

Nauseef, from the same upstate New York area as Ronnie James Dio and the Bouchard brothers of Blue Öyster Cult fame, had cut his teeth as part of Ronnie's early honky-tonk band Elf before joining Ian Gillan's jazz-fusion Ian Gillan Band. Post-touring duties for Lizzy, he would extricate himself along with Gary Moore and form peppy one-record rock outfit G-Force. Interestingly, Terry Bozzio almost got the gig, but not only did he demand too much money, he wanted to take his wife Dale on the road, out of the question with this gang, Phil remembering all too well how hauling along significant others on the road was part of the reason Eric Bell had flamed out of the first version of the band. "I memorised an entire Thin Lizzy album in three days," complained Terry, who had been balancing the Lizzy situation with thoughts of joining prog supergroup UK. "Totally blew them away, and they didn't want to pay me any money! They only offered me half of what I expected. Apart from that, the lifestyles were different. They're into getting stoned and trashing hotel rooms. I go more for a family scene."

The US tour dates, winding up on October 15th '78 in Pasadena, California, included further support slots to the Blue Öyster Cult, REO Speedwagon, Styx and Journey, but also headline dates, with warm-up for Lizzy including the likes of AC/DC and The Cars. Other bands sharing the stage included Climax Blues Band, Savoy Brown, The Dictators, The Outlaws and Marshall Tucker Band.

"We played a couple of shows with them and AC/DC, which was an amazing configuration of musicians," recalls Dictators guitarist Ross The Boss. "One story, we were getting ready to play, we played, and Thin Lizzy didn't like AC/DC. Thin Lizzy goes, 'Keep playing, keep playing, just keep playing, come on, I don't care, just take your time, don't…' 'We gotta get off the stage; this is a big concert here!' 'Nah, nah, screw AC/DC.' It was a very competitive situation there. We just wanted to be nice to everybody. We were the young band and we were just in awe of those guys. We were just glad to be there."

"Another thing I remember," continues Ross, "growing up, I was an incredible fan of Fleetwood Mac and Peter Green — so enamoured with Peter Green — and I'll never forget this. I walk into the dressing room and Gary Moore is sitting there playing this Les Paul, and I said, 'Wait a minute, I know that guitar.' He goes, 'Well, it's Peter Green's. Peter Green sold it to me.' I said, 'He sold it to you?! Oh my God!' I played it; it was unbelievable, so amazing. That guitar is probably so valuable. I knew that guitar looked familiar. It's a '59 Les Paul Sunburst. Today it must be worth about $500,000, $600,000, $700,000. As for Phil, weren't on the road with them long, but I talked to him for a bit about his bass, and we talked equipment. He wore his Fender bass up really high — I never saw anyone play up so high like that, especially a bass. But no, Gary was a moody fellow; he seemed very moody to me. Scott Gorham on the other hand, with his long hair and everything, he had this image going on. He was a really good-looking fella and presented a great image. But no question, we were in the presence of some brilliant guys."

"I definitely remember those guys," laughs James "JY" Young, guitarist for Styx, asked about Lizzy. "First of all, four guys in the band and the two crew guys they had were sharing one hotel room, somehow; I don't know how. There was a bill in Evansville, Indiana where it was Ted Nugent, Styx and Thin Lizzy, and they were the opening act. They were just a bunch of guys from across the Atlantic Ocean who were trying to make their own name in America like so many bands from the British Isles before. You know, Phil Lynott and I hit it off nicely, and ultimately they became the opening act for the first batch of shows we did on our first full headline tour of arenas in North America, which was the Pieces Of Eight album. At the end of that, Phil was mad because he didn't feel they were getting treated right. He and I never spoke again after that (laughs). It was great to start the tour with them anyway."

"You know, we're all profoundly competitive," continues James, not one to blame Phil, "because otherwise you have no chance to succeed. You've got to want it more than the next guy. Everybody thinks they should be headlining, and some people really… you know, it gets them worked up and it gets them angry, and that's part of what got them there in the first place. So I can't say bad things about it. It's the nature of the business. Everybody on the football field… you can get hurt by the littlest guy on the field if he hits you in the right spot in the wrong way."

After the US jaunt, the novel Phil, Gary, Scott and Mark line-up proceeded to Australia, most significantly playing with well-regarded AC/DC-styled veterans, The Angels (known as Angel City for their successful early '80s run stateside) as well as Wha-koo, John English and Sport. With typical Lizzy luck, the flight overseas was delayed five hours due to a bomb scare and band and crew got so inebriated, two of the crew were kicked off the plane at the Honolulu stopover, prompting them to be fired by the band as well. Once in Australia, Phil's behaviour became more erratic, giving bad interviews and acting the prima donna, treating back-up bands badly, resulting in further deterioration in his relationship with the comparatively more professional Gary Moore.

Returning to the UK, Brian Downey (who said he surprised the guys by having lost a lot of weight, as well as cutting his hair short) would play his first returning gig with the band on December 17th at the Hammersmith amidst a good few rave-ups by The Greedy Bastards, who one night were supported by U2. Thin Lizzy's Hammersmith stand unfortunately went badly, as reviews would attest. The show was hobbled by bad sound and missteps, including Gary getting handed a guitar with no strap, resulting in a beat-down on the roadie by a clearly embarrassed Moore. Still, the band managed to debut a spate of still unreleased material, including 'Black Rose', 'Waiting For An Alibi', 'Get Out Of Here', and a manic Moore solo track called 'Back On The Streets', sung by Gary.

Also toward the end of '78, Phil gets to play some footie at a charity event at Wembley, along with Chris O'Donnell, Frank Murray and a couple of Boomtown Rats, as well as serving as a judge at the Miss World Competition, which wound up garnering quite a lot of press exposure for Phil, orchestrated by the band's capable press agent Tony Brainsby.

On a more personal note, Phil, wanting his first child to be born in Ireland and to become a Catholic, sets up Caroline, then all of 19 years old, in Dublin to wait out her pregnancy. Shortly thereafter she buys, at auction, a house called Glen Corr, near Howth, while Phil also gets into the game and buys a similarly expensive home, Walled Cottage in Richmond, Surrey.

Similar to Paul "Tonka" Chapman's relationship with UFO, Gary Moore had been in and around the Thin Lizzy orbit for years, helping out here and there, just being a buddy. As discussed, his first solo album, Back On The Streets had just emerged, featuring some co-writes with

Phil Lynott, and Phil was working on a solo record as well, so the songs were flowing, as was the communication between these traditional old Dubliners. Thin Lizzy was riding high on the success of the band's incendiary *Live And Dangerous* album, and it was well on time for a follow-up, this time with the wrinkle of a new line-up to add drama.

The album that was to become *Black Rose* was recorded in two studios, EMI Studios in Paris and Good Earth Studio in England, and the result is a batch of the band's best songs, all over the emotional and stylistic spectrum.

"It was done for tax reasons at the time," relates Moore with respect to picking France as a recording spot. "They wanted to record out of England so they wouldn't have to pay so much tax. But the studio was pretty much the same. It was EMI Pathe Marconi, which was a well-known studio at the time. I do remember when we got there, Cliff Richard was there and we had to throw him out because we wanted to start and they were running over, so we had to throw him out of the studio (laughs). It was a pretty good studio though."

Quipped Phil at the time on the Paris decision, to Record Mirror's Ronnie Gurr, "Partly the money thing, and also the attitude of the French. It's like they take everything one stage further. I'll take you to this club later on and you'll see just what I mean."

The legendary Tony Visconti was tapped once again for producer, Thin Lizzy ultimately being one of his few hard rock credits over the years. Engineer this time around would be one Kit Woolven, who would figure prominently on the band's next two records. "Marconi Studios in Paris was absolutely huge," recalls Kit. "We did use the room a lot, because it's such a big room. It's a great sound. At the time they had such great older mics and instruments everywhere. So yes, the record was started in Paris, although there were lots of songs that had been demoed in London, before we started. But the actual album, we did most of it, all the backing tracks and everything, in Paris, a whole different time. Then we went back to London to finish it off."

"The thing is," laughs Moore, remembering the walking quirk that is Visconti, "when Phil would go in and do vocals, Tony would be like... I think he had a half bottle of brandy hidden under the console. This is how I remember it. This might be exaggerated because it was a long time ago, but I just remember he had some valiums or something and he would get really wound up because Phil would spend six or seven hours on what would turn out just to be a guide vocal. Tony would be like 'Aw fuck, we're going to do this again tomorrow?!' Because we would go home and Phil would just keep Tony in there for hours, just making up these lyrics and seeing how things work. But that was his way of working and sometimes it really worked great."

So Phil was quite a workaholic?"

"Well, you know, he was at one point. He would work so hard and as time went on and he became affected by other things in his life, he lost that. But certainly in the early days, he was a real workaholic, yeah. But Paris… that's when the heroin started. I wasn't into all that. Yeah, some of us got out more than others. Still, we did a hell of a lot of the album there. We finished it off later on in Tony Visconti's studio and Tony was great. It wasn't easy for him with a couple of smackheads and me. Things got quite difficult for him at one point. He held it all together."

For the cover art, it was good to see Jim Fitzpatrick back and in control, after the dog's breakfast that was the *Bad Reputation* sleeve. "*Black Rose* was, of course, a painting; there was no photographic aspect to that at all," begins Jim. "Done with acrylic — always acrylics. Works best, and they last. I have *Black Rose* at home, and it looks just as good as when I painted it. The reason I have it at all is because, literally, Philip carried it back home under his arm, to give it to me. Most are missing. My biggest loss was *Chinatown*. I lost all that artwork en route to Dublin somewhere, along with a gold album, literally, a gold album, for my cover. So a lot of valuable stuff was lost, or stolen."

"The brief for *Black Rose* was pretty simple," explains Fitzpatrick. "They tried a photographic version. 'Waiting For An Alibi'… you have to remember, I'm not a Thin Lizzy historian, so I'm only guessing. But I remember Philip sent me over a cover, and I think it was for 'Waiting For An Alibi'. They were all sitting on the floor with a very dead black rose in the foreground, where they tried to spray-paint the rose and it pretty well died immediately. So Philip asked me, could I do an artwork version, and so that's how *Black Rose* came about. I had the black rose drawn up for him in great detail as a pencil drawing and I conferred that and did a painting of it. But halfway through I thought, it needs a bit more, and that's where I came up with the idea of putting the blood on the rose, which related to a poem by Joseph Mary Plunkett, one of the leaders executed in 1916. He wrote a poem that began, 'I see his blood upon the rose.' That's where that came from."

"Philip knew exactly the reference," continues Jim. "We were all educated the same place in the same age. The Irish education system was very, very good; you learned classical poetry. You have to remember, *Black Rose* came from Dark Rosaleen, by James Clarence Morgan, who was a Jesuit, and Dark Rosaleen, or *Black Rose*, was his allegory for the Spaniards coming across the sea to rescue us from English imperialism. They were Catholics, and the English weren't, so that was the edge there. But Philip was aware of all these cross-references when he was doing this stuff."

This rich conceptual image, as applied to the idea of Thin Lizzy and the Irish anchor of a title track... it was almost not to be, given another preliminary idea featuring a rose tattoo on a curvaceous female's hip, an image more suited to, well, Rose Tattoo.

"Yes, it started off that way," confirms Jim. "There was a lot of debate at the time about sexism and that whole political correctness thing going on, but it didn't affect me in the sense of that I couldn't give a hang one way or the other. If I wanted to do it, I would do it. But we were dealing with a very quasi-mystical kind of album, and very quasi-mystical imagery, and to stick the rose on a girl's thigh, I just decided I wasn't going to go in that direction. I was focused on the rose itself, make that an object. I always felt, when I was over in London, when I saw my work, if it didn't jump out of the record shops, then I knew it wasn't working. You have to remember, when you went over to London, around Dean Street, where Lizzy's office was, you'd have whole windows, like three or four of them, wall-to-wall of whatever design. When I saw *Black Rose*, I remember thinking, that really does it, you know? It just hits you. Even though it's quite a subtle image."

As regards the back cover illustration of the band, the label had demanded at the last minute that he conjure something quick. Jim was quite pleased with his portrayal of Gary, Brian and Phil, to whom he applied a dash of Little Richard, remarking that the look, with Phil's hair covering one eye, was suspiciously later adopted by Prince. Jim figures, however, that he made Scott look too feminine. Tied in with the visual theme of the album, Polygram's John Burnham got the idea to boost enthusiasm for the record by buying up a bunch of black roses and taking Phil around to present them to all the girls in the office. It turned out to be the sort of PR coup that helped the staff remember the record fondly amongst the shuffle of releases they were charged with selling.

Black Rose, issued on April 13th 1979, kicks off with a gorgeous hard rocker (and subsequent hit single) called 'Do Anything You Want To'. After a bit of a kettledrum thrum from consummate drummer Brian Downey, the new guitar team gets down to work, offering the record's first harmony solo. "'Do Anything You Want To', that was a crazy-ass song," laughs Gorham. "I remember when we actually played that onstage, we had to wheel out these big old fucking kettle drums and Gary and I would have to play these things. Immediately after you get done with the kettledrums, you've got to go into that long harmony line. So you had to time that absolutely perfectly, throw the sticks away, crank up your guitar and get right onto that harmony line and play perfectly. It was a fucking bitch. I was never so glad to drop a song in my life (laughs)."

"Yeah, the kettledrums," laughs Moore. "We did it on the video, and it was on the record and it just went from there. So we ended up having a couple of them on stage just as a visual thing. It wasn't my favourite thing in the world. Because you had to transfer quickly onto guitar."

The track ends with a brief but touching and convincingly sorrowful near-eulogy to Elvis Presley, Phil expressing both surprise and grief through the simplest statement of fact. "Well, it actually reminds me of an Elvis Presley song," muses Moore. "You know, 'I can't help falling in love with you.' 'Take my hand...' (sings it). That's where he steals the melody line from. It's right there. But Phil was a big Elvis fan; all of us were. He even did a song dedicated to him called 'King's Call'. He's very clever. But a lot of bands do that. You take the first two lines of the song and then you rewrite the rest (laughs). That's what Peter Green used to do. He'd say, just take the first two lines of your favourite song and take it from there."

Asked about the track, Kit says, "The timpani drums or kettledrums on there... you know, they were in the studio, so it's like, 'Good, let's use those' (laughs). They became a key part of that song, and also a key part of the video that went with the song. I know he was mortified when Elvis died and there are all the various references to Elvis in his songs. On 'Do Anything You Want To', of course, there's 'The king of rock 'n' roll is dead' and all that, and then we did 'King's Call' on his solo album, which was a tribute to Elvis."

"I thought he was pretty good," ventures Moore, asked to sum up Scott Gorham as Moore's co-guitarist. "I mean, when I joined the band, Scott's confidence was really, really low. I remember him telling me that he felt he had been sort of pushed aside a lot of the time by Brian Robertson and he lost a lot of his confidence. I tried to sort of pull a lot of that out of him again, encourage the guy and we started working on stuff together. Because it was somebody new in the band for him, I think it made the whole thing fresh again for him and I enjoyed it. But I don't think it was quite that simple. Because I was so used to not playing in that situation, being the leader of my own band or being the one guitar player. I think it was never going to work the same as Brian and Scott. At the end of the day, that was the classic Lizzy line-up and that's the one I enjoyed listening to the most, if I was really honest with you. I enjoyed being in the band, but it's like anything, if you remove one component the whole thing can change. I think we did some nice tunes together but again, the songs weren't up to what was going on before it either. There were a couple things there but it wasn't like a classic Thin Lizzy album, *Black Rose*, in many ways — it wasn't like *Jailbreak*."

"Well, I don't know about that," ventures Gorham on Gary's supposition about his state of mind. "I don't know about my confidence level. I was aware of how good he was at that point. Which was good for me, because I had entered this comfort zone, and I think when he entered the band, I knew I had to step my game up quite a bit. So it was a big challenge for me. I had to step up to the plate even closer. So I actually quite enjoyed that. I thought the *Black Rose* album was great; I thought Gary did a really good job on that. There were some great songs that came out of that."

Scott gives cause to the departure of Brian Robertson from the band. "You know, in the beginning, Brian was one of those... you've got to remember, he was 18 years old, right?

Never really been out of Scotland. But this guy could really play. He really had something there. He would be coming up with these lead breaks that were just killer. You'd sit back there and go, 'My God, where are these things coming from? The guy is great.' But he had that Scottish tradition thing in him that he really had to get drunk and play the part and all that. I really think that started to affect him and it started to affect his playing, to the point where Phil just didn't want to work with him any longer. Really, it was me that kept Brian in the band. I kept arguing with Phil that, this is the way we started, we've created this sound together, we can't just break up this, what I was always calling the magic circle. It always felt to me that once the magic circle was broken, it was over. Which it wasn't. But that was the way I was thinking at the time. So I kept talking Phil out of it. Then Brian would do something, or pull something stupid, refuse to play on songs or whatever. At one point Phil had just said, 'That's it, I don't care what anybody says, either he goes or I go.' Well, at that point it's no contest, isn't it? So it's 'okay, Brian, you're gone' (laughs). It was a shame to see, but you know, it is a business out here. As much as fans and all that don't like to think of it that way, you have to be as professional as you possibly can. There are responsibilities you have to keep up, and it's a lot of hard work. If you can't come up with all three, then you can't be in the band. Or you shouldn't be in the band."

'Toughest Street In Town', *Black Rose's* second track, offers more spirited melodic hard rock, maybe with a bit of a punk vibe. Still, the smooth deliveries and the sturdy, time- honoured '60s-based chord patterns make it a timeless rocker. As well, this is as good a track as any to represent Phil's admirable skill with vocal phrasings, his ability to string a line with complex cadence across a riff that gives no clues as to where the words should go.

"That was a riff I had before I joined the band and we built it up from there," recalls Moore. "The middle eight was a riff that Scott had hanging around. The title was mine and again, I lead off some of the lyrics. I would write some of the lyrics for the first verse and a chorus, and Phil basically filled in all the holes for me. So that's how that one came together. But the main idea was something I had. I think I wrote it in New York actually, the riff, funnily enough. Good place to come up with a song like that (laughs)."

If the album was shaping up pretty heavy, Phil so much as put it down to the drugs and the booze. "The thing was that hepatitis left me as half the man I was. I had to lay off the drink for a year and obviously that was bound to change me. That's why *Bad Reputation* and *Johnny The Fox* were a bit more laid-back. Being straight made me a bit more reflective, but live it's always been about 50,000 watts and the kids going wild. I used my poetry books as diaries, but it's still about those 50,000 watts and really the two sides both exist quite normally within me."

'S&M' is an experimental track to say the least. Funky to the max, the song recalls the verse of 'Johnny The Fox Meets Jimmy The Weed', while the chorus thumps with all manner of bass throb. Incidentally, this is the first of a few tracks (also 'Waiting For An Alibi' and 'Get Out Of Here') on which one's ears perk to Phil's gnarlier, more attack-oriented bass sound. It's not quite Lemmy or even Steve Harris, but really, this is the first album where Phil's fat-stringer shoves its way occasionally into lead position.

Says Gary, "I think he was writing 'S&M' when he was in the studio. Because we were cracking up over some of the lyrics; sometimes we would just joke about putting lines in. But I remember he would just go in and start singing the melody. He'd have a good idea about a melody in his head and he would build it up slowly, as other guys might have a song finished before they came in. That wasn't usually the case with him." The band throw in a crunching heavy break late in the sequence, before a scrappy single lead solo continues the black and blues party. The band collapse into another bit of chorus and then Downey takes a drum solo. Strange one here, for sure.

Brian Downey, like Ian Paice with Purple, is often the unsung hero of these Thin Lizzy records. "Brian's got a really big knowledge of the blues," says Gary, offering an assessment of Downey, in the context of playing with him again in 2007, in Gary's solo blues configuration. "That's why it's great to have him on my new album. Because it's the first time we'd ever made a whole album together, outside of Thin Lizzy. He's a great barometer for what's right and what's wrong. I wasn't playing for him, but I was very aware that he was there, so I made a special effort this time to make sure it was right. Brian grew up on the same music that I did. We started with the blues boom and got into the older blues after that. But I met the guy when he was 14. I was opening up for his band. He had come up from Dublin and I was from Belfast. He was in a band called Sugar Shack, which was probably the only blues band from Dublin at that time. There was a much bigger blues scene where I came from, in Belfast, and we just hit it off. He grew up liking the same drummers that I liked, like Aynsley Dunbar and Mick Fleetwood and people like that. So that, coupled with his Irish feel, the Celtic thing — it's quite a unique style actually."

Asked similarly to sum up Phil as a bass player, Moore ventures that, "Phil had very good coordination. He's kind of like Sting, really, plays the bass like a guitar. For Phil to do his vocals together with the bass playing, that's not easy. So those two things together... it takes a special person to do that with that kind of confidence and make it sound as smooth as that. He's very good at that. He could come up with funky riffs on the bass. But then he used to write a lot on acoustic guitar. He didn't write on the bass. He had a beat up old acoustic at home, and a lot of his bass playing came from the guitar, really, just play it with a pick. Like 'Dancing In The Moonlight'. I remember when he wrote that — he wrote it on an acoustic guitar, and he transferred to the bass later."

Black Rose's ambassador single (issued in advance of the album by two months, its b-side being 'With Love') came next, 'Waiting For An Alibi' ("a gamblin' song," said Phil) being one of the great Lizzy anthems of all time, a tough yet tender rocker with an anthemic chorus and sophistication for miles. The solos, the twin leads, the plugged bass riff, the transitions... this is a gorgeous and balanced track, rewarded for its charms by rising to No.9 in the UK charts, and No.6 in Ireland.

Closing side one of the original vinyl is the album's first of two ballads, 'Sarah', fully poppy and casual for this band, not to mention full up with strange guitar tones and... harmonica!

Lyrically, the track reflects Phil's transition into fatherhood, Sarah being Phil's recent first daughter, with a second, Cathleen, to arrive in July 1980. "If people go, 'Oh, since he's had the kid, he's written 'Sarah' and 'A Child's Lullaby', the guy's gone a bit soft. The thing that people don't realise is that with having the kid now, I'm far more protective. So if someone slags me now — or if, for example, the Ayatollah in Iran, now I'd fucking kill that bastard if I got me hands on him, because he could start a Third World War and my kid could be living in a fucking wasteland. I'm far quicker to get annoyed over a bastard like that than I was before I had the kid. It bugs me now. Before, I'd hear about a child molester, never bugged me too much. I'd say, 'Man, that's real tacky, attacking kids.' But now, the thought of someone attacking my kid fucking drives me crazy. I'd want to hang the bastard. It's making me twice as quick to go off the mark with the temper, and be angry, and protective — as well as making me very soppy and that. So when they continually play up, 'Oh, he likes to be seen as the hard man, the romantic' — there's other parts to me. I'm a lot more complicated than the paragraph you read about where they're summarising Philip Lynott the romantic, the lover, the hard aggressive man, the father. I suppose I do live up to that to a certain amount, but I have noticed that now I keep, especially in interviews, very protective."

Comments Gary on this lightest of Lizzy ballads, "You probably wouldn't know this, but that song was actually going to be on one of Phil's solo albums and it's actually about his little girl who was born about that time. I wrote most of that song, 85% of that song and he wrote most of the lyrics. But even some of the lyrical ideas, was my idea that it should be about his kid basically, which is a really weird thing to have happened (laughs). The song wasn't recorded as a Thin Lizzy track at all. It was recorded with Mark Nauseef on drums who stood in for Brian Downey on one American tour and then he became the drummer in G-Force later. Then Huey Lewis played harmonica and Phil played bass and I played acoustic guitar; it actually was put down on acoustic guitar with a drum machine, and then we added a lot of stuff after that. So it was actually going to be a solo thing for Phil and it was put together over quite a long period of time. So that was completely different from any other Thin Lizzy track ever recorded."

"And that was all DI'ed guitars on there," continues Moore. "I thought we came up with some really good guitar sounds. We spent a lot of time getting the guitar sounds on that. I just sat with Tony. The other guys weren't even there when I was doing the guitar on that. I just sat with him and we did it together, with about seven tracks of guitar: I like more of the ensemble playing. 'Black Rose' is probably my favourite track, but I was playing all the guitar on 'Sarah', which is probably the best showcase of my playing on that record. Because it's only my guitar on that track. Like I say, that was meant for a Phil Lynott solo album, but I think he ran out of *Black Rose* things so we had to put it on that album."

"But you can well hear yourself; it's very different from Thin Lizzy. 'Waiting For An Alibi'... I love that. But again, the solo is just sort of split in two and it ends up in a harmony again. So my main solo track on the album would be 'Sarah'."

Apparently the band was a little reserved about using 'Sarah'. They thought it was too conventional. "Yes, as I said, I thought it was going to be on Phil's album. But he liked the song and I liked the song too. To be honest with you, I wasn't sure it should be on there, but it kinda ended up on there because maybe they needed some extra material."

Gary says Huey Lewis is on this track, "again, because it was going to be a solo thing. I think he had just happened to be in London playing with Clover. This is before The News and all that. He just happened to be around. But Huey was a big friend of Phil's, because they had done a lot of shows together. Clover used to open for Lizzy quite a lot. In fact, when I was playing in the states one time, I was on a bus and I bumped into Huey. He was on a bus on the same freeway. They got on the CBs and I pulled over, and he invited me to come up and play with him the next night. They were doing 'The Boys Are Back In Town' in their set at that time. I came onstage (laughs), and it was the weirdest gig. Because I remember all the guitars were in flight cases because he wanted it really, really quiet onstage. I'm like, what the fuck is this?! So strange. He had the mayor and all his family sitting there. It was like the equivalent of a Cliff Richard gig back in England. It was all so polite and everything was very low-key backstage. I thought, what happened to rock 'n' roll, you know? Very strange, but he was nice guy, Huey, I always liked him."

The ubiquitous Don Airey, now with Deep Purple, had a small part in the construction of 'Sarah', but then he left the building. "I played string synth on it," recalls Don. "There was a guy there from a band in London called Clover, and he was hanging out a lot, he was known as Huey Louie then. They said, 'Oh, he's going to play harmonica' and when he did, I said, 'That's it, you don't really need the strings.' Of course it's Huey Lewis, but it was Huey Louie when he lived in London. So they decided to use the harmonica and not the string synth. That's the only time I ever played with them. That was at Morgan studios in north London."

But nonetheless, Don was within the band's orbit, having played with Moore before than and after. "I remember the first time I met Phil," relates Don. "He lived around the corner from me in West Hampstead, and Gary Moore had come to see me. We were just writing some stuff, and he said, 'Oh, Phil lives around the corner. Let's go see Phil.' So we went to Phil's apartment. The door was wide open, and in we went. This was about 11 in the morning. There was no one there. I was just very impressed by what I saw. There were books about art and books of poetry. It was very tastefully done out, unlike most musicians that I was acquainted with. I thought, 'Oh, this is some guy.' Gary said, 'Well, let's just sit down. He must've popped out and he'll be back in a second. Let's sit down.' So there was a zebra skin on the sofa. So I sat on the sofa, little realising that Phil was underneath it fast asleep. As I sat on him, he jumped up and he appeared underneath this zebra skin, and he said 'Top of the morning to ya, boys' and that's how I met Phil."

As regards Moore, Airey comments that, "he's very meticulous about his music. He knows what he wants. He's probably the most brilliant guitar player I know — I'll have to say that. I don't think he always gives himself a fair chance, to be honest. I wish he'd just play and not worry so much. I think he worries too much these days about what he's doing. Whereas in the old days when I knew him, when we were young, he used to just let fly, and it would just be glorious, really. So I miss that side of him."

Side two of *Black Rose* opens with a crunching classic called 'Got To Give It Up', a torrid tale of drug dependency capturing all the power of the blues without using blues conventions, even if at one point Phil adds an amusing disco lick to his bass part. An intriguing wrinkle in the vocals is the way Phil's pronunciation of the word bottle can sometimes sound like bible, as well as the double meaning whereby bottle is used to represent the deteriorating mental faculties of the semi-autobiographical narrator. Additionally, for most the track, it seems like the intention is to portray mother, father, sister and brother as alive, distant and concerned, but then at the end, given the impassioned and fatalistic deliver of Lynott, that coming home to mama implies a reunion in Heaven.

Explains Scott, "It really is an ode to 'I've got to give the drugs up.' I think that is more of a psychological thing, coming from Phil, knowing, at some point or another, the drugs are going to do you some big-time damage. So you've got to give this shit up. I wish he would have listened to his own words. It still makes me angry when I think about him, that he didn't listen to himself, or that he wouldn't listen to anybody else."

"'Got To Give It Up' came together more in a conventional way," recalls Moore. "We would put the track down and then we would go back. Phil always had this thing about double-tracking or whatever. Anything that could be double-tracked would be. So with the guitars, as soon as we got a track down, we would double it and build it up in that way. Sometimes he wouldn't have any lyrics. Sometimes he would just go in there and light up a big spliff and say anything that came off the top of his head; he would just create it on the spot sometimes. Six hours later he would say, 'Yeah, that's okay; that will do for a rough vocal.' He would call it a scratch vocal and then the producer would be going crazy because he thought it was a master. Then he would come back in and do it all again. He had his own way of working. It was done over a few months, that album. Like I say, we did some in Paris and some in England."

I asked Gary why the riff in 'Got To Give It Up' has an almost scraping, grinding quality to it. "There might have been some flanging on there. I know what you mean. Also the bass had a flanging effect on it, nearly on the whole record. He always played through this particular effect, Phil, so sometimes things sounded bit funny."

'Got To Give It Up' could be called a heavy metal song, but as usual, Thin Lizzy infuse so much more into a raucous rocker. It reminds me of a discussion within the band on whether 'Angel Of Death' was good enough to put on *Renegade*, given its standing too close to rote metal. A good attitude to have, as Scott attests: "Yeah, absolutely. We never, ever put ourselves in the metal stakes. We always considered ourselves a hard rock band, which to me just entails a little bit more on the songwriting side, rather than just heavy guitar riffs going constantly through all the songs."

"Tony was becoming increasingly irritated at Phil's drug abuse," recalls Kit, offering a story related to this seminal Phil confessional. "Whereas I don't think it was that bad. I do remember one time, when we were doing the vocals on 'Got To Give It Up', and I think Phil had a joint in one hand, a bottle of Courvoisier, a few lines of coke out in front of him, while he's on mic, you know? Singing, 'I've got to give it up' (laughs), and Tony just turned around at me and just went, 'I can't work with this sort of hypocrisy.' Tony has been documented later as saying that he couldn't stand to see Phil killing himself. Which is probably also the truth of the matter. There was definitely a clash of egos; I mean Tony has quite a strong ego, and Phil had a very, very strong ego, and I think Phil wanted a bit more control. Doing *Black Rose*, Phil came to me one time and leaned into me, with Tony sitting on the other side of me, and Phil whispered to me and said, 'I want you to produce the next album.' I said to him, 'Let's get this one finished first.' A bit awkward with Tony on the other side of me. Tony's is on one hand saying, 'I don't know if I can work with this band anymore,' and Phil is turning to me and saying, 'I want you to do the next album.' Phil wanted me to do the solo albums anyway."

"I'm being a bit cynical with 'Got To Give It Up'," Phil told Harry Doherty. "How many times do you say you're gonna give something up and you don't? It's that perpetual thing where you can't break the habit. I mean, I'm trying to be really honest in the song. Like on 'With Love' too. I wanted to achieve total honesty and also write a love song, and I say, 'This Casanova's days are over, more or less.' It's the 'more or less' that's the honest bit. It shows the human elements, the wanting. When I was writing those songs, those were the moods I was trying to capture. I did mean what I said. It's honest contradictions. If my life was a simple black and white, if it was just straightforward, it would be easy to write songs. I wouldn't wrestle with it. But it's not like that at all. It's all so much more complicated. 'Got To Give It Up' is to do with trying to give up bad habits, when you know that you don't really stand a chance. But it's not just me. It's relevant to a lot of people. I try to give these things up. I really do try; with all the sincerity I can, for brief periods, to give it up. I don't condone drugs, really, but I know why artists take drugs. They take them to experience, to go to the edge. Why do people climb mountains? To go to the edge. People always want to go to extremes. If you go to the edge, you must be prepared to fall off. And a lot of guys have."

"I want to develop more as a songwriter and as an artist of some sort," added Phil. "I want to get better and better at it, and I honestly believe that I am improving. But whether I actually move at the rate of speed that people want me to is another thing. Graham Parker hit it right on the head — Squeezing Out Sparks. That's what it's all about. What I can tell you is that the band is going through a really creative period at the moment. Things are very positive for us. Everybody's talking about Thin Lizzy as a band that's been around a long time, whereas I think that it's just the start, 'cos Gary's in the band now. I don't feel that I should defend *Black Rose* for nobody. *Black Rose* is the start of a change. I can hear a definite change on *Black Rose*. Our last recorded album was *Bad Reputation*. There's a hell of a difference between that and *Black Rose*."

Back to *Black Rose*, another buoyant, spirited rocker is next, 'Get Out Of Here' slashing simply but with joy, Phil's stacks of variously recorded staccato vocals representing a nice foil to the straight-line chording. Again the track possesses the energy of punk, but played by professionals.

"I think that's something they wrote together," says Gary, asked about the co-credit between Phil and James "Midge" Ure of Slik/Rich Kids/Ultravox fame, Ure soon to be Thin Lizzy's touring guitarist. "Because again, Phil used to hang out with a lot of different musicians. Like, we used to hang out with the guys from the Sex Pistols and stuff, and if anybody happened to be around while he was writing a song, if they were friends of his, and if they contributed anything at all, he would give them a credit sometimes. I mean, Brian Downey, drummer, didn't really write anything, but Phil would give him a lot of credit on songs which worked really great for him. Because when *Live And Dangerous* came out, Brian ended up with a bunch of songs on there. Which was great, because Phil took care of Brian that way and that was nice. After the band folded, that meant Brian always had money coming in for years afterwards. Because they went back so far, he wanted to take care of him, which is a cool thing to do."

'With Love' is much more of a high-minded ballad for the band than 'Sarah' was, written a little desperado-desperate, like 'Wild One' for example, or 'Southbound'. Comments Moore: "'With Love'... it's good that you mentioned that. Because I think that was recorded originally as a solo track as well. There might have been a couple of versions of that. At that time, Phil had this idea of getting all his pals together. There was a guy called Jimmy Bain, and Jimmy wrote a song called 'Flyaway', and I had 'Parisienne Walkways', and we had all these songs lying around. Phil said let's just get a pool of songs and then we'll decide what to do with them after. He had 'Fanatical Fascists', which ended up on my record and I had 'Parisienne Walkways', which he then wrote the lyrics for and did the vocal part for that. So we were just putting things together. So there were a couple versions of 'Parisienne Walkways', there were a couple of versions of 'With Love', all done in Tony Visconti's studio, Good Earth. Then I think as time went on he thought, well, this will work on a Thin Lizzy album and it had become a Thin Lizzy track. So both 'With Love' and 'Sarah' were definitely two of those songs."

Lyrically the song is a wry or ironic look at love, a sister track to 'Don't Believe A Word', as it were, Phil calling it, "a song about all the Dear John letters in the world that end, 'with love,' but aren't."

Adds Jimmy Bain, "I was working with Phil on his solo record at the time and it just so happened they were shy a song for the *Black Rose* record, and we had recorded 'With Love' for his solo record, and it ended up going... I was playing bass on it and he liked what I played, so he didn't put bass on it, and that happened on a few tracks. We were very similar bass players, but he liked something I did and he'd just play something else. So that ended up on *Black Rose*. I was down in the sessions when they were doing it, but I wasn't hired to play on a bunch of songs. It was just the one song and it was originally for something else, which is why it went on there."

Black Rose closes with its erstwhile title track, 'Roisin Dubh (Black Rose) A Rock Legend'. Reactions to this one have been mixed over the years, myself tending to take the naysaying view on it, despite my championing of this album as a whole, perhaps the usual consensus on it. *Black Rose* is a moderately large epic, incorporating all manner of traditional Irish melodies into a progressive metal feast for the ears. Still, the concept comes off a bit forced, leaning into the vibe most have come to agreement on with respect to *Chinatown*: that it's a forced album that on paper looks good but... something just isn't right.

"Well, we wanted a song that was going to identify all of the nationalities within the band," offers Scott. "So there's Danny Boy, I think there's a Scottish reel in there, there's the American side that is in there. That was mostly Gary and Phil that came up with that one; I just wrote a tiny bit on that. But it was one of those epic deals that really is a blast to play live. Gary had put a few bits in there, guitar-wise, which at that point, they were quite technically challenging for me. But he and I sat down together and we just worked these things out; we made it work. But there's a lot to learn in that song. Some of those are like stock, sort of Irish tunes in there, and I'd never actually played those, so I had to go in there and actually learn all those melody lines, plus figure out the harmonies to all these things. So it was a pretty challenging song. But it's one nowadays, you know, when we get up and play 'Black Rose', it's probably one of the most satisfying songs to play in the set, just because there's so much going on in there."

Adds Gary, "On the title track 'Black Rose', I wrote the Irish-sounding,

Celtic-like, jig-type pieces in the middle. I got very involved in the arrangement of that song with Philip. We worked pretty closely on it. Phil had the idea as I remember, and the riff for 'Black Rose' and he worked together with Tony because it was quite a big arrangement. I think his idea was to represent the different people in the band at that time."

"Because Brian Robertson was Scottish, he thought of doing it with him at one time, so there's a bit of 'Will You Go, Lassie Go' in there, which is a Scottish traditional song. But then you've got all the Irish stuff plus a bit of 'Shenandoah', the American side which represents Scott, I guess. So he was playing on his little thing with all the people in the band, representing their nationalities and stuff. That was one of the things. But then it was also a mythical Irish Celtic legend sort of thing, Cuchulain and the kings and the warriors from Ireland, which Phil was very fond of; he was very into Irish mythology and Irish poetry."

And into the Wild West as well? "Well, I don't know about the Wild West; the Wild West of Ireland, maybe (laughs). But yes, 'The Cowboy Song' and stuff, that gang mentality with 'Boys Are Back In Town'. But a lot of it was rooted in Ireland because Ireland is a lot like cowboys anyway (laughs)."

Much synergy in this one, as Phil fully made use of his own — as well as his new/old guitarist's — deep knowledge of Irish roots music. As well, on top of allusions to 'The Mason's Apron' and 'Whisky In The Jar', the band tried to pay extra tribute to Scott by trying out a few more American references, although the attempts came out sounding "corny" according to Gorham. In terms of the track's philosophical thrust, 'Black Rose' was full up with Irish history. A laundry list of Irish artists, writers and musicians provides a look at the island state's rich heritage, most important among them, Cuchulain, the original Irish cowboy figure from the dark ages of the eighth century.

The "black rose" idea, as alluded to by Jim, refers to the traditional Irish vision poem figure of a shrieking, sobbing female apparition, the most famous expression thereof being Dark Rosaleen, central figure of a poem by the same name written by James Clarence Mangan (a.k.a. Morgan, as Jim has cited) in the 19th century.

"I've always viewed our band as something rather special," Phil told Andy Secher. "Sure we depend on a lot of rock 'n' roll structures, but I've always tried to make sure that we have a lot of different influences in there too."

"Scott is from California, but the rest of us are from around Dublin, so we've tried to include some of the music we grew up on — traditional Irish tunes — in our format. 'Black Rose', for instance, is our interpretation of an old Gaelic poem called Roisin Dubh, and for us it's just natural to mix Irish melodies with more conventional rock 'n' roll. We've been at this game for over eight years now. I think it's taken all that time for us to understand that if you can just make music that you really believe in, rather than always trying to live up to everyone's expectation, then you've accomplished something that can be viewed as real success."

"We've been through a lot of changes in this band," continued Phil (demonstrating no understanding of the Thin Lizzy catalogue whatsoever!) "Back on albums like Fighting, which came out in 1975, we were really trying to just blow people away with our energy and volume. Then with albums like *Johnny The Fox* and *Bad Reputation*, which were our last studio records, we tried to slow things up a bit and show off our musical diversity. We thought that a broader style might help us with album sales, but we've come to realise that our major strength is our ability to play good rock 'n' roll, and that's what we return to on *Black Rose*. We put a lot of extra effort into its creation, and in a lot of ways I look at it as the ultimate statement of the band's musical ideal. It's just got to be the album that will really solidify our position in rock 'n' roll."

"I've always been somewhat anti-establishment, I guess. Hell, being Irish and being black forces you into a position where you have to fight back against established principles. Even if I didn't necessarily want it to, my music, I suppose, would have to reflect my upbringing and background to some degree. There's a lot of hostility there, which comes across in our music, but there's also a lot of love for Ireland, and more than just a touch of old-fashioned romanticism. I'm a poet as well as a musician, so words are very important to me. I always hoped that even when our music is at its loudest, there's some lyrical message there that people can grab hold of. I try to write about things that the ordinary guy can listen to and say, 'Yeah, I've been through that.' But I don't feel that I have to walk around with a cross to bear just because I'm black. All I can really hope to do is show a few people that a black man can make it in any field if he really wants to. I'm very proud to be black, and I'll fight for the cause if need be, but people like Stevie Wonder and Bob Marley are saying far more about what it's like to be black than I am. Thin Lizzy is a band of the people, whether they are black, white or green, and when we play rock 'n' roll, I hope we're creating a language that everyone everywhere can understand."

The NME's esteemed Nick Kent, whether he understood it or not, certainly didn't like the sum total of *Black Rose*, deeming the album, "not the masterpiece Lynott believes it to be. In fact, after numerous plays, I can only conclude that *Black Rose* is nothing more than another Thin Lizzy album, certainly no greater than *Johnny The Fox* or *Bad*

Reputation, and depressingly bereft of anything that can lift it above the gash and thunder that will always make Lizzy a worthwhile band to check out. No, *Black Rose* is eminently listenable to those already enamoured with the enterprise, but fails to break any new ground. The 18-month sabbatical has provided nothing more than a new variation on the same damn themes. I have few doubts that *Black Rose* will be the first album since *Jailbreak* to receive a real critical drubbing."

"*Black Rose* has the sound of music beginning to take on the ominous form of tone and formulae caught up in diminished echoes," continues Nick. "It will be wildly successful — of that I have no doubt — probably in both American as well as here, where its success is virtually assured anyway. But in the back of my mind, I believe Phil Lynott has got more to offer as an artist and what follows on from *Black Rose* will dictate either a going-through-the-motions super-professionalism or a real attempt to deal with something with more substance. I do believe Lynott will go for the latter."

Back on the extracurricular front, recall if you will, that Gary had on his hands at that time, his second solo album, technically first, given that '73's Grinding Stone was credited to The Gary Moore Band. Back On The Streets, issued on MCA, would get to No.70 on the UK charts. Produced by Gary and Chris Tsangarides, the album would include as players, Brian Downey and Phil, as well as utility man Don Airey.

The album was a hodge-podge of funk, jazz-fusion, rock and blues balladry, main points of interest from a Thin Lizzy perspective being three- fold. One was the newly shared hit 'Parisienne Walkways', a slow ballad on which Phil and Gary both sing. Second, Phil finally gets his way and puts the dreary, pointless version of 'Don't Believe A Word' to record, again, both he and Gary singing. Arguably coolest is sizzling punk rocker and Phil Lynott composition 'Fanatical Fascists', which, unfortunately Phil doesn't sing on, but hey, spot the 'With Love' chord sequence. All told, despite the dog's breakfast of ideas and styles of the album, there was an endearing quality to its hyperactivity (most manically exemplified by the title track), a vibe from Gary that we also hear on his next record, the self-titled G-Force album, but also way back to Moore's acrobatic, anti-commercial Skid Row records.

"Yes, and there wasn't any tour for Back On The Streets," says Gary. "The Back On The Streets tour was the *Black Rose* tour. Because what happened was, I was finishing the Back On The Streets album, and 'Parisienne Walkways' came out at the same time as 'Waiting For An Alibi', so we had two singles in the Top Ten, before we went out on tour. So it was a really good time for the band and me. I didn't play a set or anything. We just played 'Parisienne Walkways' in the set, that's all."

"We played all the big places, but that was before they built some of the bigger arenas here," says Gary, estimating Thin Lizzy's touring reality in 1979 and 1980. "But three, four, 5,000, whatever, medium-sized from where you come from but that was pretty big over here. What you'd do in those days was, you'd do a couple of nights in Hammersmith if you're a big band rather than play Wembley. You'd do two nights in Hammersmith Odeon which was 9000, if you add those up. So we could draw quite a few people."

But Gary would soon be replaced by Midge Ure. Then both Midge and the short-lived Manfred Mann's Dave Flett would be followed of course by Snowy White, who would be on board for Thin Lizzy's next two albums, *Chinatown* and *Renegade*.

"I left because the band was falling apart because there was too many drugs going down," explains Moore. "It was just becoming a mess, and people would deny that, but I was there, man. I wasn't used to working in a band where you'd start a solo and the bass player was playing the wrong chords or he'd start singing over your solo and you'd get in a row onstage and stuff like that. It was just becoming stupid for me. I wasn't really in a position to do anything about it because nothing would change. I spoke about it but nothing ever changed, you know? Obviously there were problems there. But I don't want to disrespect people, especially after all this time. It's not a good thing and I don't want to go back. But if you ask me a question, I'm going to tell you the answer and the honest answer is, you know, the party after the gig was more important than the gig for certain people in the band. That was just not the way I wanted to work — very frustrating. I left in the middle of the tour. So it wasn't like I was telling the guys, 'By the way guys, hope we're still friends.' There was a lot of animosity between us at that point. Midge... he was just a friend of Phil's and Phil had to get somebody quickly. He obviously wasn't the most suitable replacement. It was a completely different style. He was only there to finish the shows."

Adds Scott, "As far as the band was concerned, Phil was always the consummate professional. His whole life was Thin Lizzy. I mean, he went out and did maybe a solo album here or there.

But it was always Thin Lizzy for him. He played Thin Lizzy. But he was always on the airplane, always there for rehearsals. He always got on the plane for the tours, the whole thing. It was just all the in-between things that let him down. When you have a problem like that, you start treating people in not the greatest way. You start to get a little sicker, things start to give out on your body that are out of your control, and you have to quit the tour. Maybe you don't want to, but the doctor is telling you you've got to go into the hospital. So it was things like that. If the band was being let down, it was because of those reasons."

"Gary was cool," reflects crew principal Frank Murray, struggling with the question of Gary's place in Lizzy's pecking order. "Gary always wanted to make himself a solo person. He never quite got the commercial acclaim that Philip was getting. But by then, because he had some modicum of success as a solo guitar player, and he had a bit of a reputation as well, Gary could often find it hard to be in a band and take leadership, let's say, from Philip. They would rub each other the wrong way with that. Philip always had the upper hand in that respect. I think Gary just got frustrated. He would up and leave."

It seemed very much however that Moore was in the right on this one. He would watch how professional Journey was, how manic AC/DC would be on stage, giving it their all to the crowd. He would see the Doobie Brothers making it so big in the states that they had a private plane for the band plus one for the crew. This he would contrast against Lizzy constantly being late for gigs, planes, limos, due mostly to Phil's drinking and drugging, his strife with Caroline back home, and his lack of consideration toward making everyone and everything wait until he felt like emerging from his hotel room, usually worse for a long night's wear.

"I never really worked out the relationship between Gary and Phil," reflects Kit Woolven, "Gary seemed to like tormenting Phil. If he could have a dig at him, he would. I think he'll only put up with it because Philip really wanted Gary in the band, because Gary was an amazing guitarist. I mean, truly amazing. He's one of the few guitarists I've ever seen where you can literally hum him a song, and he will play it. Like some pianists can. Gary was very instrumental on all of the guitar melodies — very much so. In terms of working with Scott, that's something they would work out between themselves. They would pretty much go in and work that out between them while we were doing other things. Then they'd come back in and put their parts down, and it's pretty much a done deal, that they had worked out their bits. But I know Gary was very helpful with Scott in working a lot of the parts out."

"He only got to a certain point," continues Frank, on the supposition that Gary was known to wind Phil up, defend his territory as it were. "Maybe the last time he came into the band, and maybe because Philip was not on the ball as much, because Philip might have been under the influence. But with a healthy Phil or anything like that, he wouldn't have taken any guff (laughs). Also, it's easy to be in the right when you're dealing with someone who's taking hard drugs. Because you can tell them that they're being unprofessional and you can pick holes in them and all of that stuff. It's an easy thing to do. If you are on hard drugs, it's pretty hard to have any comeback in denying any of it. So to some extent, Gary might've been right in that."

Before Gary leaves Thin Lizzy this time, however, a spate of tour dates are indeed logged, the band beginning a US leg in early March, supporting Nazareth (the album having been recorded in January), followed by a headlining UK leg beginning March 29th, leading up to the release of *Black Rose* in April. Mainland European dates commence on May 6th (with a riot in Gothenburg, Sweden), with Phil getting food poisoning in Belgium from drinking sour milk, resulting in the cancellation of the band's last seven scheduled stops.

June '79 features the release of 'Do Anything You Want To' as a single, backed with non-LP track 'Just The Two Of Us', a spirited, punky hard rocker in the rootsy tradition of 'Toughest Street In Town' and 'Get Out Of Here', but with some nice jazzy chords thrown in for colour. The single hits No.14 in the UK and No.25 in Ireland. As well there was a second trip — taken by Phil, Scott, Gary, Mark Nauseef and Huey Lewis — to the Bahamas in 13 months, two weeks in total, over which the track 'Jamaican Rum' was recorded for a Phil solo album that would actually soon come to fruition — 'Spanish Guitar' also getting manhandled for Gary Moore as a solo artist. The presence of Nauseef did not mean that Brain Downey's status of the band was once again in question, Downey having opted out of the trip to rest at home in Dublin, to gear up for the next leg of dates.

By late June the band were back in the States, supporting Journey, including a stand as part of Bill Graham's cocaine-fuelled Day On The Green Festival, with Journey, The J. Geils Band, UFO, Nazareth and The Rockets, after which Gary got into an argument with Phil in the band's trailer and stormed on out of the band.

"I've never been sacked from any band," fumed Moore, in a BBC Radio One interview. "I left Thin Lizzy about two weeks ago. It is true that I failed to turn up for a gig. I was very, very upset with the way things had been going at the time. There were a lot of personal problems between Phil and myself: I didn't feel that he was performing up to the standard that the band deserved and I felt there were a lot of things wrong with his tuning onstage plus personal things that I really don't want to go into. The reason that they're saying I was fired is because they're so annoyed that I walked out in the middle of a tour. The thing between Phil and I is just very intense. It's either very, very hot between us or it's not so hot. I got very hurt about some of the things I heard like, 'Scott has always been the lead guitarist in Thin Lizzy.' That's just crazy. We actually had to drop the title track of the new Lizzy album *Black Rose*, because Scott couldn't play it live. I'm very sorry for the fans, but as a musician I have certain standards to keep up and there is no way I could've gone on with what I was hearing next to me on stage. I think that people who pay to see a band deserve higher quality music than they were getting."

"I must say," chimed in band manager Chris Morrison, "the last time Gary Moore left Lizzy was the day before a tour and I nearly went bankrupt. However, that was a long time ago and I haven't any particular resentment towards him. But I think he's really let down Phil, who spent a lot of time just helping him out as a friend with his solo career."

Incredibly, Phil, Scott and BD (with two Brians in the band, the drummer was sometimes called this or simply Downey) limped through a handful of dates as a three-piece (evoking for Brian and Phil memories of the original band, no doubt!), after which Midge Ure joined the lads on the road, his first date being July 18th in New Orleans. Downey had been against the three-piece idea, but it was decided that given Lizzy's track record of cancelled US tours, skipping out on any number of dates would have been career suicide. Tramping through the south, the band's next big show was at the World Series Of Rock in Cleveland, where they shared the stage with co-headliners Aerosmith and Ted Nugent, plus Journey (tour mates virtually throughout this leg), AC/DC and Scorpions, a seminal late '70s proto-metal event if there ever was. US leg over in August, Lizzy experience their next line-up change in advance of the band's next career event, a scheduled September tour of Japan.

"I had earlier met Scott," begins Dave Flett, guitarist of choice on these milestone dates, Flett having proven himself through his work with Manfred Mann's Earth Band. "There was a music show called Top Of The Pops and it was on every Thursday night. Lizzy were playing 'Rosalie', if I remember correctly, and we were playing either 'Blinded By The Light' or 'Thunder Road', as Manfred Mann. Anyway we were on the same show together and we got chatting, and Scott and I kept in touch, and I would beat him in darts now and again. A couple years later when I heard Gary Moore had left, I knew that since I knew Scott, I knew I would at least get an audition, so that's what I did. I got through to the management company, found out when they were holding auditions, and just got in there with an audition. That's how it all began."

"It was some big rehearsal room on the outskirts of London," continues Dave. "I had a '58 or '59 Les Paul. But I remember that they had had a couple of auditions that morning, and they said, 'Come on, we'll have a beer first.' I remember, they were having a giggle, because I don't remember who the last chap was, and he had wangled his way in for an audition. They were just starting, and Phil said, 'Okay, what do you want to play?' He said, 'Well, you guys just start, and I'll jam along,' and apparently this guy had not even learned a single Thin Lizzy song. So they were joking, 'Well, Dave, I hope you're better than the last guy.' But I'd done my homework. Obviously, being in Britain and playing guitar, Thin Lizzy was an inspiration in that style of guitar playing, and although I hadn't played tracks, I knew how the tracks went, so when the audition was coming up, I got all the albums, went to a friend's cottage for a couple of days and learned everything. So I was very determined, when I got to the audition, I wouldn't let the side down. I thought, even if I didn't get it, I wouldn't be wasting their time or mine."

And what does one play at an audition for Thin Lizzy? "I believe we did 'Jailbreak', 'Still In Love With You', maybe 'Rosalie'. You know I felt pretty good about it, because after two or three numbers, Phil put together sort of a proper stage set-up, and he said, 'Let's try this,' and then they came out with two tracks that they were going to be playing in the future that hadn't been recorded, possibly 'Sweetheart' and 'Didn't I'; it was two tracks and they were just getting those together. So the fact they were doing that, and we were working on guitar with Scott, I thought well, I guess they must know that I can play."

"First of all, the guitars have got to be set up pretty well," continues Dave, asked about the particular challenges of being parachuted in and playing Thin Lizzy's famed twin leads. "Because if you're a wee bit out of tune with a keyboard or something, your ear sort of hears it, you can sort of bend the string a fraction to try and get into pitch. But when you've got two guitars, playing harmony, and especially if you're bending notes as well, you've got to be spot-on. If somebody is bending a note, you've got to have the bend at the same time. Although it's harmony, it has to sound like the same person is playing it. But it's great; it's truly enjoyable playing the Lizzy harmony lines, because they're well thought-out. Although they're simple and straightforward, they're extremely effective. Challenge-wise, we did 'Waiting For An Alibi', and there's a part, where Scott takes a solo, and then coming out of the solo, it comes into that twin guitar part. You're just sort of playing, and then Scott's playing away, and then you have to jump in and join him, and there's a lot of hammer-ons and seeking the right place far up the neck, playing pretty quickly. You had to be on your toes for that one. That was a wee bit... well, I had to keep on my toes for all of them."

I wondered if Dave had noticed what the vibe had been in the Lizzy camp concerning Gary's flame-out. "Gary had obviously been a very good friend, and I think for a while, making *Black Rose*, it really worked. I always loved Gary's playing — he had something extra. But I think because he had spent so many years doing his own thing, with The Gary Moore Band and different versions of that, solo albums, I think although *Black Rose* worked, I suspect that when you've actually been on your own, I think it's a bit like when you've been growing up in your parents' house and you leave home and go and find your own apartment, and then something happens, disaster strikes, and you've got to go back and live with your mum and dad for a few months (laughs). Once you've been out on your own, it's nice to be back there with your mum and dad — it's very familiar — but it's never quite the same again. So I think it was inevitable that he wasn't going to stay with Thin Lizzy for any length of time."

Contrasting Moore's work on *Black Rose* and that of Scott, Flett figures that, "Scott is an extremely underrated guitar player, because he's very solid, and when you think of Thin Lizzy, first of all, you often think from the guitar player perspective, Eric Bell back in Ireland, and then Brian Robertson because of his sound, and then you say Gary Moore. But Scott's got a very nice, simple, melodic style, and most of the time, he's always got some phasing going on, a very slow chorus/phaser on his tone. So with Scott, you've always got a fuller, thicker sound, whereas when you hear Gary's sound, when he's got the neck pickup on, it's just really mellow and bluesy and nice, but when he clicks the treble pickup on, it's really biting and cuts through, where Scott would put a small amount of chorus on his guitar, and that sort of takes away the hard edge, just softens it, makes it slightly mellower. But for example, the *Black Rose* track, that's all Gary, playing the Irish jig."

Clarifying the circumstance of his period with the band, Dave explains that, "Gary Moore left while they were still mid-tour in America, and then Midge Ure from Ultravox, who had the same management as Thin Lizzy and had been doing a couple odds and ends, some tracks with Phil, he came in. Because he played keyboards and a bit of guitar, management said, 'Gary's gone; we'll get Midge in there.' The idea was to get them out of a jam. As soon as they came back, the auditions started, because he wasn't going to be continuing with them. But I toured Japan with them. I think we had seven or eight gigs, Tokyo, Osaka, the main ones I guess. But yes, Midge Ure was the keyboardist, and then for the encores, like for 'Rosalie' and things like that, Midge would come off the keyboards and Scott, myself and Midge, just for the encore, would play guitars, just for the big rock 'n' roll finale. Then we did a couple of Christmas gigs, north of London, in this huge old abattoir. But it was a big, big gig, about 100 miles outside of London. We did that, and we did one in Manchester, and one other; I think we did three Christmas gigs."

Asked to characterise Ure, Flett figures, "Midge was a nice guy, Scottish guy, but it was very much... how should I put this? He wasn't part of Thin Lizzy. You heard things printed here and there, but he never was part of Thin Lizzy. The story is Gary left in the middle of the tour, Midge jumped in to help them, and that was it. He was just getting Ultravox off the ground and I think Visage was the band he was actually involved in when he was helping Lizzy, so that was his focus. He didn't dress like a rock 'n' roll guitar player. He dressed like he was the keyboard main man in Visage. But you know, nice guy, never any problems, got along quite well."

"But yeah, basically, they were in the middle of the tour and there was some big blow-up and Gary just left. So Midge literally got on the Concorde that night or that afternoon, and flew right to the gig and learned a few songs and just took over Gary's spot. It was either get somebody in right now who might know the material, or else cancel the tour and throw a lot of money away and disappoint a heck of a lot of fans."

During his tenure, Flett didn't see much evidence of drug use in the band. "I mean, smoking a bit of pot and stuff, but there was nothing like... no powders going on. I went in there, did the auditions, got down to work. The guitar playing duties came down to myself or Snowy White. So Snowy was playing with Pink Floyd on *The Wall* tour — he was involved in that, so I guess they took the opportunity to say, okay, let's take Dave out to Japan. He can certainly handle it and we'll do that. So basically it was short-lived. I was in there, rehearsing every day. As far as drugs are concerned, there are no drugs in Japan (laughs). If there did, you'd be in a heck of a lot of trouble. Then we got back, and Phil was in the studio doing his *Solo In Soho* album. Popped in there here and again, people were working, and then I got the call, 'Will you do these Christmas gigs?' so I went and rehearsed again, and that was pretty much it (note: these were make-up shows for pulling out of the Reading festival). It wasn't like I was with them a long period of time and doing a lot of socialising. So as far as drugs were concerned, yeah, there were a few beers and joints going around, but that isn't what I would call drug use at all."

Where does Dave weigh in on Phil's reputation as Thin Lizzy's drill sergeant? "I don't think Phil was that much of an out-and-out authoritarian leader. He was just a very, very charismatic guy. He gave you leeway: 'Dave, you can play the guitar, you know the gig.' We just got on with it. There was only one time where, when I got to Japan, the second gig or something, I ate something that gave me a wee bit of food poisoning. I was nauseous, dizzy, throwing up all day, and I got to the gig and I looked yellow; he said, 'Just hang back there, stand in front of the drum kit, and just play solid. Don't worry, just get through the gig.' It was a really concerned understanding from him. But of course once the gig started, and the thunder flashes went off, and Scott and Phil were running up the skywalk, there was no way I was just going to stand in there like an idiot, so I guess the adrenaline took over and off we went (laughs). Those guys had been doing it for a long time — you just go to work. You do what you do, get up; you'd make sure you're rested. There was no crazy lunacy around at that time. You showed up, did the gig, gave our best, a few drinks afterward, and it was pretty good. No major rituals or anything like that. They're just rock 'n' roll guys."

The band did in fact play those two advance *Chinatown* songs — 'Sweetheart' (with quite a few different lyrics) and 'Didn't I' (really loose and jammy) — live in Japan, Dave soloing rapidly, admirably, braying synth from Ure sounding like an intrusion... "Yes, and as far as playing with Thin Lizzy, that was a really good feeling for me, that I was actually playing new Lizzy tracks that no guitar player had been playing before. It was quite nice, somewhat of a compliment, that they felt confident enough in my abilities that we could go and perform these new tracks."

"The one interesting thing about the Japan trip," continues Dave, "was, while we were there, the championship sumo wrestling was on television all the time. When we were in Tokyo, we had finished the gig, came back in the car, and I remember walking out to go back into the hotel. There was a huge sumo wrestler in a kimono and his hair all up in a bun and some needles through the top. He was marching, sort of pacing up and down, outside the front of the hotel. He seemed to be quite disgruntled. Apart from what he was wearing, a big person in Japan really stands out, because they're not known to be a tall nation. Then he got angrier and angrier, and we stopped and looked for him, and then we realised, another taxi had come along to get him somewhere, and someone who was taking care of him was making mistakes, because the next time a cab came along, yet again, he couldn't get in it. It was like a small Toyota, and I think that's what was pissing him off. It was about the second or third, and this one, he didn't even try to get in it. Sumo wrestler and big was putting it mildly. But yeah, remember, it was Lizzy's first time in Japan. That was another thing that I was pleased about, because they'd never been there before. They wanted to make a good impression, so it's great that everything went well. The Japanese people were extremely polite and extremely welcoming. But because it was the first time there, they didn't do the Budokan. They weren't sure what sales would be like. So we did a couple of really big theatres, I believe."

"I think it comes down to the best man got the gig," continues Flett, on how it worked out that Snowy White would come to be the next Thin Lizzy guitarist. "There's no sour grapes at my end. I went to Japan with them, I did the British gigs, and Snowy is a wonderful player. If you're going to analyse everything, I guess my playing is in the same vein, very much like Brian Robertson's and Gary Moore's. Snowy is a bit different. Instead of more rock/blues, he's more of a tasteful type of blues. People have said he's almost like the sixth member of Pink Floyd that you never heard about. Because all the Dave Gilmour tone, and in-between tone, was very much a tone that Snowy used a lot. So I think, if

I had been Phil and Scott and Brian, it would have been quite nice… obviously, I was okay to have been there and I could have filled the spot, but I think Snowy just brought something different, something not quite in the same blues/rock, Brian Robertson, Gary Moore vein — a different feel. I think it was probably a good move."

But how did Snowy come free from Pink Floyd to be able to switch bands? "Snowy was basically helping out playing during *The Wall*. There was actually a huge wall, and bit by bit the roadies would come out and the wall would come down (laughs). So Snowy was like a second guitar player there in the background. So he had to fulfil that commitment. I think at the end of *The Wall* tour, Floyd stopped for a year or two anyway. So after that was done, everybody was probably having a well-deserved break anyway. Again, he was never a full-time member of Pink Floyd anyway."

Closing out 1979, Gary Moore saw the release of 'Spanish Guitar' as a single, backed with an instrumental version of the same song. What's interesting however is that Phil's vocals were scrubbed from this new issue, with all the vocals being handled by Gary alone. Moore would also show up on Cozy Powell's Over The Top solo album, issued in the fall, as was a Thin Lizzy single pairing 'Sarah' with 'Got To Give It Up', in three different picture sleeves, the track rising to No.24 in the UK charts.

Further on the Lizzy alumni front, Brian Robertson surfaced with his first Wild Horses single 'Criminal Tendencies', backed with 'The Rapist', the latter non-LP, while Phil took time out from working on additional solo material with a visit to the Kingston Crown Court to deal with a raid on his house at which time a pot plant was found growing in his conservatory. An additional supply of pot was found in his Mercedes, and a quantity of cocaine was found in his jacket draped bedside.

4

CHINATOWN

"Snowy was none of those things"

Aside from a new guitarist called Snowy White officially slipping into the ranks of Lizzy in February, the first half of 1980 was more about Phil as a solo artist, although Lynott also managed to marry Caroline Crowther, with Scott serving as his best man.

Phil's *Solo In Soho* would be issued on April 18th, but before that, Brian Robertson would strike with his first post-Lizzy record, with his band Wild Horses, who would cut a swath of terror across the rock scene in a two-record flash, as much of the mayhem caused by ex-Rainbow bassist Jimmy Bain as it was Robbo.

"Jimmy, what can I say about Jimmy?" muses Kit Woolven, engineer and producer who would go on to work with both Wild Horses and Thin Lizzy. "Good fun to work with, doesn't muck about, but again, another one with a few too many drug problems. Which was the problem when we did the second Wild Horses album. That was very, very difficult, with Robbo and Jimmy. There were just so many drugs going down. But Jimmy is a good lyricist, very melodic, and that's why Jimmy and Phil got on very well, on the solo stuff. But making that second Wild Horses record, *Stand Your Ground* — very, very difficult."

"They had great delusions of adequacy, those guys," figures guitarist/keyboardist Neil Carter, in Wild Horses for the first album, but out by *Stand Your Ground*. "They were good fun but again, they were terrible wasters, both him and Brian Robertson. They were characters, let's put it that way. They were great, strong characters, both of them. With hindsight, it's always a learning process. In life, you need people like this. I've worked with some real characters through the years and I can look back on it now and think that they were a bit of a nightmare but it was great fun. I hadn't seen Jimmy for years, but I saw him, when I was playing with Gary Moore, when we were playing with Rush, funnily enough. We were in Los Angeles, on one of the tours I did with Gary. I hadn't seen him in a long time. I don't know what they do now. They always seemed to jump about. They must all still enjoy doing it. That's all I can say."

Once out of Wild Horses, Neil would end up in UFO for a productive run, that being a band often compared with Lizzy... "Thin Lizzy and UFO, entirely different animals, really," says Neil in disagreement. "If you actually look at the two groups, Thin Lizzy is almost like a different style of rock music. You've got that Celtic influence. You never get that with UFO which is essentially a very British rock act, with American leanings — because they spent a lot of time in America. There were slight Americanisms. But Thin Lizzy, not at all and very much not a British band. Phil Lynott was an Irishman, completely different, although I can't put it into words. I don't ever remember Phil Mogg talking about Thin Lizzy. Because UFO were geared more towards America and Americana."

Then after UFO, Carter played with yet another Thin Lizzy guitarist, Gary Moore, Carter being somewhat surprised at how the hard rocking material during his tenure turned out to be something Moore would dismiss and even disown in later years. "I know, he has, yeah. It's very strange. I mean, I'm sitting here looking at all my gold albums for all that stuff we did in those years, and I just can't believe that he dismisses it. We had a chat a couple years ago about it, and it's almost like he's slightly embarrassed by it. Yet it set him up to do what he does now (ed. Gary was still alive at the time of the author's conversation with Neil)."

"It's paved the way for him to becoming... well, after we finished *After The War*, he went straight on and did *Still Got The Blues* and that's the album that actually pushed him into the next strata. But he was pretty big at the time that I was with him. The thing is, is that it never crossed over particularly. We toured America quite a few times, and Canada, but he never really made any headway in the States particularly. That's the difference between him and UFO, I suppose. UFO always did quite well in certain parts of the States. But Gary essentially did very well in places like Scandinavia and Germany, where UFO did moderately. But I mean, I've got gold albums from all those territories, really, really successful albums, by Gary Moore. I've got one silver album from UFO and yet I've got twenty something gold albums for Gary Moore."

"Gary's stuff has done so well over the years," continues Carter. "Like I said, the songs... 'Empty Rooms' has paid for my house; it bought my house. So it amazes me that UFO has so much stuff over the years, but like I said, there has been so much wastage that has gone on. I walk into one of our record stores like Virgin or HMV and there's this catalogue of UFO albums coming out. I don't actually know where the money goes. Who gets the money? Because we certainly don't. It amazes me. But 'Empty Rooms' has been great. I wrote that when I was on tour with UFO. There was quite a lot of stuff I was writing with them in mind that ended up with Gary. Because it was at that time that Gary approached me to join him and that's when I jumped ship and went off with Gary."

"The first one has much more energy," says Wild Horses drummer Clive Edwards, asked to characterise the tight, two-album catalogue of the band before it all went pear-shaped. "All those songs had been played live. You know, we'd gone out and gigged it. That was the set, really. There was only a couple of minor changes to arrangements although suddenly new arrangements popped up on the day of recording 'Street Girl'. It's like, 'Oh, we've got this new idea,' and I think it was possibly an idea that had come up with Jimmy and Trevor Rabin; there's that half time in the chorus, which I'm not particularly keen on. In the verses it's got this sort of backing vocal thing going on, and if you ask me, I've got the demo where it doesn't have that, and I must say I prefer it, straight 4/4. But that's really the first album. The first album is our live set, minus a few tracks, like 'The Kid'. Brian did all of the mixing and stuff like that, with Trevor. I think Trevor hadn't really produced that much before. They are quite strong, dominant personalities, but in the end, Brian — hard to control. You had to coax… and a lot of it is reverse psychology with those people. You know, if you say to them, 'I want this,' you won't get it. So you have to say, 'Well, I don't want that,' and then they will start doing it the way you want them to do it."

"Brian is much more that way than Jimmy," qualifies Clive. "But Jimmy is quite a strong personality. With Dio he wouldn't have had the clout — it isn't his band — whereas Wild Horses, it was Jimmy and Brian's band. In fact that's one of the differences between the two albums. Jimmy's influence is much stronger on the second album, production-wise and songwriting-wise. Obviously by then, Jimmy had worked a lot and had some access with Phil, and so his status within the band was higher. I think with the first album, Brian was more of a dominant character and Jimmy would go along with it. Also, the single, 'Flyaway' (credited to Bain/Lynott), that suddenly came out of nowhere. It's an old song of Jimmy's, and it was like we're in the album, and next thing, you come into the studio, 'We're going to do a new song today called 'Flyaway'.' 'What the fuck is that?' So there were a few little curveballs tucked in."

"The second album was completely different. Production-wise, they had Kit Woolven, and obviously Kit worked a lot with Lizzy and Tony Visconti, and he would be much more of a producer's producer. Trevor is very much a musician, rather than a producer, and he fitted in with what Brian and Jimmy were doing in early days. Whereas Kit was actually a producer, and there's no point doing an album, especially coming out of working with Lizzy, and not have his sound on it. You can hear a totally different take on sounds — drums, guitars, stuff like that. The songs are much more sophisticated, but the thing is, is that none of them were played live. Which for me personally, I always prefer to have at least gigged the songs a little bit. Certainly some of them anyway."

"Some songs were great when you just put them together and you record them. But a lot of songs, by taking them out on the road a little bit, they morph into 'Yeah, that song should sound like this.' That's just a natural thing of playing a song live, and that didn't happen on the second album, so it hasn't got that. Like I say, the first album, it's almost like punk rock, a punky feel, that kind of energy. The second album didn't have that rawness and energy."

"Brian would never talk about Lizzy," continues Edwards. "I think it was a bit of a sore point. He never really got over the fact that he had fallen out with Phil. That Phil had found it impossible to work with him. I talk with Brian, you know, all the time, and quite recently, we were talking about that, and I said, 'Fucking 'ell, Brian, think. How bad must you have been, to have broken up the A-team? You've got a great band, everything is going great, *Live And Dangerous*, hit singles, everything was great, why would you break that up?' The only way you break that up is if you have a major problem. So Brian hadn't really thought of it like that. So Brian wouldn't really talk about that much in the Wild Horses days. It was, as I say, a sore point."

And Clive's take on why they broke up the A-team? "Well, the answer was that Brian was absolutely unmanageable. Brian got the sack from Motörhead for drinking too much! That's a gold medal in my books. You know, what did he have to do to get the sack from Lizzy? He refused to play all the old songs. He wouldn't play any of the old stuff because he thought it was shit. Brian was a bit of a monster, most of the time. Especially when he was drinking, and he was drinking all the time. So basically, Phil had had enough, and Lemmy had had enough. It's typical, you know. Brian at the time was just an awkward bastard to work with. Everybody loved his playing, and he's got so much goodwill going for him, everyone goes, 'Oh, I'd love to see Brian.' It's just, Brian had a lot of people wanting to work with him, but he had a self-destruct mechanism going on — musically as well as mentally."

"We did quite a few gigs with Wild Horses," recalls Steve Dawson, bassist for Saxon. "In fact, we did some rehearsals in a famous place in London called John Henry's, where all the bands rehearsed. There were quite a few rooms in there and Wild Horses were rehearsing in the next room, and they inevitably didn't do much rehearsing, but did a right lot of drinking.

Jimmy Bain and Robbo were always coming into our rehearsal room and saying, right, let's play Led Zeppelin or let's play Cream, and we couldn't get any rehearsing done when they were there (laughs). Jimmy Bain — a brilliant bass player that I respect totally; completely brilliant guy. I remember, we did some gigs with Dio a few years ago, and Jimmy was playing the bass for them again. We were speaking after, and he really made me laugh, because we were talking about him drinking and everything, and he said something along these lines, '80 to '83... dirty. '83 to '85, clean' (laughs). This just went on and on and on until you just got to where it was just dirty all the time (laughs)."

"Only sort of like loosely," answers Clive, asked if he ever worked with Phil. "Like around his house, in his studio, or with Jimmy. So it would be myself, Jimmy and Phil. Worked on quite a lot of stuff with Scott. Actually, I did some stuff with Scott and John Taylor from Duran Duran. None of it was used. I think Scott was trying to get a solo album deal, but he didn't get the deal, so the songs are on tape. I've got copies of all of it. Some of the stuff with Jimmy and Phil morphed into a few of the solo record things, but quite loosely. But they're cassettes. Some of the stuff goes on for hours. Jimmy would be out of it, Phil would be out of it, and it's just early days writing, just going over fiddles and chorus lines, and Jimmy would just sing for hours. Phil used to do it as well. They would get themselves into the right mood, basically." With respect to Phil's home studio, located down by his garden, Midge Ure used to joke that it was the only 7-track studio in the world, given that it was an 8-track set-up with one bum track that never worked.

"I don't think Phil would decorate, no; he would get somebody in to decorate," laughs Clive asked about how Phil kept his home. "Phil was very much DIP, rather than DIY, you know, DIY being do-it-yourself, Phil was 'Do it, please.' So, I'll tell you one thing, when *Solo In Soho* had come out... you know the front cover, he's got like his coat on, and his collars are up or something, well there were these big cardboard cut-outs that were going in the shops, and he had one, and he put it in his front window, so as you come through the gate, unless you knew it was there, you'd look, you know, 'Oh, there's Phil.' Because it was a full life-sized cardboard cut-out, and he had that in the front room. But the place was decorated nice. It was a family home. Caroline lived there and I think later on she moved out and was over in Ireland a lot. Later on... because Phil was a philanderer, we all know this. He couldn't keep his pants, you know, zipped up for very long. He always used to say to me, 'Clive, don't do as I do, do as I say,' and, 'don't do what I do.' But yeah, with Phil, it was a bit of an open house. You would go around there, 'Oh, there's Scott;' there would be Billy Idol; there would be Phil, Darren."

"Always something going on. Phil was always a very open guy, really. He wasn't much of a quiet person; he liked to have people around him and he was always out and about. He knew everything that was going on. He knew most of the new players and would check them out. He was always full of encouragement to young players and young bands, much more so than the other rock stars. You wouldn't get that with David Coverdale or something like that, in their lofty castle. Phil was out on a regular basis, and would be, like I say, very approachable to people, and would always give some encouragement to musicians and bands."

"Phil was quite unique, because he was a storyteller with his lyrics," continues Edwards, asked about Phil intellectually speaking. "You know, I would compare him to Phil Mogg as another great lyricist (note: Clive later drummed for UFO), but they're very dark and they're lyrics — they're not stories. You can't listen to a UFO song like you can 'Dancing In The Moonlight' or 'The Boys Are Back In Town'. I just listened to 'Cold Sweat' recently. It's a story! The guy's putting money on a horse, and I think that comes from the Irish limerick thing, or the Irish folk songs, where they all tell a story. Because that's what music is all about. The tradition of that has stayed alive in Ireland, whereas in England, pretty much, all the old folk songs are stone dead. You know, no one sings 'John Barleycorn must die.' So I think that's probably one of the biggest influences on Phil's writing, was that storytelling element. It set him apart from everybody else."

"Nobody else wrote stories, or very rarely. Maybe Townsend did in Tommy or something, but then they don't really work as well. You never listen to Phil, a Lizzy song, and say, 'Oh, there's a story going on here.' It just comes over and it doesn't get in the way, whereas somebody else tries to write a story and lyrics, and it would probably get in the way of the chorus or the verses. But Phil had this knack that he could do it, and he must've been well-read to have had that. But I never saw him reading that much."

On the subject of Phil's musical tastes, Clive says, "I never spent lots of hours, just me and him. He would say he loved Elvis, but I didn't spend ages watching him play all the Elvis stuff. When I was around, he would only play what he was working on, or what he wanted to work on, or something he knew — because Phil was in the here and now. Elvis would've been what he grew up with, and that's what influenced him, and that's why it was important to him. But you know, you don't have time. He's writing this new album and all you're doing is listening to what you're working on, so you listen to the demos, come up with new stuff, you're listening to mixes of the new album, and the only other stuff you're doing is listening to who else is doing what, so you're abreast of what's current. You can't be listening to 'Hound Dog', not when you're trying to write a new album. So he would be listening to the new Queen album, new bands. I never heard him play old stuff."

Back to Clive's and Brian's wild band, aside from the aforementioned 'Flyaway', two other tracks on the first album maintain added relevance to the Lizzy story. One is 'Dealer', which is credited to Bain/Robertson/Gorham, and the other is 'Blackmail'. Explains Lizzy expert and Robbo archivist Sören Lindberg, "The material Brian brought forward to Lizzy over the years, most of it was more or less used. The only song that comes to mind is 'Blackmail'. That I know he demoed with Lizzy, but it didn't really fit the Thin Lizzy format. Phil Lynott had trouble getting that song in his head. And I know for sure that Brian Downey once said that he couldn't get the timing into his head either. So it didn't really work."

"It's a song that Robbo wrote in the mid-'70s somewhere," continues Sören, "and basically, when Lizzy rejected it, he tried it with the Steve Ellis Band, and they recorded it. He also did a solo demo of it, which was never released, which is actually very good. It's probably the best version of all of them and then he obviously did it with Wild Horses. I don't know if most people know this, but Wild Horses started out as very much a Jimmy Bain solo album, where Jimmy started recording five, six tracks, with Morgan Fisher from Mott The Hoople. What happened was, with Robbo losing his position with Lizzy in '78... Robbo was already involved with Jimmy's solo album, sort of playing guitar and whatnot, but at that point it became more of a band thing. So obviously both of them had songs that they did together. The credits on the album say Bain/Robertson on every song, but that wasn't really the truth, because like I said, 'Blackmail' is a lot older, and it's actually one of Robbo's own compositions."

"I don't know if I really want to discuss that one. No, not really," says Robbo, asked for an assessment of Jimmy. "As far as I know, he walked out on Dio after being given so many chances. Again, he was involved with the drugs, with Phil. I didn't appreciate that at all. You know, I took him in as my best mate, sort of thing, and it turned out not to be that. I know he says that, because I was asked in one interview, 'Would you ever put Wild Horses back together again?' I said certainly not. Not a chance. He came back and said, 'Oh, I don't know why Robbo would say that.' Very well, if he doesn't know, then he's obviously back on the drugs (laughs). I mean, it's painfully obvious what went down, even though he apologised about it. But it was unacceptable to me. Because you give your friendship to somebody and you get kicked back in your face. I don't deal with that well. I'm a pretty open geezer."

"He's from Scotland as well," says fellow Scot Jimmy, as explanation as to why Brian turned out such a hell-raiser. "I met him when I was in my band Harlot, before Rainbow, and I stayed pretty close to him. After I got the boot from Rainbow I went straight back to England the next day. He had been in some skirmish and he couldn't play with Lizzy for a while. They were using Gary Moore, so him and I got together and we clicked and wrote some songs and went in and demoed them. He was with Thin Lizzy's management and my best friend was Phil Lynott as well. So I had this idea that him and Robbo had had this head-to-head thing that was never ever going to be sorted out. Basically it worked for me because Phil was basically telling me that 'If you're going to work with that creep, good luck to you!' But I liked it. It was craziness, but we managed to get a record deal and put out a couple of records, one of which was produced by Trevor Rabin. I liked it because I got to sing and we wrote all this stuff. It was a lot of fun and it was a little crazy too. At that time when we were in London, you couldn't get arrested if you were playing anything heavy. It was punky and rebellious and we were playing the wrong kind of music at the time. But it was a lot of fun."

"We used to go down to Blitz club, for instance," recalls Woolven, on Phil's enthusiasm for modern music, "where there was a lot of New Romantic, and then sort of crossing over into punk people, hanging out there. Phil really embraced all that sort of thing. A lot of other bands at that time were very discouraged, or very anti- the whole punk thing. Phil really did sort of embrace it, saying you had to look forward and you had to go with all this new stuff. Which was good, yeah. When we were doing the *Black Rose* album, when we were in Paris then, when we were working on the sessions on *Chinatown*, and when we were working on the solo stuff together, very often it was just Phil and myself in the studio for days at a time. We would go out after the session, in the evening and meet up with various people, members of the Sex Pistols, and of course there was the whole Greedy Bastards thing."

Swing completely the other way, and there's Phil cavorting with punk's prime adversary, Yes! "Chris Squire and myself did a track with him," recalls Yes drummer Alan White, "with some ridiculous name, something that just came out of the blue, that was dreamed up by, I think, originally Phil, but then we spent about seven hours in the studio. It was called something like 'Silly Willy' (laughs). It was a really, really silly song. I wish I could find a copy of it. This was possibly middle of the '70s, maybe a little bit later. It just came out of Chris' friendship with Phil Lynott. Chris knew Phil better than I did, because he lived in the same area as Phil — Virginia Water — in England, so they were more friends than I was. I just saw him occasionally and said hi. But I was around, and we just went into the studio and just worked it — a bit of lunacy, actually. I think Phil played guitar, and Chris played bass, and I think Phil sung it. It was a really silly piece of music, but it was fun at the time."

"It was probably in the early '80s," counters Squire. "Phil used to come visit with his family, and when I had a studio in my house, we put down a couple of tracks. One was called 'Little Silly Willy', I remember that (laughs). It was a tongue-in-cheek kind of song. There was another song that might have been called 'Hurricane' or something like that — some weather condition (laughs); I can't really remember much about that song. Phil was a great guy. Of course, as we all know, he was a dyed-in-the-wool drug addict, but he was a lot of fun as well (laughs). Yeah, we had some good times and we had some creative times together. I'll always remember him fondly."

The track in question was none other than 'Don't Talk About Me Baby', which indeed contains the "little silly willy" bits. The song would show up on Phil's second solo album, *The Philip Lynott Album*, however with different players, including Gong's Pierre Moerlen on drums.

Like Kit Woolven, Jimmy was also there to lend witness to Phil's affinity for punk. "Yes, well, I went and worked up at his house a few times and Sid Vicious is sitting in there or Johnny Rotten was over, or Rat Scabies. We did the Greedy Bastards and that was a good indication of a marriage between punk and hard rock, with the Thin Lizzy guys and myself and Chris Spedding, and it was really good. There was no problem with it. Just musicians getting together, it was all good fun. The punks... I think they maybe liked rock but they didn't really care for it because you had to actually play your instrument to get away with playing metal music. It wasn't like you could just record and get by with it. Johnny Thunders did it but he was a bit of a cross between one and the other. He was a bit heavy and a bit punk. There was more envy than bad blood, and Phil Lynott was just one of these guys that everybody liked and it didn't matter who you were; if you're black, white, green or blue, everybody loved him and he loved pretty well everybody, too and he crossed the border with the music."

But any success Wild Horses had wouldn't have had anything to do with punk. It was more likely that the band received a bit of a boost from the New Wave Of British Heavy Metal movement exploding at the time. Because there was Wild Horses, stacked with veteran players, sure, but a feisty new hard rock band as well.

"Absolutely, yeah," says Jimmy. "Iron Maiden got signed around the same time we did. There wasn't a lot of deals going around with the punk thing happening. I think Maiden were one of the first ones, and it looked like they could just go and take on the world. They had great management and great players and had a great attitude to it, and they've proved over the years they've done exactly that. Back then it was just playing down the Greyhound on the Marquee and stuff like that, and any other little bits and bobs of gigs you could get anywhere else. It was still few and far between at that point. But the thing grew pretty quick when it got started, and you could tell there was a lot of talent in England. There's always been a lot of talent, and kids just wanted to get a chance to get away from their problems and stuff. There was a lot of great bands who came out of that time. I was happy for everybody that got a chance to get in the studio and record."

"As far as us playing live, we had Sweet Savage support us; that was Vivian Campbell's band. We toured with Ted Nugent in England and Scotland supporting him, and we played a couple shows with Rush at Bingley Hall in Stafford. The other shows we would do we were just playing on our own with some local bands. Oh yeah, Def Leppard supported us in Sheffield a couple weeks before they got signed. But we weren't very heavy metal, Wild Horses, but we were happy to get tagged in with whatever was happening just to get a bit of recognition. So I was happy about it. We were trying to get something that would get us over to America. Almost like The Faces — not metal but more like good time rock 'n' roll."

"Phenomenal guitar player," adds Jimmy, on the subject of Robbo. "I love working with Brian, just one of a kind and I think he was one of the biggest influences people like Steve Clarke from Def Leppard had. He just adored Robbo and the style, which is definitely rooted in the blues. Brian was just a super guy. Maybe I think him and I drank a little too much, without exaggerating on it. We did get drunk a lot. Scottish people do when they get together. But we were friends too. We shared an apartment for a long time. We were never that far away from each other, and it was a perfect partnership for a while. After a while it just got to be a bit much with the drinking and I got fed up with it and tried a couple other things, but it never worked out as good as the original."

As regards Def Leppard, it wasn't just Steve Clark that was enamoured with the band. Joe Elliott is on record as a huge fan, plus... "Yeah, Thin Lizzy, definitely, the two guitar thing," says guitarist Phil Collen. "Definitely an influence on the Def Leppard end of it. I loved Thin Lizzy, especially the early stuff. I loved the fact that they were 'a gang.' But obviously as soon as Phil wasn't around, it was more like the Stones without Mick Jagger. It wasn't that gang thing that happened to be Scott Gorham, Phil Lynott, Brian Robertson, and Brian Downey on drums. I do remember, interestingly enough, I was in London, early '80s, and Fast Eddie just left Motörhead, and somebody had asked, 'So what do you think? Who are they going to get?' Brian Robertson! Funny enough, ironically, he was going to join and obviously they get a better player, but it was like, well I don't like him anymore! They're not a gang anymore. That whole thing, Thin Lizzy for me, I really enjoyed the gang thing. The songs and the context of it was pretty cool as well."

Flash forward three decades to modern times and another Def Leppard guitarist, Viv Campbell, actually moonlights in Thin Lizzy. "He loved it," says Collen. "It's like a dream come true. For all of those reasons, and more so for Vivian, because he's Irish, and Thin Lizzy evoked that spirit of the   Irish artist, the songwriter, the rebel, all that stuff. Phil Lynott was great, and in every respect, he was probably the only black man in Ireland at the time, and so he had a real thing, a real special band, and so for Vivian to be part of that, I think growing up in Ireland and seeing all of that stuff, was absolutely a dream come true."

As alluded to, Jimmy Bain (Viv Campbell's co-worker in the classic Dio line-up) had a hand in Phil's *Solo In Soho* album as well as *The Philip Lynott Album*, Phil's second and last solo record, issued a couple years later. *Solo In Soho's* April 18th release date was preceded by the single for the irresistible 'Dear Miss Lonely Hearts', backed with the pure reggae of the title track. 'Dear Miss Lonely Hearts' was in fact played by the Thin Lizzy line-up of the day, namely Phil, Scott, Brian and Snowy White, the lads showing up in a number of spots, as did past touring drummer Mark Nauseef.

"I think that was partly written with Jimmy Bain," recalls Scott with respect to 'Dear Miss Lonely Hearts', the lyric of which parallels the theme of Nathaniel West's seminal short novel Miss Lonelyhearts. "I've always liked that song. It sounds like it's in hit single country. I think we only did that song live a couple of times. In fact, I even have a recording of it, from RDS in Dublin. Phil does a whole speech and all that in the middle of it, but beyond that, I don't think that song really lasted too long in the set. As you can see, it got confusing there, didn't it? Are we doing this for Thin Lizzy or is this for Phil's solo stuff? What's going on here? You know, what would happen a lot of times, is that in the writing stages, we would all bring our things in, and especially with Phil, he would bring something in, and we'd go, 'You know, Phil, I love the song, but I think it's more of a solo song.' Rather than him getting upset with that, for him that was more ammunition for his solo stuff. So that's basically how he gathered all his solo material. It all ran through Thin Lizzy first, but when it got the rejection, it went on to the 'to do' solo pile."

"But the trips to the Bahamas, that was purely for Phil's solo albums," continues Scott. "I mean, Phil was so into being Thin Lizzy, that he didn't even bother getting other musicians. Most of it was done by the guys in Thin Lizzy (laughs). But it was all done on Phil's dime, with the solo album, and a lot of the time, to be quite honest, we just sat on the beach drinking Bahama Mamas (laughs)."

Explained Phil in the press pack for the album, "Me and Jimmy Bain of Wild Horses got together one night and he had this chord sequence that I came up with the hook line for it, which was plaguing me and plaguing me. So one Monday I was reading the problems page. For some reason they always put Marjorie Proops in on a Monday, and I came up with this idea. It's about a situation where people would write into a hearts page and the chick would give the wrong reply to each person. The lyric was written out in Nassau, where we did a few backing tracks and where we did a song called 'Jamaican Rum', a Calypso thing just to get that authentic feel."

Into early June, Phil's playful, versatile album would yield another single, 'King's Call' being an impressive Lizzy-grade ballad commemorating the death of Elvis. The single, which reached No.35 in the UK charts, was backed with gritty rock 'n' roller 'Ode To A Blackman'.

"Everyone says it sounds like Dire Straits," wrote Phil. "I jammed with them over Christmas at the Rainbow and I said, 'Look, I'm in the studio, why not come down?' Mark Knopfler liked the track and came down and played guitar on it. He's the type of guy who wouldn't play on somebody's stuff unless he thought it was good. The only other sessions he's done have been with Dylan and Steely Dan, I think. It's about things like Elvis or Dr. Martin Luther King. It's just how I felt on that night that Elvis, the King, died."

"I didn't meet Mark Knopfler," says future Lizzy member Darren Wharton, also a staple of the Phil solo stable. "He came out to the house for a drink with Phil, and I remember he just brought Phil a copy of his new album, which had just been out three weeks and it'd just sold half a million. Phil just had the knack of finding top people."

"I just loved doing those," recalls Kit. "They were wonderful. Having people like Mark Nauseef, Mark Knopfler, Huey Lewis, Jimmy Bain, and of course, all the Lizzy guys were there, in and out (laughs) and Darren of course played lots of parts. He played a big part in the solo albums, the second one particularly. But working with Mark Knopfler was very embarrassing for me. Because Mark wanted to use his characteristic repeat echo on his guitar, which is a very, very simple trick to perform in the studio. And due to a technical hitch that we had in the studio, and the fact that there was a tremendous amount of pressure on us all, 'My God, this is Mark Knopfler,' and we wanted everything to go absolutely perfect, spot-on. We were using a Revox tape machine with vari-speed, for the repeat echo, and it just wouldn't work. We could see the signal going into the machine, but nothing was coming out, so we changed all the leads, still nothing is coming out, we changed channels on the desk, still nothing coming out."

"Mark Knopfler was getting irritated by this time and just wanted to get on and record, and eventually Mark said, 'Look, I'll just play — you sort out the problems later on' and he did, and we did it and it's fantastic. But later on, trying to sort out what the problem was, it was a really stupid thing, a silly little thing called a hum shield, that comes across the head on a Revox tape machine. You can't see it just a glance at it, but the hum shield had come across, and the tape-op put the tape on the wrong side of the hum shield, so it wasn't actually going across the head, and that's why it wasn't working. It's a really silly mistake."

Other highlights to the *Solo In Soho* record included the sensuous pop of 'Girls', the controversial synth rock of 'Yellow Pearl' (inspired by the Yellow Magic Orchestra, whom Phil and Midge were introduced to in Japan), and the funk of closer 'Talk In 79', on which Phil gives a quick state of the world address on the subject of post-punk while Nauseef rips it up, giving his deft percussive answer to Brian's performance way back on 'Boogie Woogie Dance'.

Recalls John Vasey, who worked with Lizzy and Phil solo in the studio as well as with Lizzy live, "I first met Phil when I was 16 years old, I am 55 now. I met him at a friend's house, Miles Landesman. I had moved from Sydney to Ireland when I was 13 and did the last two years of school in Northern Ireland. Years later, when I worked for a sound company, TASCO, I was sent to a Thin Lizzy show with some replacement equipment. Some of the English road crew could not understand Phil's Irish accent, which I had no trouble understanding and I ended up as a sound engineer for the band. In 1979 I left the sound company and Phil called me and asked me to work for Thin Lizzy. I helped get the studio built at his house in Kew and then we worked on the *Solo In Soho* record and *Chinatown*. I also worked as a sound engineer on the shows."

"My first child was born during this time and towards the end of the year I decided to move back to Australia," continues John. "But the home studio was built in the garage of the house in Kew, opposite Kew Gardens. It was an intimate space where the guitar and keyboard parts were added to the rhythm tracks that were recorded in Good Earth studio in Soho. I did the guitar and keyboard tracks for the *Chinatown* and *Solo In Soho* albums. Midge Ure also used the studio for some Ultravox songs. His house was comfortable. Chalkie Davis, a photographer, lived in one of the spare rooms for some time. I don't recall any particular decorations other than an elaborately carved coffee table and yes, Jimmy was there — Jimmy was a young talented performer when I knew him."

Of particular note on *Solo In Soho* is 'Girls', due in no small part to the spoken word in it. 'Girls' was slated to be a Wild Horses single, but then Phil whisked it away, even considering calling the album Girls. "This is Bobby C Benberg (a.k.a. Bob Siebenberg) on drums and I wrote it with Jimmy Bain," commented Phil. "There's no bass on it, just bass Moog, string machines and piano. It's very slick, and it's got a nice tune. I got a lot of girls into the studio, an English girl, a French girl, a Northern Irish girl and a Swedish girl, and I got them to read set pieces that I'd written. Then I took extracts and made it into one piece that cuts in and out of the song. It's a great experimental track for me, the same as Midge's. Now that I've experimented with keyboards and Moogs, I know what I can do and I'm no longer scared of them. Before this, it was the great unknown."

"Oh, Phil Lynott was just unbelievable," remembers Jimmy. "I worked and wrote on a couple of his albums, but on Solo In Solo, I wrote 'Girls' and 'Dear Miss Lonely Hearts' with him. Phil did things really sort of differently. For example, I played a lot of Minimoog and keyboards on the first record. What he would do is just give you an idea of what to play. For example, the song 'Solo In Soho', I played the melody line on Minimoog. There were no drums on it at all, just a click track. He had no idea what he was trying to do, but he had it somewhere in his head and it just developed as it went along. On 'Girls', we did that song, and the drums that guy from Supertramp played, we didn't put that on until the end. So the whole track was completely done with vocals and a basic, very simple drum machine, and then they brought the drummer in at the end to play on it. So the whole track was almost complete and we put the drums on last. It was like 'whoa!' You would play something to him that you thought was really mediocre, you'd just be pissing around, and he would pick up on it."

"He was testing the water a bit with *Solo In Soho*," continues Jimmy, implying that the second record was an example of a freer Phil. "He did try a lot of things that I think worked out pretty good, like the title track. When I went in there I started working with them on that from day one, and I was trying Minimoog or something like that at the time. I had no clue how the finished song was going to be because he didn't have a demo of it. He had an idea and he just related that to me as much as he could, and what he played, but I had no idea how the song was going to go or how it would end up. I just saw the thing grow. Each day it was getting more playing on it, and that was the way he was with the solo stuff. It was testing new waters for him. It wasn't a set thing with the two guitars and the drums and everything like that. He could do things he wouldn't have got to do with Thin Lizzy, and that's why he loved it so much. It was very diverse with whole kinds of different music going on there. I loved working with the guy. He was a genius."

"I like the ones I wrote," laughs Bain, asked for favourites. "'Dear Miss Lonely Hearts' and 'Girls'. I liked particularly 'Girls' because there were a lot of girls on that talking and stuff from different places in the world. As I said, we had Bobby Benberg from Supertramp playing on it. I also liked 'King's Call' a lot."

Remembers Kit on the plush and dramatic Elvis paean, "'King's Call' was literally started off... Phil had a white Falcon guitar. We plugged it in and it had this wonderful, warm tone, and he was just strumming, and that's how it started, right there in the studio. Phil started strumming these chords, we recorded some of it, and then over a few days it developed. Then over the following weeks it eventually became the full song, with everything involved."

With not a whit of reservation, one would have to say that either or both of 'Dear Miss Lonely Hearts' or 'Girls' could have been smash hits of a stature more grand than anything Thin Lizzy had ever written...

"Of course!" says Jimmy, who soon found himself dealing with the same frustration in the Dio band. "See that's the thing, when he did the video for that — I didn't find out this until later — I saw a video and it's Thin Lizzy playing on the song and it wasn't them playing on the record! If he'd used the people that maybe did the actual song, he might have had a completely different audience for it, but because it was a Thin Lizzy thing, everybody thought it was another Thin Lizzy song and it didn't have the same impact."

If the credits are to be trusted, Bain's wrong about that. But the point he's making can be allowed to stand. There was indeed a full production video made featuring all of Thin Lizzy playing the track, a track that was from *Solo In Soho*.

On why Phil was making solo music in the first place, Jimmy figures, "You know, I think what happened was, Thin Lizzy wasn't really happening, and their management Morrison O'Donnell... Phil was the main man. They had Wild Horses, they had Thin Lizzy, and they had a couple of other people as well, but Thin Lizzy was No.1. Then Phil turned the management onto Midge Ure and Ultravox, and then the management took over managing that, and then Phil wasn't No.1 anymore."

Although the first part of 1980 was taken up with record-making and the pondering of a solo career, Lizzy did get out in early April for a considerable spate of Irish shows (support from Tearjerkers), giving Snowy his sea legs, with Midge Ure also on board, slowly transforming Lizzy into a band that uses keyboards regularly.

Says Scott, "How we found Snowy was Phil and I went to a Pink Floyd concert at Madison Square Garden, and this guy, up on the Pink Floyd stage, came out, spotlight hit him, and he played this fucking killer solo. Phil and I turned to each other, and said, 'Who the fuck is that guy?! It ain't Gilmour. Who the hell is that?!' We went backstage, and hunted him down and he said, 'Yes, my name is Snowy White,' blah blah blah, and the next time I saw Snowy was when we were looking for a replacement guitar player. We were down at Pinewood Studios, and who's down there playing with Cliff Richard of all people, but Snowy White? That's when I asked him if he would come down and have a jam with us. 'We've got all these no-hopers down there trying to get in the band; we just need to get somebody in there we can have a good time with.' Not thinking that he would be in the band or anything. He came down, and within about four or five song, Phil and I looked at each other and said, 'Hey, you wanna be in the band?' (laughs)."

"There was a patch of time when I wasn't doing very much for a year or two," explains Snowy, strangely yet perennially dismissive of his experience with Lizzy. "I did this request to go and do a gig... an open air festival with Cliff Richard, who was looking for a guitar player. It really wasn't my cup of tea, but I said yes. We were actually rehearsing and I bumped into Scott Gorham, Thin Lizzy's other guitar player at the rehearsal place. He remembered me because he'd come to see the Animals tour in Madison Square Garden a few months previously. He said, 'Wow man, we're looking for a guitar player. Can you come up and play with us and see how it works out?' I said, 'Well, I can't now, because I'm busy.' So he rang me up about a week later and I went along and they asked me to join."

"I was in two bands at once at one point," continues Snowy. "I was with Thin Lizzy and Pink Floyd, 'cause I said, 'Well I can't do any albums now, because I'm going to America. I'm doing The Wall shows with Pink Floyd in America and that doesn't finish for a few months.' Phil said, 'Well we'll wait till you get back.' So I was back from America for about two days and I went straight into the recording studio with Thin Lizzy to record the first album with them. But, I had to take a break from that to do The Wall shows in Earls Court with the Floyd, so I was sort of with both bands. That was 1980 when I did that. 1980, '81, and half of '82, I think was when I was with Thin Lizzy."

The Devon-born Terence Charles "Snowy" White would actually be the first Englishman to officially join the ranks of Thin Lizzy, and at this point, into his 30s. White had been the epitome of the silent musician in the back as well as a straight session man, having worked with Cliff Richard, Peter Green, Al Stewart, Steve Harley, Pink Floyd keyboardist Rick Wright, and of course, Pink Floyd proper, in the fall of '76, signing on for the band's American and European tours.

Before the next leg of Lizzy's record-less dates begin however, Midge

Ure, always a bit of an amusing question mark within the fold, would be replaced by Darren Wharton, who is now with the band again 30 years later.

"Phil was never one to sit on his laurels, really," says Darren Wharton, explaining his introduction into the band. "He was always trying to push the band with his music, as you can probably tell from his solo albums. He was always trying to experiment and grow. For me, it was sheer chance that Gary Moore left during an American tour. Phil, at the time, didn't really have many options. He flew Midge Ure in to play the keyboards and a little bit of guitar, and just because he wasn't really a keyboard player but a fully-fledged guitarist, he sort of jumped into a bit of keyboards as well, as they were needed, when Phil found them appropriate. They obviously liked the texture of them in the band. So after that tour Midge went off and joined Ultravox, and Phil decided that he wanted more of a permanent keyboard player in the line-up, and obviously that was my lucky break."

"So when the American tour ended," continues Darren, "first on the list was to find another guitarist, which they got in mind with Snowy White, and they also decided that it would be nice to have more of a permanent keyboard player fixture. I was working in a club in Manchester where Phil used to go and have a drink, a place called Dino's, and there was a guy in there, really to see me play. I was playing grand piano in there. I was only 17. So this friend of Phil's called Joe Leach saw me playing, and had been with Phil a couple of nights before and heard that he was looking for a keyboard player and just approached me, really."

"I did know Joe. He was like a friend of the family, and he knew people that knew my family. So he had my phone number, rang me over, and said, 'How do you fancy an audition with Thin Lizzy?' That was it. I said yeah, brilliant. Took me down on the train, and I met Phil and Scott in Good Earth Studios the day they recorded 'Chinatown'. Phil was actually putting his bass part down on 'Chinatown', and asked me to play the descending line on a Minimoog (sings it), that sort of triplet type-feel. I thought it was a really easy one to play on the keyboard, so I played that first time, and then he asked me what football team I supported, and it was United, and I was in. I was in the band (laughs)."

"Scott took me down to the pub, and we seemed to get on really well, and the week after, I was in rehearsals in Shepperton for the European tour. But first I had to learn some of the songs in the set. We were due to start rehearsals at Shepperton, so Phil gave me a list of thirty songs to learn, and when they came back a week later and he said, 'Well, which songs did you learn?' I said, 'I learned all of them.' So we just went through the set and that was it. The week after that we were in

Scandinavia."

"On the album, I ended up playing on about three or four songs," notes Wharton, "including 'Killer On The Loose', only texture stuff. Phil got me down again for three or four days to do some more recording, so I was on a few tracks there. They were still talking about whether they were going to add a keyboardist on a semi-permanent basis. But I think the sheer fact we got on so well, Phil just decided to keep me on board."

"When Darren got into the band, it was a real keyboard season, if you will, at that point in time," recalls Scott, on the subject of Darren's hiring. Indeed, for the Scandinavian tour, he was the typical heavy metal band hired gun keyboardist, hidden in the back and having to plunk out his parts in near darkness. "As you know, we had Midge, because Gary had just kinda flown the coop, left us in the lurch. Phil really liked that idea, figuring it was a little bit more of a modern sound to have the keyboard in there, not like as an upfront instrument, but an instrument that adds a lot of colour and mood. So Phil let it be known to his pals in Manchester that he was thinking about this idea of adding a keyboard player, and some of his buddies up there knew of this whiz kid, who was really young. He was only 17 years old when he came down to us, shaking like a leaf (laughs), scared to death. We could see that he was really young but still put him on the keyboards there while we were doing some recording, and he just so impressed us all, that we started to use him on this show here and that show there."

"We actually started to write a couple of songs around him so he could show off his talent. Then after a while we realised that he could also sing well, so he was like a multi-talented guy who was really young and we felt that we might be able to mould him into our way of playing, so that's why we asked him to join the band, and he's been there ever since."

"In the beginning I thought, what the hell do we need keyboards for?" continues Scott. "This is a guitar-based band. The whole reputation of the band has been based around guitars, but as soon as I started to hear what Darren could actually do and started hanging out with him and what a really cool guy he was, I was all good for it. Especially when I started to hear some of the things he could actually do inside the songs; yeah, I warmed to them really quickly."

Chinatown would be called that, says Darren, partially because that's where it was recorded. "Right, well, we recorded it in Soho in London, which is basically right across the road from Chinatown. Knowing Phil, he probably didn't come up with the idea for the album until he went into the studio. But being in those surroundings, right in the middle of Chinatown, obviously gave him the inspiration."

Asked to sum up Kit Woolven, the co-producer of what would become the band's tenth studio album, Darren goes with, "Really nice guy, easygoing, diplomatic type of guy. Kit was just a really good engineer, basically, and a good friend with all the band — I'm still very friendly with Kit. Looking back, I was naïve. It was difficult to know at that point how far Kit really was involved with actually producing. It certainly wasn't taken out of Phil's hands — it never was. There was always a great deal of Phil, and Scott and Brian, in the actual make-up of the songs, and I think the producer's role, especially Kit's point of view... I didn't work with Tony Visconti — I imagine that was a different scenario — but working with Kit was more of a guiding thing, more of a co-production really. You couldn't really say that Kit produced *Chinatown*; it wouldn't really be fair to say that. But Kit had very important input. That was a time when Phil wanted to be more in control of the production, and wanted somebody there to mould his ideas to make it work."

Lining up with Phil's framing of the *Chinatown* album in interviews, Kit agrees that there was a toughness there that wasn't as prominent on past records. "They were always a very good rock band with very strong melodies. After they did *Black Rose*, I produced *Chinatown* with them, and Phil was very much into the whole sort of metal thing. He wanted to make a harder-sounding album, a more in-your-face album, basically. Which I think is why he wanted me on board. Because it's my sort of thing and not Tony Visconti's, and it had gotten to the stage where Tony was finding it harder and harder to work with them. I was Tony's engineer at the time, and Phil wanted to work with me, and so it worked out well."

Contrasting further the record with *Black Rose*, Kit figures, "They had a different guitarist for a start and I don't think Snowy was particularly ideal in terms of... Snowy didn't add to the metal side of it, because Snowy is more of a blues player. Yet Phil just wanted the whole thing to be more upfront, more in-your-face, more like a rock band live but on record. *Black Rose*, there were a lot more commercial songs on it, like 'Sarah', for instance. But it was hard to do, very largely because there was a tremendous amount of making it up as we went along. Philip was trying to write on mic — there wasn't a whole bunch of pre-production done, as such. In fact, as I can remember, none (laughs)."

"Which always makes it harder," continues Kit, "and I think that particularly got to Snowy, who is used to a more organised or regimented approach to recording and music in general. I think it frustrated Snowy quite a lot."

Yet Snowy didn't have any material as such. Fortunately, the guys had 'Didn't I' and 'Sweetheart', but other than that, responsibility for the songs was put upon Phil. "Yes, and I think he wrote on bass, mainly," says Kit, "but he did occasionally write on guitar. We did the record at Good Earth, which is in Soho, which is Chinatown, in London. Which is how the whole thing came about, including the title Solo in Soho. We ate Chinese food every day (laughs), but other than that, no real significance, really."

"*Chinatown* was a strange album," figures Scott. "It never felt that the production side was all that great. The drug thing was kicking in, in a big way, so we were mentally having a hard time. So it was a tough album to actually get through. It's one of those albums that I rarely listen to, a Lizzy album anyway, but that would be one of the last ones. But both of those records, *Chinatown* and *Renegade*, they're really tough to remember, just because I was going so heavily through the whole drug thing. I listen to a lot of that stuff and go shit, I don't remember recording that stuff. Some of the actual guitar work on there is pretty intricate, and I'm thinking, how'd the hell did I ever even get that one together? (laughs)."

Chinatown, issued on October 10th 1980, opens with a statement of defiance, 'We Will Be Strong' striking a deft alchemy between Lizzy as melancholic pop and Lizzy as aggressive, driving hard rock with a punk edge. Its overall sense of desperation — essentially hope toward strength in the future rather than confident affirmation of strength now — smacks of Phil's heavier solo statements. All told, the track's subtle blends points to an increased sophistication in the band, perhaps due to Snowy, but weirdly, a sophistication within a track that was easy to dismiss as covering tried and even tired themes. Still here come the twin leads and one wonders why everybody talks about Snowy and his bluesiness and ill-fit for Lizzy — the *Chinatown* album in total might just house a greater quantity and quality of Lizzy leads over and above any much more celebrated record from the band.

"'Chinatown' is one of those songs you really have to concentrate on when you're playing it live," says Scott, of the record's snarling, hard rocking title track, which hits like a hammer next. "There are so many fucking bits to it. 'Oh shit, here comes… oh, wait a minute, here comes another one!' It keep you on your toes."

Keeps Brian Downey on his toes as well, this one serving as the record's drum showcase, in parallel to the title tracks of the last two records. "I used some double bass drum fills on 'Chinatown'," notes Downey, "Then I use them obviously on the drum solo on 'Chinatown' live. When I started playing with Lizzy I just had a single bass drum; the double bass came later when Scott and Brian Robertson joined and then I had them always after that, through that Robertson and Gorham period. But it's just for some solos and some breaks. One of my main inspirations for this — favourite players in fact — was a guy called Pete Gavin, who played with a band called Heads Hands & Feet, back in London in the '70s. We did quite a few gigs with them, and I got to know him quite well, fantastic double bass guy. He had a great feel for drumming as well. Not many people know about him. I saw him playing at the Lyceum in London quite a few times and he always did a spectacular solo. I got his album, and he plays a solo called Pete Might Spook The Horses — really good solo, double bass stuff. Also Ginger Baker is a big influence, as is Louis Belson, jazz player."

"The title track, 'Chinatown' was taken to a few different studios to get the right sound," adds John Vasey. "The opening drum sounds were worked on laboriously to get the sound Phil and Kit were looking for. Kit had been Tony's engineer and had moved up to co-produce the records when Tony was not available. He gave encouragement when needed and had the patience to produce the records. Tony owned Good Earth studios. His advice was always welcomed because of his depth of experience. It's funny, I remember Snowy was called Captain Sensible by the band as he did not have the same aspirations as a rock 'n' roller that Scott and Phil had. Brian and Snowy were family men who worked in a rock 'n' roll band."

Brush Shiels — Skid Row bassist and mentor to Phil — says that the intro to the song is a bass exercise he had shown Phil back in the day when he was teaching him to play the instrument. After discussing the lift of the exercise for the track a decade later, I asked Brush if he could hear other places in the Lizzy catalogue where there were licks that had come from him, Brush tellingly replied with typical Shiels edge, "If you can hear anything on the Lizzy albums that didn't come from me, you let me know (laughs)."

Another highlight of the title track is Phil's exacting pronunciation as well as his menace, framed on what is roughly a blues-structure of a song, but twisted into metallic form, the end result being rolled steel due to Downey's ceaseless and circular groove. 'Chinatown' features one of three Snowy co-credits on the record, the others being 'Sugar Blues' and 'Having A Good Time'. Fitting the framing of Snowy's tenure with the band, Scott says of any of the heavier stuff, "that was mostly Phil and myself. I don't think Snowy really felt comfortable with all that. I always got the feeling that Snowy might have felt that he was betraying the blues, if he started to write any heavy riff. So yeah, that was left up to me and Phil. But you know, saying that, Snowy could come up with a lot of really cool parts in all of the songs. I don't think he actually ever initiated them, is what I'm trying to say."

'Chinatown' would see issue as a single (backed with a live version of 'Sugar Blues') fully five months before the release of the album, the track rising to No.21 in the UK charts, buzzing around concurrent releases by Wild Horses, Gary's snappy outfit G-Force, as well as Phil as solo artist, as Lynott hit the press trail to trumpet *Solo In Soho*.

Supporting the gritty story of *Chinatown* is the Chinese dragon of explosive colour used for the cover art, not to mention the Chinese lettering. "We had a lot of different ideas for *Chinatown*, and I did a lot of sketches for it," explains artist Jim Fitzpatrick. "It started off with *Chinatown* in flames — Philip had that idea. I did one drawing that was of an elongated dragon with all the flames behind him, in a Chinese type of pagoda style. But anyway, Philip loved the dragon idea. So he got me to focus on that, and forget all the rest of that stuff, just focus on the dragon, do something extraordinary. That's what I did. For the back cover, he didn't even see it. That just arrived and they bloody loved it. Because I was going so fast. I had no time to run roughs by him. Because in those days, you couldn't just e-mail a scan. There was no e-mail, no scans, so you had to literally post it, or send by courier, you know what I mean? It was a much longer process. Now everything is just spontaneous. It's brilliant. He didn't get any notice of what I was going to do. I just said, 'Look, I'm going to make a beautiful back cover for you, and I'll leave room for titles.' He said, 'I think the record company ought to put photographs on the back.' I said, you could put them across the bottom or something and that's the dragon's head for the back cover. One of my best pieces of work. It's why I want it back, right? If it ever turns up anywhere."

"No idea what happened to it," continues Jim. "The record companies said they sent it, but I never got it. It wasn't like now where you have tracking numbers and cell phones. This was just put on a plane, a courier service. There were no mobile phones to talk in great depth. To ring up the record company to find where the album cover was, it would cost you a bloody fortune." As is wont to happen with such strong graphics around a record, the label splurged for ancillary promotional items, including silk, embroidered jackets, promo posters and flashy store displays, spending upwards of £50,000 once all was said and done.

Back to the record, 'Sweetheart' is brisk and melodic, some of its twin leads featuring a "synth guitar" type sound while Phil rhymes cutely, his lyrics lacking focus, this time seemingly more about the sound of the words. No soft songs in sight, next is 'Sugar Blues', like 'Chinatown', a juiced, riff- strapped monster unrecognisable as blues but subtly framed as one.

Recalls Kit Woolven, "'Sugar Blues' came about, because they'd just come back from the Bahamas, and Phil couldn't believe all the sugar bars out there, people just drinking these incredibly over-sweetened drinks, and really, it was down to that sugar rush, you know? But also, there was obviously a tongue-in-cheek, slight twist on it where it's slightly about cocaine as well, and sugarcane. But it did come about because they saw people just drinking these really highly sweetened sugary drinks."

Scott brings the analogy closer to home... "No, I'll tell you what it was; there was this restaurant/club that we always used to go to, in Twickenham, after we would record, a place called Crust. That's what he was referring to. It was a South American restaurant, and they had drinks called things like the Brain Teaser and the Mind Dynamite, that kind of thing. We would bring people in and buy them, and say, 'Hey, have a Brain Teaser,' and see if the guy could walk out the door straight afterwards. So Phil might've got an idea off of that, drinking these absolutely wild drinks that they were concocting there.

Downey can be heard loud and clear on this one as well, filling the spaces with fluid single stroke rolls and such. "Brian, is brilliant, an incredible drummer," says Kit. "Brian has just an amazing feel for a rock drummer and instant — Brian would always get it right. Particularly with Lizzy, the backing tracks, we would always record the backing tracks as per live in the studio. It would be bass, drums, and two guitars, to get down the backing tracks, and if there was spill there, there was spill there. We would then, very often, re-dub guitars or whatever, but very often the actual backing tracks were that take — you know, we used the sort of live in the studio take. It was very rare that we didn't. I can't actually remember an instance where we re-took because Brian had to do it again, unless he busted a stick or went through a skin or something. He was always just spot-on every time."

Side one closes with 'Killer On The Loose', yet another borderline metal rocker, Phil's voice beginning to take on that rasp of his last years, a rasp that was sometimes combined with a slight nasal clog, as one can hear on the song 'Chinatown'.

The song received some unwelcome publicity, due to the concurrent case of the Yorkshire Ripper gripping Britain at the time. "What happened there got so blown up with the newspapers and all that, that it was ridiculous," explains Scott. "Unfortunately it was in Liverpool or Newcastle, one of those places, that we were playing one night, and 'Killer On The Loose' was in the set, but unfortunately, that night, when we were playing, allegedly, a girl got raped, outside the venue or near enough to the venue. I guess there must've been some journalist who didn't like us or whatever, because he came up with this whole story that, you know, how callous can Thin Lizzy be, people being injured and raped outside of their concert, and they're playing songs like 'Killer On The Loose', glorifying death and rape and murder, and the whole thing. At first we just said, 'Oh, fuck this guy,' but then the radio stations started to ban us and people wouldn't play it, and so we just put out a press release saying, we understand, we are sensitive to this whole thing, and we're dropping the song from the set. Until we came back here, and with a new set together, that song hadn't seen the light of day for what, well over twenty-five years. Which I always thought was ridiculous."

"Chinatown is a seedy part of London late at night," defended Phil. "I was there recording, so I got to meet many characters. A lot of the hookers were very paranoid about the killer who was on the loose. I wanted to write a warning song and the way I thought it could be most frightening was to become the part of the Ripper in the vocal. Obviously I don't condone the rape of women."

Speaking to Hit Parader's Liz Derringer, Phil said that, "Right now there's a killer on the loose, and I wanted to write a warning. Like an actor would assume the part, I assume the part of the killer and I state things that I don't actually believe. I got a lot of flack in England, because some people thought it was glorifying rape or writing a sexist song." Speaking about the album's character in general, Phil added that, "What with me getting the solo album out of my system and the band going through that long wait to find a new guitarist, we wanted to do an aggressive album. This time, everyone wanted to play rock 'n' roll. We've only scratched the surface of what we can do, because we are a new band."

"I think one of the best tactics that can be used is fear," said Phil to Liam Mackey of Hot Press on the topic that wouldn't go away. "There were two things that really annoyed me: a) They wrote to everyone except me, and b) I didn't like the idea that they were setting themselves up as the censor for Thin Lizzy supporters, whereas up to this, they'd probably never listened to a Thin Lizzy record at all. They didn't credit the fans with enough intelligence. Okay, they might wear denim, they might wear leather, headshake, drink beer, hell-raise, but they have fun. To say they're unintelligent. Like, these people come up to me and for every interview I do, like, there might be some guys who might know everything about the band, but these fans ask questions that go right to the heart, right to the subject matter, although some of them miss the point as well."

On a technical note regarding the track, Kit Woolven recalls that, "The guitar solo on 'Killer On The Loose', the end of Snowy's guitar solo, the last note just goes up and up and up until it disappears. He just keeps stretching the note and keep stretching and stretching and stretching, and I remember that was quite amusing, because we did this thing where I convinced Snowy that if we put a string-winder on the machine head, when you got to the end of the solo, if I slowed the tape down and at the same time, wound up the string-winder on the machine head, on

Gary Moore and Phil Lynott whose long-standing musical relationship continued throughtout Lynott's life, irrespective of whether or not Moore was in Thin Lizzy.
(*John McDavid*)

This shot perfectly illustrates the band's backdrop that caused some costernation on the 1977 North American Tour where they supported Queen.
(*John McDavid*)

Scott Gorham was an ever-dependable
part of Lizzy from the moment he joined
in 1974 and continues to fly the flag
today with a reactivated Lizzy honouring
Lynott's legacy.
(*John McDavid*)

PHIL LYNOTT (Thin Lizzy)

Above: Lynott press photo. A priest in waiting?
Below & right: In more familiar guise, looking
anything but reverened.
(*Chris Hakkens*)

More action shots of Scott Gorham including playing the kettle drum
during a live performance of 'Do Anything You Want To."

Scott: "I remember when we actually played that onstage, Gary and I would have
to play these things. Immediately after you get done with the kettledrums, you've
got to go into that long harmony line. So you had to time that absolutely perfectly,
throw the sticks away, crank up your guitar and get right onto that harmony line
and play perfectly... I was never so glad to drop a song in my life."
(Kari Lehtinen)

Above: Skid Row guitarist and long-time friend of the band Gary Moore had a couple of stints with Lizzy, but always seemed destined for solo success. After making several rock albums, including appearances from Lynott, he ventured into the blues where he found his greatest success.
(Kari Lehtinen)

Below: Lynott, Moore, Gorham and Downey at full throttle.
(Keenan Neighbors)

There have been few bass playing frontmen in rock of real note. Phil Lynott was as good as they come. As Scott Gorham observed, "Phil didn't actually need a lot of tricks up there. He was one of those kinds of guys that when he walks on the stage has that magnetic quality. He just absolutely took command of whatever audience was out there. He had the audience right in the palm of his hand. He did it time after time."
(*Keenan Neighbors*)

"I've always been somewhat anti-establishment, I guess. Hell, being Irish and being black forces you into a position where you have to fight back against established principles. Even if I didn't necessarily want it to, my music, I suppose, would have to reflect my upbringing and background to some degree. There's a lot of hostility there, which comes across in our music, but there's also a lot of love for Ireland, and more than just a touch of old-fashioned romanticism. I'm a poet as well as a musician, so words are very important to me. I always hoped that even when our music is at its loudest, there's some lyrical message there that people can grab hold of. I try to write about things that the ordinary guy can listen to and say, 'Yeah, I've been through that.' But I don't feel that I have to walk around with a cross to bear just because I'm black."

(Kari Lehtinen)

Left: Publicity photo of Snowy White, who had been touring with Pink Floyd before he joined the band in 1980. He contributed to *Chinatown* and *Renegade*.

Below: Scott Gorham with Darren Wharton who brought keyboards to the Lizzy sound for *Chinatown* and remained with the band until the end in 1983.
(Robert Cakin)

Left: John Sykes helped steer the ship on its final voyage during a period where both Gorham and Lynott were battling with drug addiction.
(Anna Svendsen)

The final Lizzy line-up that recorded *Thunder & Lightning*.
(Wolfgang Guerster)

that particular string, while he is stretching it, we would get this whoop effect, that just went up to the ceiling, you know? Which we did of course, and of course the string was going to break, which Snowy thought was quite alarming, so... it's not particularly a production technique, but it was interesting at the time. But I thought 'Killer On The Loose' was a great song for a single. 'We Will Be Strong' was a candidate, but I really pushed for 'Killer On The Loose', because it fit with Phil wanting to be harder. It was sort of the start of English heavy metal — heavy metal was the catchword at the time — and it was a rockier approach for Lizzy. That song hadn't had the same melodic niceness to it as most of the other songs."

'Killer On The Loose' was issued as a single on September 9th, in advance of the album's unveiling by a month. Its distinction is the inclusion of one of the great Lizzy b-sides, a confident, professional non-LP track called 'Don't Play Around', yet another heavy song from this era. 'Killer On the Loose' would get to No.10 on the UK charts, the song also issued in a double 7" version that adds a live version of 'Got To Give It Up' and 'Chinatown'. No more singles would be forthcoming from the record in the months after its release.

Over to side two and we get a White/Lynott co-write in 'Having A Good Time', a brisk pop metaller mixing acoustic guitar and power chords while Phil scats a manic mouthful of party lyrics. "I think it's just Phil having a rant, really," laughs Kit with respect to the side's second track, 'Genocide (The Killing Of The Buffalo)', yet another grinding metal rocker for the record, Phil's phrasing in full flight as he articulates over typically high-end Lizzy melodic decisions. Breaks are also of well-crafted construct, turning the song into something of an epic.

'Didn't I', the ballad debuted back on the Japanese tour with Dave Flett, is *Chinatown's* only truly light moment, as the album clocks toward 'Hey You', another gritty hard rocker, despite its spare reggae intro.

"Every night I changed the lyrics because I haven't got what I'm know I'm trying to say," noted Phil concerning 'Hey You'. "It's about how when you leave your hometown everybody goes, 'You've got it made now man, you're off.' When you get to London you haven't, you've just solved one set of problems for another. I'm trying to get that, 'Hey you got it made, your record's in the hit parade' and they don't realise your problem now is getting the next hit or whatever. The amount of kids that go, 'I wish I was you, you've done everything!' I think, 'Jesus, if you only knew the problems I fuckin' have, trying to maintain and improve!'"

Was *Chinatown* any sort of improvement, really? Most critics and fans didn't think so at the time, considering it just another Thin Lizzy album albeit a fairly heavy one. Distractions were many. Perennially and increasingly, there was drugs, but there was also yet another guitarist, something that always chipped away privately within Phil who rued any weakening of the sense of gang within the band. But there was also the solo album, for which he seemed to do more press than for Lizzy.

"I think they were okay with it," muses Kit, upon turning the record in to Vertigo. "At that time, I believe Lizzy's management, Phil's management, Morrison O'Donnell, had done a deal with Vertigo, where, pretty much, we had total say in the production of the album, and as much as what we provided, they still had to accept. It was sort of like a production deal, because my deal was with the band and not the record company."

Continues Kit, "Phil could be your best friend and your worst enemy sometimes. Depending on his mood. You couldn't muck around. You could muck around with him but you couldn't muck around with him. You could have a good laugh one day, and then another day... there were lines that you couldn't cross, with Phil. He was very much in control of the whole Lizzy thing. Lizzy was Phil, without a doubt. He controlled every aspect of it, from the artwork down to the stage set design. He was always there in every aspect of what the image was; it was down to him. He took that job very, very seriously. Sometimes, due to his excesses, he could become quite awkward with certain things. I knew stuff was going on, but I never actually personally saw anybody doing smack. But it was pretty obvious. Especially on to the second solo album, where Phil kept falling asleep in the studio and starting to become very, very unreasonable. That was very largely down to the amount of smack he was doing and I'm sure and we get from Kit more of the standard framing we seem to hear from everybody concerning the conundrum that was Snowy White."

"Lizzy was very much sex, drugs and rock 'n' roll, not necessarily in that order, but it could've been (laughs). Snowy was none of those things. Snowy didn't drink. He might have a weak beer, but he certainly didn't do any drugs. He did rock 'n' roll (laughs), but he wasn't into the partying side of it. Snowy wasn't into hanging out after the session; he would go home. After the session, the other guys... Downey also would very often just go home. He would hang sometimes, but the nature of drums is that you get them out of the way early on, and that's done. But Phil used to like to party and Snowy wasn't into all that. But as a guitarist, he was very, very confident."

"Snowy's very quiet — but then so is Brian Downey very quiet," said Phil. "But quiet guys are the hardest to understand, because when they say no, they mean no. They say it quietly but it's as strong as somebody screaming, like me. Snowy'll go, 'No, I don't want to play the song that way,' and shows the strength of character. Obviously, we've gone for a little more security — someone who wanted to be in the band, and who wanted to have a say in the band but not just use it for his own benefit, who wanted the band to be a band."

Painting a rosy picture, Phil was, because in the few interviews Snowy has ever given about his time with Thin Lizzy, as alluded to, he's dismissive of his time in the band. It's frustrating that he won't own them, because most would say his two Thin Lizzy records are the greatest creative achievements of the man's career. Writing and recording albums with Pink Floyd would trump doing the same for Thin Lizzy, but he wasn't doing that — Snowy was a touring guitarist, a supporter of songs already (magically) penned by others. Solo albums... although Snowy would likely point to these as the most satisfying writing and playing of his life, few music-watchers would. No, both *Chinatown* and *Renegade* are rich, rewarding listens for lovers of classic rock and most Lizzy fans, and Snowy's twin leads, his solos, and any of his writing therein enclosed... he should be very, very proud of it all.

An obvious parallel to this situation would have to be Viv Campbell (later a Lizzy guitarist, in fact!), who will be remembered foremost for his classic writing, recording, soloing and riffing on the classic Dio albums, and not for his... whatever it is he does on those plasticised Def Leppard records as the new guy, no matter how many units have been shifted. Yet Viv is dismissive of what is near unanimously thought of as his greatest work, never to be topped. Ergo, there goes Snowy as well, perhaps worn down by all the vague and tepid, half-hearted criticism of his supposedly half-hearted life in Lizzy, both in the studio and on the lackadaisical stage.

And that always came next — Snowy didn't look right. Yet... more to the point, Snowy brought Lizzy's look into the '80s. Attendant with Snowy's behaved hair and aristocratic, intellectual facial features, Scott cut his hair, out came the skinny ties and bomber jackets, reduced in size went Phil's afro. Bottom line, Thin Lizzy replaced 20% of their '70s hippie rocker look with a post-punk pertness, and Snowy was an integral part of that presentation.

Underscoring this — and despite how heavy *Chinatown* was — is Brian Downey's take on the times. "Again, our influences weren't being touched by the New Wave Of British Heavy Metal. In fact, I wasn't aware of it. That name came after the band broke up. I mean, obviously there was still the same hardcore bands around at that time, but the punks were going more... there were bands coming along like Dire Straits and the Boomtown Rats who weren't really punks at all, but you had this new wave image. That seemed to be creeping in more than the New Wave Of British Heavy Metal, into our consciousness and Phil met Mark Knopfler a few times. Don't forget, as well around that time, Phil was writing songs for his own solo album which was going to be recorded, and he was making friends with people who he wanted to play with on this particular album, people like Billy Bremner, who was playing with Rockpile, a new wave band. Those kinds of bands we were going to listen to more so than the new hard rock bands that were coming out. So that had a bit of an influence."

"Once Snowy White came into the band," continues Downey, "Snowy was a very lovely blues guitar player, a big blues fan; he knew Peter Green very well and was into all that sort of stuff. We had lots of potential because of the fact that we knew that Phil wanted to do his solo stuff, so we didn't know exactly what direction he wanted to go in. Some of his tunes used to end up on Lizzy albums, and in fact some of the Thin Lizzy tunes would end up on a solo album. When he met Mark Knopfler, who came down to play on 'King's Call', he asked me to play on that track as well, so all of this was happening in the studio at the same time as Snowy joined the band, and there were lots of influences mucking around, on both the solo album and *Chinatown* as well. So that whole period was a bit experimental."

"We had obviously split up with Gary Moore. Gary had gone on, and when we got Snowy, we knew that Snowy was a fantastic player, but he was completely different from what I expected. He struck me as being more introverted than Gary had ever been. Gary was really out there giving it his all, and Snowy was a bit more laid-back, and a bit more bluesy than we expected, which was fine by me. But I think at the end of the day, that particular album, *Chinatown*, was a great album to listen to, but again, it just didn't have what it took to get in there and really make an impression, you know? Not saying that the line-up was at fault, but it was just a case of being slightly… things were winding down in the hard rock sphere, and these other bands seemed to be having more of an influence than we expected."

"But there again, it's just another case of, you just go along with your instincts and just play as best you can, and that's what we did. But we seemed to be swallowed up in the releases around that period. It didn't really make it into the charts, and it got knocked critically in the press. So it was just unlucky that we were in that position, you know?"

Asked who, then, might have been lobbying for all these heavy songs on *Chinatown*, Downey replies that, "It was never really a lobby as such. We all knew that Phil was a fantastic songwriter, and we used to just leave it more or less up to him. Now don't forget, other guys were coming in with… Scott had one or two ideas, but Phil was really the main songwriter in the band. We never really questioned too much his input into the band. We never said, 'Look, Phil, the song doesn't really suit.' We tried everything, and that was the beauty of the band. We tried anything that he had written, and honestly one or two were discarded, others were kept on, it was never a question of saying let's go in more of a hard rock direction. We had an unspoken rule that we would try anything that was suggested, by any members of the band, and give it a go. I think because we had the hard rock imprint in our history, it was not a case of saying look, we should go more hard rock. We just let it evolve the way it should evolve. It was never a case of consciously saying we should go more hard rock just for the sake of it. We tried everything that Phil had, or Scott or Brian and myself would come up with; we tried everything, and some stuff was discarded and some stuff wasn't."

"So here we are, with the new album, by yet another line-up, introducing guitarist Snowy White," wrote Hot Press' Dermot Stokes, in a typical perfunctory *Chinatown* rumination. "You could say it's true to form in being very good, but playing safe. Form and content have become, to a degree, standardised. Frontiers, both musical and lyrical, are left alone. But past performance from Lizzy is such that you can bet that if this unit welds on the road that their next will mark a progression from *Chinatown*. In the meantime, this one is pretty good to be going on with."

"Lizzy basically have taken the chassis of *Live And Dangerous* and grafted on a new body — the might remains. It's like seeing Jack Palance play a bad guy. Time and tide, compulsion and commitment, skill and technique, they kept the powder dry. Lizzy are old hands. It's dead easy for them. The one real disappointment is the lyrics, where Lynott throws away unfulfilled possibilities. You get the odd line where the easy rhyme has been taken and doesn't fit too well, for example. While the essential image of the song is as strong as ever, as in 'Chinatown' or 'Genocide', the lyrics don't always get right to the core — don't have the power of the playing. Well, what the hell."

"They're there and in good form, and that makes the world just a little bit better. People who wrote Thin Lizzy off last year are going to have to cancel the post-mortem for a while. They may have abandoned the idea of being Bob Dylans, but they can still plant the boot where it matters. It's worth adding that Van Morrison had his uneasy patches too, before he got back onto the running board."

The release of *Chinatown* in the fall of 1980 was accompanied by a tour of Japan, Australia and New Zealand, followed by US dates into November and December, supported by Code Blue. Phil must have been feeling flush, because for his mother's 50th birthday, he bought her a house known as White Horses. As well, Phil gets Philomena out of the nutty Clifton Grange Hotel, buying together, Asgard Hotel, Howth, for the sum of £235,000.

"Well that's about as far afield as we got," reflects Scott, on reaching out to Japan and Australia. "We never got down to South Africa, you know, for pretty good reasons. Because of the apartheid going on, Phil being black and all that, it wouldn't really have gone down too well. But the one place I do regret that we didn't get to was South America, which was still wide open. The rock doors were opening up at this point. I don't think it was going full guns back then in '80, '81, '82, but you could see the door was opening. But we just never made it down there. So yeah, I mean, I've been to Japan something like seven times, Australia three or four times, but that's it."

On December 8th 1980 John Lennon was gunned down in front of his residence in Manhattan. Coincidentally, earlier that day Phil, frankly, not one to cite the Beatles as much of an influence, had penned the lyrics to what would be one of his greatest non-LP tracks, 'Somebody Else's Dream', eventually used as the b-side to a song called 'Together' from his second and last solo project, *The Philip Lynott Album*. A haunting ballad that would have fit well on a Lizzy album, the track opens with Phil's half whispered, "damn, damn," and then repeated, a memorable launch to the introspective lyric to come.

"There's a time when you are the generation you're singing about and then there's a time when you're not," Phil mused, in conversation with Hot Press. "Lucky enough, I never wrote songs for my generation; I always wrote songs for me. So when I had a daughter I wrote a song about my daughter, when I was feeling low in Soho, I wrote 'Solo In Soho'. Even on the new album (unissued at the time, and not to be included once it did emerge) there's a song called 'Somebody Else's Dream' which I wrote when I felt I was becoming too much their image. But then I realised that everybody in some form or other is doing it, whether it's the guy going to school and being presentable or the guy at work trying to be the person they want him to be. I would definitely say I enjoyed being a rock star more five years ago, being well-known, than I do now. It gets a bit over the top when guys are saying to you, 'Can we come and photograph your house?' and the Sunday World wanted a shot of me with an apron on. Another article I did for the Sunday World I was throwing snowballs — 'Could you throw a snowball this way Phil? Could you look mean?!' Or the Daily Mirror wants to talk about Leslie Crowther and the kids. I mean it's fuck all to do with the music, or the particular album I'm promoting, which is why I'm doing the publicity in the first place. I do believe that, as the line in the song says, 'Do the people have the right to know it all'?"

Into January 1981, and it was off to the Bahamas yet again for Phil's solo career this trip producing 'Little Bit Of Water' and 'Fatalistic Attitude', which would indeed show up on *The Philip Lynott Album*. Then it was off to mainland Europe for a fairly extensive *Chinatown* tour, followed by the release of a compilation in March called *The Adventures Of Thin Lizzy*.

Notes a frustrated Jim Fitzpatrick on the record's comic book-styled artwork, "Philip wanted me to do *Renegade* and *Thunder And Lightning*, but the record company didn't. I think it's that simple. You hear so many different stories. You listen to what they are saying, but none of it makes sense, because the dots don't connect. But the classic one was *The Adventures Of Thin Lizzy*, which was done by a comic strip artist and the one thing I can do bloody better than anybody else are comic strips.

Philip would've known that from the work I did for Captain Americas, a restaurant in Dublin, which had massive comic strip-type murals. But he said, 'Jim, we couldn't afford you.' At that point, record companies weren't spending money. So they got some English comic book artist. It wasn't somebody great like Frank Bellamy, which I would've loved and gone wow. But it was some pretty second-rate guy. But for *Renegade*, you know, I did a beautiful cover for *Renegade*, of Phil lighting a cigarette in the dark, I think. But things just weren't gelling at the time."

The hits pack went gold in the UK, vaulting all the way to No.6 in the charts. Meanwhile, also in the spring, Wild Horses issued a single, as did Phil, the synth-driven 'Yellow Pearl' paired with 'Girls'. Early March saw the release of a single by Steeleye Span's Terry Woods, doing a cover of Jimmie Driftwood's country classic 'Tennessee Stud', on which Phil sings, plays bass and produces.

In April, Vertigo issued the Killers Live EP, the 7" version comprising 'Are You Ready', 'Dear Miss Lonely Hearts' and 'Bad Reputation', with a 12" version adding 'Opium Trail'. The original plan was for the 12" version to be a bonus inclusion with *The Adventures Of Thin Lizzy*, but instead it was issued as a stand-alone at a budget price. In Canada, the EP was issued as a six-tracker, adding 'Chinatown' and 'Got To Give It Up'. All tracks hail from 1980, save for 'Bad Reputation' and 'Opium Trail', which were recorded live in Philadelphia in 1977.

"I was the monitor engineer for the live shows," comments John Vasey, providing a bit of perspective on Lizzy's approach to their live mix. "Thin Lizzy developed the sound on stage to be a more comprehensive sound than other acts touring at that time. Phil had stereo floor monitors and stereo side fills. This gave him a great deal of depth to the sound on stage. This meant that the two bass drums could be split between the floor monitors and each guitar player could be separated so the sound was much clearer. Peter Eustace, the front-of-house engineer, was always developing cutting edge techniques to improve the live sound. It's not true that Thin Lizzy were uncommonly loud live. Peter Eustace would mix the show to be heard. It was more that Thin Lizzy had a much fuller sound than other bands of that era. As Phil was the bass player and leader of the band the bass and drums were the power behind the guitar players. Phil was always looking for a sound that could drive the song along, almost like a lead instrument with a full range of tone."

"They still call me Ozzie to this day," adds John, asked about the way he is credited on the *Chinatown* album, namely: "Ossie Vasey — monitors and 8 track engineer." "I was given the nickname in London when I was 19 and I am 55 now. It's a bit strange to be called Ozzie in Australia. Phil used to say, 'Turn it up, Ozzie' to me and in Australia the crowd would always respond. Also on the road, we had John Salter, who was the tour manager and had lots to worry about. He was a good person that took care of all of us on the road."

"I ran into him in London in 1984 when I was there with Midnight Oil and he was still working with Phil. Gus Curtis was Phil's friend from school and was also my roommate for a lot of the touring. He was what we called a 'Percy,' which meant he was like a personal assistant for Phil. Then there was Micky Lawford, who was what we would call security today and made sure that the guys in the band were safe from the over-enthusiastic fans. Micky had previously worked for Joe Cocker when they were all deported from Australia in the 1970s. I haven't seen him since 1980."

Into May and June, and Wild Horses issue their second and last album, *Stand Your Ground*, plus a single from it. Phil's 'Yellow Pearl' rises in status, becoming BBC Top Of The Pops theme music, sticking around until 1986. On July 31st, Lizzy release a curious single pairing two covers, Rockpile's semi-rockabilly 'Trouble Boys' with a dark blues ballad by Percy Mayfield called 'Memory Pain'. Indeed, the track served alongside jocularity like 'A Merry Jingle', 'Daddy Rolling Stone' and 'We Are The Boys' in framing Phil, and by extension Lizzy, as jokey participants in British pop culture akin to where Status Quo was going at the time, maybe even Slade.

"I just remember that I don't think it was the band's favourite song," laughs Darren Wharton, recalling 'Trouble Boys'. "I think Phil sort of had this idea that it was going to be a good follow-up from maybe 'The Boys Are Back In Town', but most of the band didn't have the confidence in the song that Phil did. I remember being a little bit like, well, what are we doing this song for? (laughs). It wasn't the best thing."

Far cooler was a quick reunion of Lizzy Mk 1 (well, close enough), Phil, Brian Downey and Eric Bell putting together 'Song For Jimmy' — yes, a misspelling — issued as a flexidisc in Flexipop magazine as a tribute on the tenth anniversary of Jimi Hendrix's death. No slouch, the song (thought to be a possible inclusion on Phil's second solo record) is a groovy, heavy metal rocker, nods to Jimi to be sure, but very much as strong and strongly modern as certainly anything on Eric's classic swansong with the band, *Vagabonds Of The Western World*, at this point almost a quaint record lovingly crafted in a time of innocence.

5

RENEGADE

"What the hell is that?"

While recording what would become *Renegade*, Phil had to contend with the attention his solo album was getting, as well as chatter about him playing Jimi Hendrix in a proposed biopic. "I'm really trying to play down this whole affair at the moment," Phil told Max Blake at Trax, "simply because if it doesn't come off, then I'm going to look very silly. All I'll say is that negotiations are well underway but excessive exposure at this stage could blow the whole thing. If someone is prepared to put up the readies and let me have a go at acting, then sure I'll do it. I definitely have the ego for such a task. Any form of expression I'm into — recording, acting, videos or production. Even the layout of the album covers interests me. It's simply my creative instinct driving me on."

"I can't talk too much about it, because it could affect me in two ways," elaborated Phil, talking with the legendary Gay Byrne of The Late, Late Show in Ireland. "One, I could talk about it so much that the price that I'd be asking to do for the film would drop (laughs). It could affect me."

"See, there's two ways you can look on Jimi Hendrix, right? There's two sides of Jimi Hendrix. Jimi Hendrix as an artist, was very deep, and very involved, and he believed entirely in what he was doing, whereas the public figure, he was just like fodder for the media, you know? He indulged in everything, you see, and he'd do it by the way he lived. But as an artist, he was one of my heroes, you know? He showed to me that a black fella could be the front of a band, and be completely respected for what he did. I had to fly to America to do a screen test, not only for the Jimi Hendrix film. There's a couple of films they want me to do now.

Ever since... like, I mean, okay, Sidney Portier's life story (laughs), Joe Louis, (laughs) — if you're black, you name it. But the thing was, Jimi Hendrix is something special, and he's just one generation away from me. Already people have come up to me and said, 'Who do you think you are, you know, thinking you could play Jimi Hendrix?' I don't think I could play Jimi Hendrix well, but I do have enough admiration for the man, to be able to do it. I would like to give it a try, like I've done everything else in me life."

Byrne also gently chided Phil about buying a house in Howth, the north of Dublin...

"Well, I was looking for a place to live in Ireland, because when I moved away, I thought, well I must come home because I really suffer from homesickness. If I don't get back to Dublin — not so much Ireland, Dublin; I'm a real Dubliner — if I don't get back to Dublin within three months, then I really start to suffer from homesickness. So when we got married, I sent the wife over and said, 'See if you like Ireland,' and she did. So I sent her looking for a house, and she didn't like the south side, because the motorways all go that way, so she settled for the north side, Howth."

After telling Gay that his recent marriage had made him "faithful to one woman," Phil gets serious and says, "It has brought out emotions in me. You know, becoming a father and having the kids and stuff, and the responsibility of the marriage... I honestly didn't think I had the emotions that I have, in me, 'til I got married and had the children. Now, I know there's lots of single fellows lookin', and they're going, 'Oh yeah,' but it's amazing, when you do get married and have children, how much passion it can bring out of you, and how defensive you become of your family. Like, I never would've worried about the news. You know, I could have looked at the news and said that the world was gonna end tomorrow and it wouldn't have bothered me. But having the children, like it worries me."

"The thing is now, when Thin Lizzy started, I had a bit of a wild boy image," continues Phil. "But when all that started to happen, I went for it, because I was tired of hearing rock 'n' roll stars saying how sorry they were for themselves, how they disliked fame and how they were bothered. I jumped to it; you know, I was famous, I thought, great, the women are after me, people want to buy me free drink, they want to treat me, they want to take me here, they want to take me there, great, and you know, I really went for it hook, line and sinker. Since I got married, all of a sudden, it's not as important anymore as the actual art of making music and the art of self-expression, in which I work, because I'm very happy. My private life, I like to keep very private, and I'm very happy with me private life."

After starkly predicting that the band had "at worst" three years left in it, Phil says that, "My wife and myself have decided that I should give it a couple more years while it's going for me and go for it. But then eventually, I want to opt out of the limelight as such, and maybe jump into production. Because, for example, in Ireland, there's an awful lot of talent. There's an awful lot of people stopping that talent from getting through. Okay, the last couple of years, it's opened up a bit. But even so, you still have to go to London, if you're anyway talented at all, and that's a very harsh decision to make, to leave family, country, just in search of. It's happened to all Irish artists. I'm not just talking about the rock theatre. You name any great Irish writer; most of them had to leave the country."

"It will be different but I do find it genuinely a problem trying to define in what way it will be so," continued Phil, back to discussing with Max Blake how *Renegade* had been taking shape. "Our approach, though, is far more experimental than before. One particular effect that I'm personally working on at the moment is a box of tricks to which you can hook up an ordinary bass guitar and produces simultaneous bass/synthesizer sound. "My songs are like mini-diaries. But when I'm having a good time, I'm simply not in the right mood to set it down on paper. No, I find much easier to write about more serious matters, because then I'm in an introverted frame of mind and this allows the creativity within me to flow naturally. What I've constantly avoided is empty sloganeering. There is a great tendency these days for bands to do just that sort of thing. Punk is a prime example of this; the words sound good but have no depth or meaning to 'em. My success came because I stuck to my guns and remained true to myself. Bands who use slogans simply to get fame for its own sake are dangerous."

Renegade would arrive in November '81, sporting a provocative and classy front sleeve, reminiscent, for those into underground rock history, of a "communist" image put forth by the New York Dolls briefly in the mid-'70s. "It's not supposed to be a communist flag, even though it looks like one," groused Phil in Hit Parader. "It was supposed to be the same colour as the Dunhill cigarette pack, 'cause that's what I was smoking at the time. I have since switched to Marlboro."

Elaborating in Sounds, Phil said that the cover was, "Just about as far away from communism as you can get. The five stars represent the five people in Lizzy and the flag is just the symbol of a renegade, nothing to do with North Vietnam or anything. Anyway, how can anyone be in something as decadent as the rock business and be a communist?" Of note, there are no five stars anywhere, although there is a five-pointed star.

Furthermore Darren is not shown or listed as a member of the band anywhere, his last name appearing in the 'Angel Of Death' credit and that's it. This would tend to support the supposition at the time that the record label erred in displaying only Phil, Scott, Brian and Snowy on the back cover, i.e. that they were "unaware" that the band was now a five-piece (another version claims that they had to go with four because of the simple fit of four squares within a square). The only credit given to the players anywhere on the album consisted of their names under the individual shots — nowhere is any instrumentation discussed. Ergo, there's a sense of omission or error in all of this.

In any event, once past the rich reds, greens and metallic golds of the wrapper, the band get down to business with a true heavy metal rocker — replete with Iron Maiden gallop — called 'Angel Of Death', at the start of which Darren gets to show his "next generation" chops. We're in the punted thick of the NWOBHM now, and Lizzy has fired one over the bow.

"*Renegade* was obviously a step up for me," explains Wharton. "You've got 'Angel Of Death' which I co-wrote with Phil. It was more than just the solo, the riff. The structure of the chords, going up into the (sings it). One of the ideas that Phil obviously liked was that lead thing I had, which spurred him on and gave him ideas of 'Angel Of Death', that haunting keyboard riff. At the time, synths had just come out, and that was just a sound that the OBX Oberheim did particularly well, monophonic lead sound, going through an echo unit, and that inspired me to come up with that idea. I was playing it at sound checks, and on *Chinatown*, doing stuff like that, and Phil actually really liked it and came up with that idea, just around that riff."

"There was not much available at the time," continues Darren, focusing on gear. "There were only a couple of mainstream companies making keyboards at the time when we were doing stuff. There was obviously Moog, there was Oberheim, there was Solina String, You know, the sort of stable, there's the ARP, who don't make keyboards anymore, the ARP Odyssey, and the ARP Axxe which I was using on stuff like 'The Sun Goes Down'. There wasn't that much — it isn't like today. They were all very synth-sounding synths, which are quite analogue synthy sounds. So there were no samples involved, as far as the synths were concerned — it was all oscillator-based. Not like today, where you can play organ and trumpets and all types of things. It was all very synthesizer-sounding. That reflects in things like 'Yellow Pearl', which is very '80s music. Everybody was using the stuff, really. It was really only getting into the '90s where sample-based synths came out, DX-7, which started to change the way records were sounding, because peoples had more choice."

But Darren rightfully notes that really, within Lizzy, the fully three albums he would be part and parcel of, there weren't a lot of keyboards used. "There's really only *Renegade* that really features the keyboards as far as Thin Lizzy is concerned. *Thunder And Lightning* as well a bit, but I have no regrets on what was used — it all sounds very good for a rock album. 'Angel Of Death', we started that whole tour with that and it was a successful tour and I had a lot of people come up to me, even Vivian Campbell from Def Leppard, saying that was one of the best starts to a rock show that he'd ever seen, with 'Angel Of Death', where we had the flags flickering in the wind and the strobe machines going. So for what we had available to us at the time, and just for keyboards to infiltrate Thin Lizzy as it did, you know, I think 'Angel Of Death is a pretty strong-sounding track for the year that it came out."

Mark of a great hard rock band, and even a maker of great heavy metal, is this idea that the writers within were touchy about the subject of heavy metal, a trait found with Led Zeppelin, Deep Purple, Queen, and of course Lizzy. Ergo, there were discussions around 'Angel Of Death' — with that riff, that title, that theme — that the track was gratuitously metal.

"Yeah, absolutely," confirms Scott, who, instantly upon hearing it, couldn't stand the idea of Thin Lizzy calling one of their songs 'Angel Of Death'. "We did not want to go down the metal road. To us, the metal thing, and I don't mean this as any disrespect to any of the guys, but it seemed a little corny to us so we tried to avoid that side of it. Plus we knew that there were a lot of guys out there that did that genre so well. But it was just one of those tracks where we recorded it, listened back to it, and for a time there, it wasn't one of our favourites."

"But yeah, if anybody actually called us heavy metal, we would actually jump all over them, and the correction would start there. You know, we considered ourselves an absolute hard rock band, but definitely not a metal band. The difference, between the two genres, to be a metal band, it all depends on the riff; you know, the drum groove and the guitar riff. Whereas with hard rock, it's all about the groove and the lyrics and the melody of the song. That's why we went out of our way to explain that we are not heavy metal, we are a rock band."

"That's one of the facets of Thin Lizzy that has kept us one step away from your regular heavy metal band," seconded Phil. "That's why I try to use the words hard rock. Heavy metal is a riff made into a song, whereas in Thin Lizzy, we have a song and add the riffs and a lot more thought goes into the lyrics."

In terms of the composition, Scott says, "Phil had this riff, and then I added to the riff, and then we decided that to create a real mood, let's build this particular song around keyboards. It was like a vehicle for Darren, to let everybody know how talented this guy was, and he has a lot of fast chops in the song, and at the same time, retaining the whole melodic sense. Darren is very good with   melodies. He found it really easy to just burn the keys in a really fast way, but still retaining a lot of melody within the song. So I think that song more than any song, really convinced me that he had a right to be in Thin Lizzy."

"I personally do believe there is a Great Unknown," mused Lynott, asked about the nod to Nostradamus within this mini-epic (of note, Phil was also proud of adding an extra real life layer with the death of one's father subplot). "Satan, cults, UFOs, I pack the whole lot together. I thought Nostradamus was very near the mark; he must have scratched the nerve somewhere. How he did it, I don't know. But basically, myself, I'm a very practical person, I live day to day. So I don't go too far into it — I could find myself like, y'know, the Don Juan of Crumlin (laughs). My saving grace, or my cop-out if you like is when I say in the song, 'Do you believe in this?' So the listener has the option. Like, Chris Tsangarides who co-produced the album went to Canada where the album has really taken off, and this geezer said to him, y'know, 'Is it tongue in cheek?' Chris says, 'An album costing £60,000 to make, do you think it's tongue in cheek?' But then he said, 'Knowing Phil Lynott, it could be.'"

"I was supposed to be doing another band that was on the same management, Wild Horses with Brian Robertson and Jimmy Bain," begins the aforementioned Chris Tsangarides, who indeed gets co-production credit on *Renegade*, along with the band. "They wanted us to do this, and it all fell to pieces, and their management said, 'Look, we're not going to do that, but Phil has asked if you would come and work on the Thin Lizzy album.' I said, 'Sure, that would be fantastic.' Okay, here we go, and I'd known Phil from working with him on his solo projects, and on Gary's *Back On The Streets* record.

"So I arrived, and nobody had told Kit, unfortunately. It was quite an awkward couple of days, until he realised what was going on. So I didn't think much of that at the time, and I still don't, but there you go. But basically, they'd lost the plot. You weren't sure of the songs that they were doing, whether it should have been for Phil's solo album, or should've been for a Thin Lizzy album or whatever. So it's not a very defined area. We recorded a few new tunes, which were the heavier ones like 'The Pressure Will Blow' and 'Angel Of Death'."

"But yeah, they had written three or four songs, and Phil had asked me to come on board because they were floundering. They weren't happy with Kit, for whatever reason, and Phil had asked me to come in, well, to finish the record. We recorded a whole bunch of new stuff, and they were more of the heavier, rockier songs on the record, that I did from scratch with them, which is par for the course I guess and really, they were very mixed up. They weren't really sure about the guitar situation. Snowy wasn't impressed with the way they conducted themselves in the band, being a rock band. He was more of a sensitive, quiet guy.

I think it was a mishmash of an album. Now I can hear it and appreciate it for the music, but really it wasn't focused. It floundered from one direction to another."

Indeed, the title track was a bellwether of the sort of album *Renegade* would turn out to be, much lighter in total that the brutish *Chinatown*. Says Chris, "Yes, it was at the time, well, I don't know what this is. It's not rock, it's not metal, some of it is, some of it isn't, what the hell is that? Unfortunately, when you make albums, I find generally they have to be focused on one side or the other, otherwise the diehard fans don't know what they're listening to. That was the case with that. On reflection, now when I hear it, I think it's bloody brilliant. The songs and everything, it's just wonderful and it all worked for me. But at the time I didn't understand why it wasn't as successful as it might've been, but I think people are revisiting it again, like I have, and going, you know what, this is a nice body of work."

"There was definitely confusion, absolutely," figures Brian Downey, on the direction of the band. "As well, there was a definite crossover where you didn't know exactly which album the songs were going to appear on. I know we had a huge problem with that at one stage. In fact, Kit questioned the whole procedure and I had to agree with him. I said to Phil, 'This is completely confusing; we don't know what is for which project,' and he said, 'Well, you know, I'm not sure myself.' So the whole thing was completely up in the air when we went into the studio in that period. We didn't know what song was going to end up on what album, and I don't think Kit had a part to play in that. I think it was down to Phil and Kit, to me, was a great guy in the studio, very calm, very collected, no problems with Kit. He was just great. Again, it was just a case of working and getting on with everybody. He was equally as good. As regards, he had a few ideas and a fair bit of input into the ideas as well."

"Snowy was really getting more involved as a writer with *Renegade*," figures Darren. "There's obviously a lot of input there from Snowy, which you can tell. Phil was quite generous in that respect, that he would look to his guitarists for their input and style, which was an important characteristic of the band. So I think with *Renegade*, it included more keyboards, which was great for me, but it also had more input from Snowy. So both of us were just starting to get involved in the writing, which is evident in the outcome. The album was a nice sounding record. 'It's Getting Dangerous' is one of my favourite songs on the album. But there's some pretty good stuff on there — I really like the song, *Renegade*. But sure, as a young guy in one of the biggest rock bands in the world at the time, I must say it wasn't something that I had a great deal of control over as far as being a member of the band. Basically, apart from 'Angel Of Death', Phil would tell me what he would want me to play on the other tracks, including a piano solo there on 'Fats'. I was just lucky enough for him to use one of my ideas, really, rather than being anything like a driving force."

"*Renegade* didn't seem to be that long in the recording," continues Downey. "We had Snowy, who was a really good blues guitar player. He had a lot of feel. And the set up of the studio, I remember getting a really good drum sound, not having many really drastic problems trying to get a good sound. We went in there, and we had the bones of the songs in our head; we knew exactly what the arrangements were, so there was no problem there."

"I think the only problem with *Renegade* was getting the feel on the songs, because Snowy was a new member. We were still feeling our way with him in the band, and I think maybe that was the only problem. But his guitar playing on *Renegade*, and also on *Chinatown*, to me, was really, really good. There's no problem. A lot of people say to me, you know, after those two albums were recorded, that Snowy White didn't have the attack that Gary Moore, maybe, or Brian Robertson had. But he had his own little touch to it, his bluesy feel, on some of those songs. I really like listening to *Renegade*."

"I'd say Kit was a fine producer/engineer," recalls Scott, getting it right, because Kit is the co-producer of *Chinatown* and a co-engineer on *Renegade*, along with Chris, who also gets co-producer! "He worked long hours on that. Some of this stuff, it's hard to remember what actually went down, in the studio. I know that for a lot of the Thin Lizzy fans, both the *Renegade* and the *Chinatown* albums were somehow not received as well as some of the other albums. I'm not quite sure why that is. On *Renegade*, maybe it got a little too sedate in there at times; it got a little too polite. Not sure what it was. But I really don't know what the reasons were for bringing Chris in. But it was always good working with Tsangarides. You know, he was the kind of guy who kept the atmosphere up. Even when there were arguments going on in the studio, he kept the atmosphere clean. So good one on him, you know?"

As alluded to before, Scott says that the material was generated in much the same way as the previous album. "Phil would bring in X amount of songs for the next album, whatever the next album was going to be and we would sit in rehearsal. Once again we would get the eight-track out and record. It would become pretty obvious. It would be, 'Hey Phil, how about that one for your solo album?' There was no animosity there at all. He was never pissed-off with that. As I said, his way of thinking was, 'Great, there's one more song for the solo album.' He was almost grateful that somebody would speak up and say, 'Here, use this for your solo album, rather than for the Thin Lizzy album'."

But there's something true-blue Lizzy about *Renegade* (incidentally Snowy's favourite track from his time with the band), from its unadorned bass-drums-guitar-vocals ballad style to its elegant heavy sections featuring obscurely angled chords buttressed by some of the band's most poignant twin leads. Then there's the lyric, which adds to a rich canon of Lynott lyrics supporting the cause of the loner.

"I saw this Lizzy supporter on a bike," explained Phil in Sounds. "He's got a Motörhead patch on his jacket with the Lizzy patch on top, and 'renegade' written beneath. We were looking for an LP title at the time. Also, I was reading this book called The Rebel by Albert Camus, which suggested the idea of being a rebel from the inside. It came in a blinding flash: the idea of there being a rebel in us all."

Progressing through side one of *Renegade*, next up is 'The Pressure Will Blow', a direct injection power chord rocker which nonetheless, through its profusion of space and pregnant pausing, demonstrates the arguable assertion that *Renegade* was the highest fidelity Thin Lizzy album to date, that it was muscular, full spectrum, warm yet welled up with enough bass, mids and trebles to elicit no objective complaint, save for the resulting lack of edge or bite that adherence to the preceding principles would produce. Further impressing upon the record is a move away from the fact that Brian's drum performance on this quite metal track, for example, is soft, sympathetic, almost shuffling, laden with grace notes, again Downey proving himself the master of the light touch.

Says Phil on the lyric, "Pressure is a love song, written about this guy who finds out his girl's in secret liaison with someone else. He's telling her to leave before he explodes and uses violence on her so it's controlled anger. Some women are inclined to rub salt into wounds! I agree with you that women do tend to come off worse. That's not to say that they should, but it's a true reflection on society. Now, 'No One Told Him' is a song where the guy comes off worse. This guy is friendless. Nobody bothers to break the news to him that his girlfriend isn't interested anymore."

"'Leave This Town' is the typical love 'em and leave 'em song," says Phil on the rollicking last track of side one. "I nicked the idea from ZZ Top which is fair enough as they're my favourite band." Phil was likely prompted to lean ZZ on the lyric due to Scott's riff, which Phil instantly recognised as quite Billy Gibbons-like. For those doing the maths, 'Leave This Town', a brisk hard rocker in the 'Sugar Blues' vein, is fully the third meaty riff-mad track out of four tunes, the side's only other song, *Renegade*, also possessive of power chord heft. This solid rock atmosphere will fade noticeably come side two.

Although not until after lead track 'Hollywood', which would be the album's last near metal pose, again, Lizzy doing the genre proud justice, namely by turning in a sturdy chorus charmed through melody.

This one kicked off with Scott, inspiring Phil to write a song about the Mr. Hollywood in the band, the poser with the long hair. Another layer addressed the rivalry between Hollywood dudes and folks from New York, with Phil also inspired by what it must have been like for Scott to be thrust into the nightlife of London.

Into 'No One Told Him' and the band begins early the pensive close to the album, this one mining a rich vein of pop metal, again, the band demonstrating a maturity of craft that just might make *Renegade* the band's most professional and ironically sober album of gravitas. The song is a deep looked-over track that, surprisingly, along with 'It's Getting Dangerous' and 'Renegade', is one that shows up way up on the top Lizzy songs list of many a deep and studied fan fanatic of the band at hand.

As the side winds down, 'Fats finds Thin Lizzy crafting a conservative jazz, but to accessible, successful effect, Phil enthusiastic about this one because he got to experiment with lower more "masculine" registers of his voice. Upon first proposal, Scott had found himself resisting, but then quickly realised that the occasional oddball song has a wild card chance at becoming a hit. Plus, experimenting broke up the monotony of continually turning in the tried and true. "I wasn't keen on the track 'Fats'," seconds Darren, "although that's the one that Phil asked me to do a solo on. I wasn't getting anywhere with that. Yeah, not my favourite song in particular."

Phil noted that the idea was simply "Thin Lizzy plays Fats Waller," Lynott rising to the song's jazziness by playing fretless bass, additionally noting that the track reminded him of 'Dancing In The Moonlight'.

'Mexican Blood' is much more successful in a Tex-Mex direction, aided and abetted by graceful playing by all, especially Downey. "I play some timbales as well as marimbas on Mexican Blood," notes Brian. "Good song — I like that one," while Phil offers that, "Mexican Blood is really every cowboy plot you've ever seen rolled into one. Y'know, the one where the Mexican girl is going out with the Mexican boy who's on the run and seeing the Marshall's son at the same time, so the whole thing ends up in one great big shootout and the girl throws herself in front of the boy and gets killed. All the clichés."

Renegade closes with 'It's Getting Dangerous', an expert slice of melancholic melodic hard rock, with sinewy twin leads that again support the argument that Snowy and Scott conjured many of the most thoughtful and emotional ones of the entire catalogue. Comparing the twin leads of Judas Priest with that of Thin Lizzy, Chris Tsangarides (who had worked with both) offers that, "Thin Lizzy would probably go more into harmony lines that were written for everything that they did, whereas Ken and Glenn, it would be used occasionally. It wouldn't be, 'We have to put a guitar harmony in there.' It was just, if you needed it, 'Oh, let's do that; that would be good.' Whereas Thin Lizzy would be conscientiously writing like that."

"That's about three friends of mine I knew when I started in the music business," said Phil of *Renegade's* wistful, winding closer. "We've grown apart in different directions. Really, it's about how you grow up and become opinionated or, maybe, less opinionated or… the drifting apart of friends."

Phil also liked the idea of using the word "dangerous" again, but mindful of not looking like he was out to relive the glory days of *Live And Dangerous*. Curiously, the song's working title was 'It's Getting Dangerous For Us'.

As turned out, Kit Woolven was much more involved in what went down on this classy affair of a controversial Lizzy album than is let on through the record's scant crediting. Not one to be a credit hog (and neither is Chris), Kit remains simply bemused at his status on the record as merely one of the engineers.

"Interesting, yeah, I don't know. I had recorded *Renegade*. I had virtually finished *Renegade*. We hadn't mixed. There were still a couple, few overdubs, but not very much at all, and I was producing it. But it got to the stage where I was working on Phil's solo stuff and the Lizzy stuff at the same time and very often, in the same day, Phil would be going, 'Right, I want to do so-and-so on the solo album.' So we would be working on the solo album, get your head into that, and you want the solo stuff to sound different. Don't want it to be another Lizzy album; it's pointless. But in the same day, Phil would go, 'Okay, let's get that Lizzy track done; I just want to do this' and it was jumping backwards and forwards."

"And this was in the same studio, on the same day," continues Kit. "I would just finish doing something on a solo track, and then Phil would go, 'I want to do this one, do a vocal on one of the Lizzy songs.' I forgot how it came out, but I remember one time, just saying, 'Please, can we just work on one or the other?' Or, 'This week, we're doing Lizzy and next week we're doing the solo stuff.' Phil said, 'Well, I don't want to work like that. I want to have the freedom to jump between this, that and the other'."

"We definitely got a harder-edged sound on *Chinatown* than on

Renegade," says Kit, "but Phil led the way in the writing; Phil had the say on which way the band went. In terms of making it, we did some of that at Good Earth, we did some of it at Mickie Most's studio, outside of Regents Park. We did a lot of stuff there. We did a lot of stuff at Odyssey Studios as well. We then took the album to Morgan Studios, and that's where Chris Tsangarides worked out of, mainly. There had always been a history with Chris as well. Phil had done things with him in the past, and that's when Phil said to me, what do I want to do? 'Do you want to work on the Lizzy stuff or do you want to work on the solo stuff?' I said, I'd rather work on the solo stuff, because to me, it was more interesting at that time."

Hence Chris getting the *Renegade* credit… "I think it's because Chris finished it off, actually," affirms Kit. "I read an interview with Chris recently, in the last couple of years, and somebody was questioning Chris about *Renegade*, and he said, 'To be honest with you, Kit did *Renegade*. He handed it over to me right at the end, I finished it off, and that's it.' That was his attitude on it. He got handed it. That's because there was a history of working with Chris and we were using Morgan Studios at that particular point in time. Chris had worked out of Morgan Studios and knew the studio very, very well. That's where he was based, at that particular time. He was probably the right man for the job at the time. Chris and I… at one time, if there was a rock job, either Chris got it or I got it for a little while there."

So somehow, a dark horse of a classic Thin Lizzy album got made, the undercurrent being the increasingly grave situation with Phil and Scott and their heroin habits, the tension exacerbated by the band's second guitarist not really wanting to be there.

"As time developed and the year went on," says Darren, "there were a few comments about Snowy, people saying he wasn't quite what Lizzy should be. Because he was quite bluesy and quite laid-back in his presence, Snowy. Even though he was a great player. There was that element of him that wasn't fitting in with the Lizzy thing. When you compare him to Robbo and Gary Moore, he's quite a unique player. He's great for some things, but probably wasn't ideal for that Lizzy spot. But only in as far as what probably the fans were expecting — they're trying to replace Gary Moore or Robbo, and what Snowy had was quite unique. Plus he wasn't the type of person who was going to follow or copy other people. So I respect him for that. He did what he did and stuck by his guns. But eventually, I think the element between Phil and Snowy was that Phil wanted to mould him into a Thin Lizzy guitarist, and Snowy wasn't having it."

"I love Snowy," adds Scott. "Snowy was such a nice guy. The only thing probably wrong about Snowy was that his personality didn't quite gel with the rest of us. You know, the rest of us were these rough and ready 'out to try anything' kind of guys, whereas Snowy was a little more reserved, a little more inward. Where we were totally outward, he was a little more inward."

Sum it all up and one would have to say that Snowy's lack of energy on stage would be the penultimate nail in the coffin. The original Thin Lizzy lives on and resonates through the records, and Snowy is fantastic there. But in the context of the times, the daily interaction between band mates, and band and fans, would be through live shows. Snowy got bottled in the press for his lackadaisical stage manner, and he admits that he was often fully disinterested. He does also say, however, that part of the problem was that Phil's bass was mixed so loud, that if he moved much outside a specific spot, he couldn't hear any of his own guitar, which of course is crucial on stage for getting it right, as well as enjoying what you are doing on any level.

"It wasn't really my scene, my environment really," figures White. "When I joined we had talked about my role in the band and it was... I was going to be of one of those bluesy musicians and we were going to sort of expand a bit. But it ended up playing all the old hits really. Also the lifestyle was not really my scene. I really didn't enjoy that 'star' thing. So socially we didn't... we hardly met. If we were on tour I'd be coming down for breakfast and the rest of the boys would probably be coming in off... after their night out, you know? I'd meet them in the lobby; I'd be getting up for breakfast and they'd be coming in for their bed. So after a while I'd had enough. I think after a while they weren't too unhappy to see me go either. You know it was time. It's just a natural thing. But I wrote the title tracks for both of those albums and a couple of other tracks on the albums."

Summing up the chain of events that led to Snowy getting hired and then his departure, Wild Horses' Clive Edwards figures, "Well, Gary walked out, they had no guitarist, so they got Midge in, and they had Davey Flett — because I did Top Of The Pops with Davey Flett, on 'Sarah' — and I don't know who they wanted with in terms of long-term. I don't think Dave Flett, because he wouldn't have fit image-wise. Midge was on the books because of Ultravox. But Snowy had come in, and I think everybody quite early on felt Snowy wasn't the right man, as a player and as a person. But Snowy was doing it; he was getting paid. Snowy is not going to say, 'Excuse me, I don't want all this money. I want to go off and play with Peter Green again.' Snowy White was a blues player, basically, and I think they suffered."

"But to be honest, a lot of this can be put down to the drugs," continues Clive. "Phil's judgment...with Phil, when I got to know him, I could honestly say, love him to bits and everything else, but his judgment wasn't as good. He would be dulled a bit, make the wrong choice. I would certainly say there are better people than me to parse opinion, but I honestly watched him from a short distance, so maybe I can be a little bit more critical on it. I felt that over that period of time, I noticed that Phil would wing stuff a lot more. I think that's what happens when you're doing a lot of heroin and stuff; you do take the easy option. You just think, 'I'm bigger than this,' and every time I make a decision it's going to be right, kind of thing. It does affect your judgment, no two ways about it, and I feel that in that period of time, I saw a decline. Of course it went on, and ultimately he didn't make it. Which is extremely, extremely sad."

Reviews of *Renegade* were generally pretty negative, although time has proven the record to be a favourite of many long time fans. Rolling Stone surprisingly reviewed the album (albeit quite briefly), David Fricke writing that, "On *Renegade*, Lynott isn't up to snuff. Opening with the trademark Lizzy fury of 'Angel Of Death' (which is undermined by a cream-pop synthesizer and a Darth Vader-style monologue), the LP drifts aimlessly from the overlong half-heavy-metal, half- Dire Straits title track to the faceless super boogie, 'Leave This Town' to the cosmetic salsa touches of 'Mexican Blood'. Only the rousing chorus of Hollywood and the poignant sense of loss in 'It's Getting Dangerous' hint at the sensitive yet anthemic writing and hard rock smarts that usually separate Thin Lizzy from the lunkheads."

Snowy White wouldn't leave Thin Lizzy until August of '82, incidentally the same month that Chris O'Donnell gives up his half of the management of Thin Lizzy. To make matters worse, the hotel that Phil and his mother Philomena had bought, burned down on August 1st. To make matters better, Phil would see his second (and last) solo album issued, up into October of '82, after whetting appetites with a couple of singles for it.

Before all this turmoil however, the band dutifully performed live dates for *Renegade*, Snowy intact, but for a spell, without the services of Scott.

"My drug problem got a little too hairy," says Scott, addressing the Spanish and German shows he missed in March, with Lizzy playing as a four-piece (early UK dates were postponed). "I was in a lot of pain emotionally — I just wasn't there. Phil just came up to me during a sound check and he said, 'Man, listen, I really need you to go home and to get better.' I argued with him right off the bat. It's like, there's no fucking way I'm missing any of these gigs. I've never missed a gig before in my life, and I'm not going to start now. He grabbed me by the arm and looked me right in the eye and said, 'Scott, you need to do this. I need you out here. I need you to get better.' At that point I looked at him and went, 'Oh, right, okay' (laughs). Because he really meant it. He wanted me to get better so I could get back out there on the road. So, they got me an airline ticket and I went home and went straight into rehab for ten days or so. But he was always calling me every other day to see how I was doing, to see if everything was okay. That was the first time I ever missed a show ever, but it was for good reasons."

Chalk it up to Phil to be able to put across a show as a four-piece. Scott says it was all down to the charisma of the man. "Phil didn't actually need a lot of tricks up there," laughs Gorham. "He was one of those kinds of guys that when he walks on the stage has that magnetic quality anyway. There was a lot of anticipation in the audience, you know, when is this guy going to walk on stage? And when he did, he just absolutely took command of whatever audience was out there. I could tell you, right off the bat, as soon as we walked out, practically every night he had the audience right in the palm of his hand. Which made it easy for me, because... this might sound weird, but when you're on tour, you get really tired out there. I always knew that Phil's shoulders were wide enough and strong enough that he could actually carry the thing by himself. So it was really nice knowing that Phil was there being able to do that. He did it time after time. It was like he just never seemed to really get tired. Whereas the rest of us, you know, you would be out there for seven months or so, and your ass would be dragging. He never really seemed to feel the effect of being out on the road. He was always dragging us around. You know, 'Come on, get your ass out there, it's going to be a great gig' (laughs)."

"As far as the band was concerned, Phil was always the consummate professional," continues Scott. "His whole life was Thin Lizzy. He went out and did a solo album here and there, but it was always Thin Lizzy for him. He played Thin Lizzy."

"I enjoyed it," said Phil, rising to the challenge of the Scott-less Lizzy. "We didn't have to lick arse, y'know, say how wonderful Spain is, go on about the World Cup! But Scott's too much a part of the band in Britain. We wouldn't get away with it. At the moment, I'm just hoping... I suppose we could advertise the gigs as 'Phil Lynott plus guitarists.' I could have Eric Bell on to do 'Whisky In The Jar', and Robbo could do 'The Boys Are Back In Town. Then Gary Moore could come on and do 'Parisienne Walkways' and Snowy could do 'Chinatown' and 'Hollywood'. For the encore, I'd just leave the stage, and let them get on with it!"

Renegade didn't even get toured in the States, which likely had a part in dooming it to its No.157 placement in the Billboard charts, contrasted against the UK which at least sent it to No.38. "I feel bad that we've neglected our Americans supporters," said Phil, talking to the influential Hit Parader. "Because we're so popular in Europe, it's been a case of, 'You can either tour Britain or Germany and make a profit, or go to America and maybe break even.' Consequently, the management decided we should make money. I hope we'll be able to change that, because I don't like the word failure associated with Thin Lizzy, and when people say, 'You failed to be successful in America,' there's that word and I have to try to put it right. If I thought Thin Lizzy was so old-fashioned or so bad or so antiquated that we shouldn't be around anymore, I would be the first to leave the sinking ship. But in no way do I see Thin Lizzy as a sinking ship. We may have been heading that way for a while, but I think *Chinatown* put a stop to it. Now *Renegade* is another step forward, and the best is yet to come from this band."

Before the end of the year, Phil's lush, elegant second solo record, *The Philip Lynott Album* was released, featuring gorgeous, hugely produced classics like 'Fatalistic Attitude', 'Old Town', 'Cathleen', 'Little Bit Of Water' and arguable centrepiece to the record, 'Ode To Liberty', which featured Mark Knopfler. Whereas many genres of music that Phil thought he could master seemed woefully just outside his grasp, the epic Celtic sweep of much of this record fit the man and his psychic landscape like a glove.

"On the second one, The Phil Lynott Album, I wrote 'Old Town' with Phil and the one that Mark Knopfler played on, 'Ode To Liberty'," recalls Jimmy Bain. "I played on all that stuff, keyboards, bass, everything. That was a real buzz because Phil was a real talent and a really a nice guy. That song 'Ode To Liberty' was just one of my throwaway songs that I happened to play for him and he loved it; he thought it was just great. So it became a song through his development. It was basically three chords that I had thrown together and he made things happen."

"You see, with Thin Lizzy, they were very structured in how they recorded," continues Bain. "He was very much in control of it, but they had a producer to deal with, and the management were there and whatnot. With his own stuff, it gave him a chance to play with whoever he wanted. He did encourage people like Midge Ure and the guy from Visage, and all these new music people who were in London at the time that he was hanging with. He was such a nice person, a nice guy, that he just attracted people. I guess when he was growing up in Dublin, he was one of very few black Irish people, so he took a lot of shit for that when he was growing up. It made him really tough but you couldn't hide the fact that he was a big softie actually. I saw him stick a few guys out, and it was no problem at all. He knew exactly how to take care of them. He was a big guy too. But he was such a nice guy."

"I think what happened was when he was working with Thin Lizzy, they were scared of him," continues Jimmy. "Brian was a little put out because Phil was really this big, larger than life guy. I would hang out with him because it was great. We just started to write that way and then it developed into, 'okay, you're going to be playing bass on some of the tracks, keyboards on some of the other ones, and writing this and whatnot.' I had a blast doing it. It was great. We spent a lot of time. We must have been in the studio for four or five months on each one of his records."

"Mark Knopfler was great on that," says Jimmy, back to 'Ode To Liberty'. "I liked that one, but also of course 'Old Town', because that's made me so much money over the years, because the Corrs re-did that song, so it's almost had a second lease on life. There really wasn't a bad song on either album."

'Old Town' was indeed worthy of push as a hit single, even getting full-on video status. Indeed 'Old Town' is a special track, with Phil turning on the charm with an intimate, wistful vocal. Photographer and band insider Raymond Wright was there to see the song put through its rich visual possibilities.

"When he was making the video for 'Old Town' on the Halfpenny Bridge, this guy named Joe was working for the asset office," recalls Wright. "He was very young at the time, maybe 16. His instructions were always to come straight back to work after collecting the metal, mainly silver. You could do that in Dublin back then. Well, Joe decides he couldn't go the long way back to work. Phil's crew had the bridge closed off. He just got under the barrier and ran across — yes, ruining the shot. Phil stopped him and said, 'Do you know who I am?' Joe says no. Phil says, 'Hold on.' He gives him his autograph and says, 'Hold onto that. It will be worth something; I'll be famous soon.' So Joe goes back to work and tells his boss. Then the rest of the office ran down to see the video shoot — Dublin was like that."

"In the eighties you couldn't get near them unless you were on the 'list'" continues Ray, offering an additional vignette that helped demonstrate what Phil was like. "It didn't bother me as I had got married and had children by then. So I had to head home after gigs. Many a time I would hear he's in town. I would drive by Moran's hotel on the way home about 5:00 — Moran's was Smiley's gig and there would be a queue outside the hotel. This would be five in the day. He would never turn up until ten or eleven that night. Sometimes he would play just two songs but other times he might play for an hour. It was exciting days. To be fair on the guy, he had an aura that just pulled you in and that's the way it was. He was a babe magnet. So you know where the guys wanted to be. The Dublin girls invented the saying 'sex on a stick' and it stuck!"

"Another time I had a special poster of Phil by Johnny Morris I wanted him to autograph for me. I knew he would be in Grafton Street, which is where I found him and asked him to sign it. He always had a pen on him, but he didn't this time. I had a Biro. He started to sign and the pen went through the poster. We both cursed out loud. So I said, 'Hold on,' and to finish lightly, I ran upstairs to a hairdressers called Herman's Haircuts, after the group Herman's Hermits. I grabbed a bigger pen, told them what it was for. They all — girls — ran to the window and started to scream. He signed another card for me and then was mobbed by about ten girls. He just laughed and said he would get me back — loved every minute of it."

"Phil involved me with the second one a lot, really," recalls Darren, taking us back to the solo situation. "'Old Town', played piano on that, and played all the keyboards on that album. So it was nice. I was living with Phil in his house with Caroline, in Kew, so we were just hanging out together, just doing studio stuff, Philip working out his ideas. We enjoyed doing that album. It was a good couple of months. Jimmy Bain was a good guy, but in those days, I'm sure you've heard the rumours about the drug side of things. I don't really know too much about that. It's probably one of those awkward moments in time that nobody should be discussing too much, really (laughs)."

"But Mark Nauseef was great. I remember doing a tour in Germany with Mark. Lovely guy; he lived in Hamburg at the time, so we spent quite a lot of time working on Phil's solo album. That was good fun. Jerome Rimson (note: on *Solo In Soho*, but not the second one) went off to play with Van Morrison, so they were all really good players in their own right. It was just good fun doing different things for a change."

"I don't think Phil took his solo stuff as seriously as he did Thin Lizzy," continues Darren. "Obviously, he was very into what he was doing with his solo stuff, but without a shadow of a doubt, Thin Lizzy was his main baby. The solo thing was just like 'a change is as good as a rest,' type-thing. It just gave him a place to go musically that was taking him away from Lizzy. I think they were all just a bit exhausted with the Lizzy thing."

"It was a little bit of both," replies Darren, asked about how the solo album was dovetailing with the making of *Renegade*. "Phil was writing and coming up with ideas here and there quite a lot, and now and again he would come up with an idea that wouldn't be right for Thin Lizzy, and he would put it on the back burner, to have it available when he wanted to do the solo record."

"We started that solo album at Compass Point in the Bahamas, with myself, Scott and Bob C. Benberg, the drummer from Supertramp, Huey Lewis, and we put down about three tracks down there. 'Just A Little Water' was the first track we did, took a little break, came back, and then Phil was inviting various people onto his record. But I was the staple keyboard player with him. But we just worked on ideas when he felt like doing something. But yes, I loved 'Old Town' and 'Just A Little Water' particularly, but to be honest, I haven't listened to for long time. I don't even think I've got a copy of it (laughs)."

6

THUNDER AND LIGHTNING

"Let's trip the light fantastic on this one"

It's obviously messy that there's a Thin Lizzy without Phil, but to a lesser extent, sadly, it's also messy that the Lynott-led Thin Lizzy would close out their run with a crazily uncharacteristic studio album that pandered to the metal market Lizzy always looked askance, not to mention closing out the whole thing with a live album that most fans consider a dud.

"John was one of those smart asses, but he looked good with his long, blond flowing hair, he played great guitar, fantastic skills, lovely fellow," chuckles Robb Weir from Tygers Of Pan Tang, who would cough up to Thin Lizzy a force of nature called John Sykes to replace the slinking-off Snowy White. "Worse still, he played guitar better than me. I probably thought bloody hell, I've got to raise the bar here. I've got some competition here."

"John Sykes is a brilliant guitar player," adds Carmine Appice, who formed a supergroup with John in later years called Blue Murder. "I think a lot of the guitar players that are happening now, like the guys in Avenged Sevenfold, those kinds of bands, with their heavy guitar... I think a lot of it came from John. Even Metallica — like when Metallica had their huge album with Bob Rock, Bob had all our Blue Murder sounds sampled. John had a certain big giant sound that he could get, and I'm hearing that sound in a lot of bands. He was also a great songwriter, great at riffs, melodies, even lyrics. But John had a management team that was bad. He had some marketing guy from Capitol, and he had his stepdad, and some lawyer. There wasn't like really one guy manager with a plan. They listened to John too much and they didn't have a plan. It's like this is what you guys are going to do."

What this adds up to is a guy that arrives with lots of baggage, lots of bluster, and, into a Thin Lizzy where the two leaders of the band are hurting, running on drained batteries, and ceding some level of control to a strong personality. Sykes was, and is, definitely that, proven time and again, such as when he would move on to Whitesnake, where David Coverdale wound up plain scared of the guy.

"No, he's not afraid of him," disagrees producer Keith Olsen, who worked with John in Whitesnake. "David was hurt, and he wasn't listened to, by John. John hurt him deeply, and so it was one of those things. John has reaped the benefits of writing and co-publishing all those songs, on an album that sold 22 million copies. You know, it's one of those things. The first thing I would do is say, 'Thank you, David, for allowing me to write with you. Want to do it again?' (laughs). But egos were huge."

As is illustrated by the following story... "We were doing this one version of 'Here I Go Again', and I really wanted eight notes in the verse, (sings it). So Dave and I got John on the phone and I said, 'John, could you just grab the guitar and come by? You can plug into the studio amps. I just need eight notes on two verses.' He says to me, 'No Keith, I can't do that. I would need my entire backline, or I would have to fly to England.' Coverdale looks at me and I'm going, 'It's just eight notes! It's just jung jung jung, to give it a little more push forward.' He would need his entire backline or he would have to fly to London to do it. So I said, 'It's eight notes!' (laughs). Anyway, I could see this call wasn't going anywhere and I said goodbye. I looked at David and said, 'You want to try some eight notes?' So I called Dan Huff. David had never met Dan Huff. Dan was the number one session player at the time in LA, and he was probably doing three or four sessions a day, commercials and stuff like that. I mean, making really good money as a session player. So I called him, and he stops by at 9:00 on his way to a 10 o'clock session, with a guitar, not even in a guitar case.

He plugs it into my amp that is sitting there in the control room, with the speaker in another room, he hears the song once and he goes, 'Okay, jung, jung, jung,' and I said thanks very much. Unplugs it, and he says, 'You know, I'll just send you a bill.' All of a sudden, it was, 'Oh.' David, 'Oh,' that special... you know. So I started introducing him to extra people here and there."

So a guy like that can take over, and in conjunction with a heavy metal producer guy in Chris Tsangarides, who had also produced John in Tygers Of Pan Tang and recommended him to the foundering situation... well, Thin Lizzy would be twisted into something quite unrecognisable, certainly a million miles away from the introspective, melancholic band that made *Renegade*.

"Well, I think that was down to me a little bit," laughs Chris, taking the blame for taking Lizzy metal. "I came along and I was into the whole New Wave Of British Heavy Metal and having worked with the Priest boys on Sad Wings Of Destiny, and Tygers Of Pan Tang and so on, and bringing in John Sykes from that world as well, it tended to beef up the sound. For the first time on a Lizzy scenario, we decided to make it lean more into rock, with fast, heavy guitars, loads of solos, which was a style that was happening around us. It wasn't from the band's perspective — I think they were just making another one of their albums. But from my perspective, as a big fan of all that, I was definitely going for that style, which, being that they were established, obviously they're not going to sound like any of the newer bands. But the sensibilities and the production values I brought along, and John with his heavy-duty guitar and fast breaks and shredding, whatever you would call it, made it sound like that."

With respect to hooking old school up with new school, Chris explains that, "it came about because I was at Phil's house in Dublin, watching a live video we had made on the *Renegade* tour. He said to me, 'Honestly Chris, tell me what you think about Snowy.' We watched it and I said, 'Well, quite frankly, I love Snowy and I think he's a brilliant guitarist, but I don't think his heart and soul is in this band. He doesn't want to be there. You can see it.' He said, 'Yeah, I agree with you. Any ideas?' That's where Sykes came in. He said, 'What's he like?' We had already organised to do a solo single with him, that I got together with MCA, and Phil had agreed to sing on it, then realised, and I said, 'It's the guy on that record you're doing.' 'Oh, oh, okay.' Once he saw him and got to know him and saw how he played, that was it."

"The idea of the change between Kit and Chris Tsangarides was nothing personal," recalls Brian Downey, referring to the move over three albums from Kit to Kit and Chris, to just Chris. "It was just down to the fact that we had a new guitar guy, John Sykes, coming in, which was purely down to Chris. Chris said, 'There's a guy I know, who I've worked with, in a band called Tygers of Pan Tang.' I'd heard of them but I hadn't heard their albums. But good reports about them, good reports about John as well, so obviously that was one of the reasons we had John down to play. When we heard him play, he was just great. We knew that this guy was much heavier than previous guys, maybe apart from Gary Moore on his heavier period. The guy was completely different from what we had expected, and he brought a completely hard edge to the band, a much heavier aspect. I was shocked when I heard how loud and aggressive John played, at the first rehearsal. I said well, this album is going to be completely different, because the guy had this really hard aggressive edge and attitude to his playing. Phil obviously had to compensate by writing harder songs. That's actually what happened — that whole *Thunder And Lightning* album turned out much harder than I expected."

"You can hear Sykes' influence because he's much more of a metal guitarist," says Kit Woolven, this time, as stated, not on the payroll. "He was New Wave Of British Heavy Metal, wasn't he? I mean, that's the thing with Snowy. I don't know that Snowy was ever really the right guitarist for Lizzy. They needed a bit of a bad boy guitarist, you know? Snowy is just a really nice bloke (laughs). He's a really, really nice chap. I don't know if that's the right image for the other Lizzy guitarist, you know, especially after Robbo."

On and off, September through November of 1982 found the band recording what was to become this barnstormer of a last Thin Lizzy record, at Eel Pie Studios. As somewhat of a dry run, John's solo single also emerged that month, closing off his obligation to MCA, Sykes having left Tygers, who were finding success with that label. 'Please Don't Leave Me' (backed with an instrumental version of the same), would in fact feature all of Lizzy on the track, save for Gorham. Additionally, 'Please Don't Leave Me' is a track hijacked by Phil, in that his vocal takes centre stage, over a sparse pop format within which Sykes strums politely and provides a simple twin lead, notwithstanding an electrocuted solo that is perhaps a bit much given the song's weak frame. All told, it's an uptempo version of 'Still In Love With You' best suited to *Solo In Soho*, and obviously no incinerating indication of the firestorm to come.

Prior to and even during the deal for the solo single, Sykes had been getting jerked around by Ozzy Osbourne and Sharon Arden in the duo's endless search for guitar blood. "I spoke to various people at MCA and a solo deal did eventually come together," explained Sykes to Kerrang!'s Howard Johnson, on the ramp-up to joining Lizzy. "I asked Chris Tsangarides if he could ask Phil whether he'd help out, to which he answered yes. I was supposed to go to Ireland with Phil to start working on the single when Ozzy rang me out of the blue and said he'd like to hear my playing. I thought that I might as well go for it, so I went and met Ozzy in London. I went down to London again a couple days later to play in a studio where Magnum were recording. It was simply Ozzy on his own — none of the band were there. I arranged to meet him at six o'clock teatime and I played for a while. When he heard me, he asked me to go to America and play with the band, which was in effect another audition. He didn't say yes or no. By this time I was due to go to Ireland so I went over and left things as they were. I was then asked to join Lizzy and I thought I'd take it 'cos I got on well with Phil and thus considered it the best move."

Expressing what he was about to add to the Lizzy stew, John figures, "People claim that Lizzy's peak was when *Live And Dangerous* appeared, Yet it's natural that when a band puts six years' worth of hits on an album, they'll hit a peak. Lizzy are much bigger than the Tygers and all the albums do pretty well. Everyone's said that I've toughened them up from what's been going down in the studio and that's probably true. They were a little mellow and even they themselves agreed. I think they got into a rut and I've come along and given them a boot up the arse. It sounds good now!"

"Lizzy was never a really heavy metal band, but it was especially melodic," continued Sykes. "The difference is that the guitar sounds sorted out now — the new one sounds like a heavy rock album with all the Lizzy traits thrown in. I'm buzzin' solely to have a gig again. Everything's working well and I can't wait to get back on the road."

October found both Gary Moore and Phil as solo artist with releases, "Philip Lynott And The Soul Band" even taking the man's second solo album, *The Philip Lynott Album* on the road, before quickly getting back to the *Thunder And Lightning* sessions in November. Come late December into the New Year, Phil hit the road again, playing solo tracks in Ireland, his band including from the fold Darren Wharton, Jimmy Bain and Brian Downey. The dates are underscored by the turmoil of Phil's marriage to Caroline falling apart and on January 18th, the announcement that Thin Lizzy would disband after the "farewell" tour for the new album. Indeed at one point, Phil wanted to knock it on its head without even doing the tour, but changed his mind when manager Chris Morrison informed him that without the tour, he'd be leaving the organization with a personal debt of £250,000.

Thunder And Lighting would be issued on March 4th 1983, initial UK copies including a bonus live 12" featuring 'Emerald', 'Killer On The Loose', 'The Boys Are Back In Town' and 'Hollywood', all recorded at the Hammersmith Odeon, November 26th 1981. The album would vault to No.4 on the UK charts but a mere No.159 in the US. The cover of the album features a gratuitously heavy metal scene, a black expanse of slag punctuated by double metal clichés, a guitar struck by lightning, and a studded leather gloved fist pumping gamely from the mire, signifying something like, "The NWOBHM may almost be over, but hey, better late than never."

Jim Fitzpatrick intimates that the cover and maybe the whole direction of the album was the result of Phil's diminished life force. "Yeah, if somebody would say to him, something he didn't want to do, he would tell them to go stuff themselves but now I got the feeling that the record company was driving all the design work. I did a stunning cover for *Thunder And Lightning*. It was a big carved stone, like a

Newbridge stone exploding out of the ground, and it was very dramatic, one of the best designs I did, and I was devastated when they didn't use it. I did two other designs that were very substandard, and I put them on, so they would choose the other one (laughs), but in the end he didn't use any of them, because they used a very fine Irish photographer, Bob Carlos Clarke, who is dead now, committed suicide, but that wasn't one of his best, you know?"

"This is the first time we've had an album ready that's coming out on schedule for the tour and we're stuck for an idea for the cover," quipped Phil, intimating that there was no time for good ideas. "It's proving to be much harder than we thought. I mean, check out how many groups have used a lightning bolt either on their sleeves or as a logo, Dire Straits and AC/DC being two classic examples."

On the subject of the new material, Phil added that, "We all can't wait to get on the road with this line-up because I think the album's great; there's no doubt that it's the best thing we've done for quite a while. But I've got to get back into shape physically, which is one advantage of living in Dublin. I'm so pleased that we've delivered the goods. I know they're going to like John; he's really put back a metal feel into Lizzy, a hard edge that's been lacking for some time."

The celebration of metal blaring out of the sleeve continued with the album's opener, a slashing fast hard rocker of a title track with Phil shouting at the top of his diminished range hoarsely, crap lyrics not helping the cause. 'Thunder And Lighting' would become the album's second single, issued a month after the release of the album. Backed with a live version of 'Still In Love With You', it would reach No.39 in the UK charts. Crash the track into your living room, and one instantly notices the seething noise and electricity of the mix as one is immersed in the cold bath that would become Lizzy's clanging career closer of a record.

"Chris Tsangarides is a real rock producer," says Scott. "He liked his music loud and wild. It was his idea of how that last album was going to sound. You know, guitars a lot hotter, a lot more sustain on the guitar. So I think it was more Chris that moulded the sound for *Thunder And Lightning*. He had to come up with the goods because the rest of us were out of it at that point. That album was the most difficult one for me, just because of the state of mind I was in. Both Phil and I were going through our pretty bad drug stages at that point. I don't think he and I were totally on top of our game. But with John Sykes coming in, he was fresh blood, he had new enthusiasm, and he gave the two of us a kick in the ass to get off the floor and get into this album and make something out of it. But it was a mentally and physically painful one to actually try to finish."

Addressing the idea that the album — and most definitely its banner song — seemed like a celebration of the metal the band usually looked down upon, Scott figures that, "More bands at that point were leaning towards the metal side of things, so we thought well, let's trip the light fantastic on this one, see what happens. It's why John came into the band, was to have us lean more towards that direction. In fact, I'd gone to Phil a few months beforehand, saying that, you know, I actually wanted out of the band. I actually didn't really want to do another album. I just thought we should knock it on the head, but he was the one who said, 'No, let's do the one more album, the one more world tour,' I know this kid who is a great guitar player, and that happened to be John Sykes. That's how John actually got in. We started writing the songs, and started listening to his guitar tone, and my tone changed a little bit on that one, to match was going on."

"I wasn't shocked at all; I knew what we were getting into here," continues Scott. "You know, I'm not sure if it was the exact right way to go and I think the sales proved it. I guess the fans maybe like that album the least, because it got heavy. But I quite liked it; I thought it was a cool album. I liked playing on it. I think some of the songs are really great."

Still, Scott concedes that the metal direction "suited John more than it did me. It threw us in a different direction than we had normally gone. Usually we were a bit more light and shade, the way we wrote the albums. This one was more in-your-face. So I guess Chris is more of an in-your-face kind of producer (laughs)."

Second on slate was 'This Is The One', which perpetuates the metal moves, leaden chords anchoring a military "one and three" beat from Brian, whose drums are front and centre on the track and the record as a whole. "I loved the drum sound on the album," reflects Downey. "Chris put me up on a big podium, I remember, for some reason. Similar to what Tony's ideas were, to get the drums totally isolated from the rest of the instruments, with no overspill, and that's why I was up on a podium. So he had good ideas as well. The studio was great as well, really good quality equipment in there, and the drum sound was great, excellent."

Young keyboard player Darren Wharton gets a writing credit on 'This Is The One', as he does on the album's next track and lone ballad, 'The Sun Goes Down'. "Darren was much-maligned," says Tsangarides. "As far as people knew what he was about, keyboard player and musical director, if you will. By the time we got onto *Thunder And Lightning*... he was first brought in as reinforcements with the keyboards. But the more we got on, he would come up with these amazing harmony parts that he would work out, that a pianist or an orchestra would play, incredibly diverse harmonies. Not just the blatantly obvious ones, between guitars. He would stack them up like you wouldn't believe, and all for the better, really."

Adds Scott, "For 'The Sun Goes Down', I just remember him laying down a really cool bed in there, creating a really cool mood so I could get in there and really put the guitars on. He inspired me on that one. Then actually that ended up being Phil's favourite song on that album." 'The Sun Goes Down' would constitute the album's third single (backed, in the UK, with 'Baby Please Don't Go'), reaching No.52 in the UK charts. A 12" version of the track features a remix done by Tim Martin in Phil's own home studio at Kew House.

"For 'This Is The One', I just wrote the middle eight, really," adds Darren, before giving his contour to the fiery new band chemistry. "That progression was mine (sings it). The riff, that was Phil's. But yeah I just remember that with John Sykes coming into the situation, there was a good vibe with the band. John had a different style, and whether or not Phil was thinking this was the way we should be going out... Some people were saying it was a bit heavy. Obviously when you get a new guitarist, it's going to change the style, as *Renegade* did with Snowy. Then Phil would be featuring John obviously as part of the new system, and that's why the album changed direction. It is what it is; some people say that it was a slightly wrong direction, but some people say *Renegade* was a slightly wrong direction. I just put it down to the guy who was doing the album, Chris Tsangarides. It was what came out. John's style, Chris Tsangarides' production, and there you go. There was a rumour that Mutt Lange wanted to produce an album for us at the time, so I'm sure it could've turned out completely different. But it felt good at the time, and that's what you do. But Chris was a lovely guy — very, very sweet man. I look back on that album now... I would've loved to work with Tony Visconti or Mutt Lange. I think Mutt would've been a brilliant producer for Thin Lizzy."

"With Sykes in the band, it was much more focused," figures Tsangarides. "For the recording session, we went to a rehearsal room as a band and we wrote songs and got our shit together, so that's why that record is a lot harder and a lot rockier, I guess. It was more focused and a whole lot more successful than *Renegade*. The heavier sound was by design. It was meant to be harder and rockier, pack some hard rock in, you know? With multi-track recording in those days, new technologies had just begun, so consequently, by the time we finished overdubbing, we still had a fresh drum and bass track which was a part of the tape where we hadn't played for four or five or six months, until the mixing stage, which accounts for a lot of the brightness and punch of it all, because of that. The idea is that the tape wasn't worn out, basically. So when that album came out, people in Europe, Germany especially, the record companies were saying to their new band, that's what you've got to sound like (laughs)."

But there is the one ballad, 'The Sun Goes Down' being a dark (!), contemplative piece, set to a metronomic tick of time expiring. "That's such a poignant, moody piece of music, that it still sends chills down my spine every time I hear it," says Chris, with respect to a track that manages to fit the vibe of the record despite its down-dressing. As noted, it's another Darren Wharton co-credit, Darren explaining that, "The writing thing in Thin Lizzy was very collaborative. Basically if you were in the room together with the guys and if you came up with something... 'I like that,' it was something like that. Sometimes you had a particular idea that you'd come to the table with, that you could sing. Other than that, if we were jamming in a rehearsal situation, Phil would always start. But Scott always has great ideas, as did John. I had 'The Sun Goes Down'. But Phil had a real talent for being able to utilise ideas if he liked them, and mould them into something practical as far as what he thought was a Thin Lizzy song."

"There'd been a lot of talk about whether Snowy was the right choice for Thin Lizzy," continues Wharton, adding more reflection on Lizzy's revolving guitar slot. "Personality-wise, he was a fantastic guy, and a fantastic player. It was just, did his style fit in with what people perceived as the Thin Lizzy sound? Some people liked it, some people didn't. So when John came into the band, it was perceived to be, 'Right, this is it, this is what Lizzy need now, this is Lizzy back on track,' more of a fly sort of guitarist. He had the hair and he had more of a rough edge, more speed, more of an aggressive player. Because Snowy didn't want to go with that, he was more of a blues player. So as the guitarist is concerned, they were chalk and cheese. So when John came in, there was a mood that this was the right way to go. John was a great young player, and he certainly gave the band an energy boost as far as the guitar goes."

"But I wouldn't say that John came in and saved the day and made everything better," continues Darren. "It was just more of a feeling of well, we're back on track now. We've got somebody who's a bit more like Gary Moore, a bit more like Robbo, a bit more the hair, the image, the style, this is more towards what Thin Lizzy should be. In that respect it gave Scott, Phil and Brian a bit of a morale boost. But in hindsight you can look back and say, was it the right direction to be going in, really? Because as a lot of people have said to me, that album had gone too heavy metal, so you've gone from the frying pan into the fire, basically. Whereas you could probably say *Live And Dangerous*, that sound, with classics like 'Jailbreak' and 'Waiting For An Alibi' — those were the classic Thin Lizzy songs.

Renegade went a bit too soft and then the last one was overly heavy.

The classic sound of Thin Lizzy is definitely the *Jailbreak* album, or most of *Live And Dangerous*. Everybody knows that. Those are all the timeless songs that we love and love to play, the lifeblood of Thin Lizzy and we build a few other songs around that in the set."

'The Holy War' (working title: 'Chosen One') delivers yet another slab of metal. After Phil's gnarly bass rhythm, Downey whacks in with an aggressive pattern drenched by Tsangarides' arch-'80s production. Up next is one of the album's more memorable twin leads, which… you can find them if you look 'n' listen, but there's so much distortion and dirt attached to them, they are summarily buried by the mayhem surrounding them.

"'Holy War' was recorded initially as just a bass and drum track that Phil had," notes Downey. "Phil had a great idea for a bass intro, and I just happened to be on the drums when he played it (laughs). I just followed the actual intro on the drums, and it actually ended up on the song. So things were happening in the studio that never happened previously in Lizzy. Outtakes were being accepted and all sorts of ideas were being thrown around. That was great, because it was a new way of approaching it."

"'Cold Sweat' was a particular riff that John had that Phil liked," says Darren of the raucous and sinister side one closer. "So that was an obvious choice where, let's use this riff because it's John's." The song was a bit of a hit, a metal invader that could never have lived and thrived had we not been within the throes of the NWOBHM. Again, twin leads are present, Sykes transforming the Lizzy trademark into something that was more picked and precise, versus the sinewy nature of Scott's configurations with either Snowy or Brian.

'Cold Sweat' was issued as an advance single in the UK in February of '83, backed with 'Bad Habits', and hit No.27 in the charts. There was also a double 7" version and a 12" version, both offering 'Don't Believe A Word' and 'Angel Of Death', live from the Hammersmith, London, November 26th 1981.

Onto side two of the original very black vinyl, and we get the origami-like 'Someday She Is Going To Hit Back', again, the wall of guitars maintained and persisting, Downey responding in kind with an over-the-top triplet fill to crack things open. Of note, the song began life as an instrumental, called 'Mama Don't Like It'.

"'Someday She Is Going To Hit Back' was one of those where they gave me a bit of rope," laughs Darren. "I was into jazz at the time. I remember coming up with all these weird and wacky harmonies — that Scott actually quite liked. There's some quite unusual chord work in that song and in the harmonies, which went from being a two-part to like a three-part thing. That, to me, was basically Scott and Phil giving me a bit more rope as far as the writing is concerned, so we came up with something a bit bizarre, unusual for the album. Those chords and those structures are very jazz-based; it was like a fusion of jazz-based chords and these augmented ninths, minor ninths, B over A major, and all types of weird stuff going on. But it transcribed into guitar harmonies quite well, so that was what was behind it. It was jazz harmonies creeping in. Whether that's a good thing, I don't know, but that's the way that came about. I don't think that's ever going to go down as a classic Thin Lizzy song, but it was a song that we all got our buzz off on, because of its energy."

"That whole track was written just purely to make sure that we kept that momentum going," notes Downey, who gets a credit on the track along with Darren and the ever-present Phil. "We were just running out of tracks and we just happened to be jamming along to this really good riff that Darren had. I suggested we put some breaks in there, and that was obviously accepted. So the results were because of input into that album by different members. Slightly different from the way we previously had recorded."

Oddly, 'Baby Please Don't Go' follows with much the same jazzy chording as well as the preceding track's flag-unfurled forward momentum. This one's chief feature is a ripping guitar solo from John Sykes that, to this writer's ears, is the man's second greatest recorded performance after his monster riff for Whitesnake's 'Still Of The Night'. The solo swoops, resolves, returns for another concentric and dive-bombed round of sound, and once it squeals out, shines gloriously as a textbook demonstration as to how a composed, considered, thought-through solo really has so much more going for it than something off-the-cuff, an idea that perhaps Lizzy had been teaching us all along with their twin lead escapades.

Scott wholly concedes ceding territory to the flash man, after a whole history of ego sub-plots with guitarists, first Brian, then going it near-alone for *Bad Reputation*, then his somewhat healthy relationship and kinship with Gary, and finally, in the two years before Sykes joins, becoming the quiet and tacit leader in a co-guitarist situation with Snowy.

"John and I got along really great," says Scott. "You know, the problem with that album is that Phil and I were right in the throes of heavy addiction at this point. Basically, on that album, I was just going, 'John, you just do whatever you want to do on this one, and I'll just grab a couple of these spots here and I'll just get out of Dodge.' I was in a lot of pain; there was a lot of depression going on with me at the time, and so that album, I don't really remember a hell of a lot of what was going on. Phil would be passing out at the console there, with all phasers on stun, listening back to it. So it was a good experience and a bad experience all at the same time. I think there was a lot of really good playing on it, but there was a lot of pain that went along with that album also."

Things lighten up for the rock 'n' roller 'Bad Habits', a song so happy-making that this writer's bar band Torque included it in our set along with the ZZ Top and Quiet Riot songs of the day! "'Bad Habits', great song, great drum fills, all left wide open to play what you want to play as well," notes Downey, who indeed fires off a most musical fill, on an album with lots of dramatic drumming.

Thunder And Lightning blazes to a close with 'Heart Attack', "a matter of me and Scott and Phil sitting down together," notes Wharton. 'Heart Attack' is essentially sister and storm cloud to 'Cold Sweat', in that both are short and sharp and quick of attack, both featuring narrators concerned about the potential doomed finality that results when one burns the candle at both ends. Coke, heroin, cold sweats, heart attacks… this is the one, indeed.

Old friend and signer of the band to Vertigo back in '74, Nigel Grainge, could see that Phil was well down a path to self-destruction. "Yeah, I went to a couple of parties that Phil was at, and actually went to the wedding as well, when he married Caroline, and there was so much dope that was going around then. It was very unhealthy. I remember seeing him a few years later. He was staying at the Sunset Marquee while we were there, and I remember, we went up and he said, 'Come up for a drink.' So we went over there to his… he had a suite there, and it looked like something nuclear had gone off in there. There was like lipstick on the walls and gunk. God, he was a madman. This would've been post-Boomtown Rats, probably '81, '82. I mean, I never really did too many drugs, but all the ones I ever did were with them. It was just rife. They were a real party group as well. It was funny; it was almost like un-cool if you didn't do it with them. On a lighter note, on a personal level, we were at a party, and he pulled some woman off me once (laughs), which was quite funny."

"Because we were coming to an end in my relationship with her, and it was just very obvious that Phil was hitting on her, and I remember speaking to her afterwards and said, 'Did you go with him?' and she did. So you know, he had no compunction of who he was trying to pull people from."

The sum total of Thunder And Lighting continues to split ardent Lizzy fans into warring camps to this day. Most decry that it's the least like a Lizzy album of any of them. But then again, many appreciators gleefully scavenge through it for scorching leads, starkly confessional lyrics from Phil, flash drumming from Brian, and the odd bit of subtle and smart Lizzy-proud melody challengingly inserted into what are bodice-rippers perhaps too uncomfortably opportunistic during this golden age for British metal.

With respect to the album's reception in the UK, as background, *Chinatown* was the first record for the band to reach only silver after a string of four gold albums and a platinum for *Live And Dangerous*.

Renegade had stalled at a middling No.38 and had not even reached silver. At least Thunder And Lighting had reversed trend and clawed the band back to silver, as well as a No.4 placement on the charts, higher than even *Chinatown*. As discussed, part of the album's modest success must be chalked up to the times, with Lizzy semi-churlishly joining the ranks of the newly (or once again) heavy, along names like Budgie, Uriah Heep, Wishbone Ash, maybe even Whitesnake and Gillan (vs. The Ian Gillan Band), and then soon to be joined by a considerably rocked-up, reformed Deep Purple.

Still, it is to the band's credit that both 'Heart Attack' and 'Cold Sweat', each an uncompromisingly steely rocker, could be hooky and even soulful, even if the title track fails in that respect, sounding hollow, desperate and average of riff on its way down to the middle of the NWOBHM pack. But experimentation is profuse enough, and then there's 'Bad Habits', which, if one squints hard enough, one can spot Phil's love for original rock 'n' roller Elvis Presley, and everything in the world is good and pure again.

7

LIFE/LIVE

"The guys were all very tired, really"

Lizzy's last loud hurrah, *Thunder And Lightning*, would be gamely toured, despite the band already having announced their impending split. As a result, press for the album wasn't. Instead, talk inevitably turned to the Lizzy legacy, as well as the idea of a final live album on which all the past Lizzy guitarists would be represented. After a couple of special appearances to debut the new line-up (BBC on January 26th and The Tube on January 28th), the tour proper would commence February 9th in Scarborough, UK support coming from Irish hard rockers Mama's Boys. The first leg was to be an extensive blanketing of the UK and Ireland, highlight being the four-night Hammersmith Odeon stand early in the tour, from March 9th through March 12th, that would serve as core tracks for the frustrating double live tombstone of an album called *Life/Live*.

Post-Ireland, Lizzy cancelled out of a few booked German dates, picking up in Denmark on April 27th for a handful of Scandinavian dates before returning to the UK for a couple of shows in May. On May 17th, the band played the first of five dates comprising a Japanese tour, with Phil suffering serious withdrawal symptoms during the inaugural Sun Plaza show, not having been able to obtain any heroin in Japan.

Come late July '83 through August 8th, there's a "Philip Lynott Band" tour of Scandinavia, otherwise known as the Three Musketeers tour.

"Right at the end of Thin Lizzy, we did a solo tour of Sweden, with Phil, doing Phil's solo stuff, and indeed Lizzy stuff as well," explains Magnum's Mark Stanway keyboard player for the tour. Mark had been invited to the band's Manchester gig by John Sykes, at which time he met Phil for the first time, at the Britannia Hotel, where Phil immediately asked him to sign on for his upcoming solo dates. "So that was John Sykes, Brian Downey, Phil Lynott, me, and another Irish guitarist called Doish Nagle. We did a lot of Thin Lizzy stuff on the tour, and Phil really liked the feel of the band and he said, 'Come on, let's form a new band,' which later became Grand Slam. There were ups and downs. When we first did that tour in Sweden, it was the cleanest I'd ever seen Phil. He put a bit of weight on, which looked good on him. He'd just come back from a holiday in Africa and he was tanned, which is weird to say about a black guy, but he looked so healthy. We did 14 or 15 shows across the 'folk parks' of Sweden, during the summer, fantastic time. As I say, we enjoyed it that much, he said, we've got to keep this band together."

Set list-wise, Mark remembers, "stuff off of *Solo In Soho*, 'Old Town', 'Yellow Pearl', which was the theme tune for the British Top Of The Pops for years. We did things like 'Parisienne Walkways' and 'The Boys Are Back In Town', 'Cold Sweat', Thin Lizzy classics like that. We also played a track that Thin Lizzy never played live, called 'Sarah'. So he was pleased to be able to play that live, which never happened with Thin Lizzy, apparently."

As regards the mercurial Sykes, "John has been a personal friend of mine since he was in Tygers Of Pan Tang and supported Magnum years ago. So the stardom doesn't come into it with me and John. We go back a long way, to when we were both broke musicians trying to make a living. I've got the highest respect for John. He's a great guy. A lot of people I've heard since, had got mixed feelings about that, but I can't comment on that, because I can only say he's a good mate and a great talent as a player.

"Phil was mad on Elvis Presley; absolutely adored him," continues Mark, asked about Phil's tastes in music. "There's 'King's Call'; I mean, mad about Presley. Phil idolised Elvis Presley. But he would so many types of different music. He did like the punk era. He liked the fashion; Phil was also sharp with fashion. We would hang around with some of these people in the West End of London, because he just liked the way they looked, and the way they dressed and everything else. So there was no limit to what he enjoyed, musically. Which I think is healthy. You know, to only like one type of music, you're missing out. There were certain things he loved about Bruce Springsteen, but he never really ran that home for me. So I didn't spot that as much as I spotted the Presley thing and he was always reading something. I know he liked biographies, autobiographies. As regards fiction and stuff like that, I don't really know. He'd always be listening to some obscure music from somewhere, whether it was something like Grandmaster Flash from the early '80s or Frankie Goes To Hollywood; he was just always listening to music — pretty eclectic guy."

"He definitely had a fascination with Elvis," agrees Laurence Archer, who would play with both Mark and Phil in Grand Slam. "Hence, if you look at some of the styling of the jackets and things like that, there's an Elvis styling going on. But yes, he was certainly a fan of the big writers, the Springsteens, the Dylans; Springsteen is one who especially comes to mind."

"He was a joker, a comedian, as well," recalls Mark. "He would like you to think one thing for a long time. It's difficult to give you a particular example, but he would wind people up and make people think he was something he wasn't. He was just a star. When he opened his front door, he put a different hat on, and just became this almighty star, and yet behind doors he was just one of the lads — he really was. There were an awful lot of hangers-on, people trying to hang around the glory of it all. But he saw through all of those. He wouldn't tolerate people lightly. He would be polite and everything, but if he didn't like you, you knew about it."

"You could tell the guy was on something, but he never actually showed me anything like that," says Sören Lindberg. "I had the fortune, when he was doing this Three Musketeers thing over in Sweden, I spent a lot of time with him, and one night he was more or less in tears, saying, 'Sören, please, promise me to never, ever, try this shit.' Stuff like that, and at that time, I know he had just gone to a methadone clinic in England, to try to kick the habit. He had all these weird people following around, trying to offer him stuff and whatnot, so it must have been more or less totally impossible for him to quit at that time. The only chance he would have had was to move out into the countryside or something."

Offering a bit of background to the casual Three Musketeers jaunt, Lindberg explains that, "What happened was, Dave Edmunds, Rockpile, was actually supposed to do this summer tour of Sweden. Dave Edmunds left the band, so the band broke up. Thomas Johansson, who was the head of EMA Telstar, he was an old friend with Phil, and he said, 'Listen, there's this three-week tour here; would you be interested in doing that, as a solo project?' Phil just went for it he said, 'Yeah, sure, I'll do it.' So he put the band together very quickly, I suppose. Obviously they must've had some rehearsals, but I don't think it was very much, to be honest with you. It was just a mix of a lot of Thin Lizzy and solo songs. I remember sitting down with Phil, and the obvious question was, 'Why did you call the band the Three Musketeers? Because there are five players here.' Phil said something in the line of, 'The Three Musketeers were actually four,' because they had d'Artagnan in there as well, and basically he thought it was a bit of a twist on the Three Musketeers, that they were actually five. Also, you have to remember that three of the band at that time were members of Thin Lizzy, so I suppose that's what he meant as well. But it was a three-week tour. I travelled along with the band, so we had some really great times together. It wasn't Thin Lizzy, or second-rate Thin Lizzy, but it was still very interesting."

"He just said it had got stale," offers Stanway, on why Phil had decided to knock Lizzy on its head. "It was time to rest it. There were talks of reforming, and so many people... I've read interviews, where people have said, 'Oh yeah, Phil asked me to reform Thin Lizzy with him.' I think in all fairness, Phil Lynott would only reform Thin Lizzy with John Sykes and Scott. He loved that band. But he wanted to rest it. It'd been a long time, and he just wanted to try new things. He had enjoyed such a wide variation of music. He loved hip-hop, he loved dance music and jazz, and he had really open ears to everything. So therefore, Thin Lizzy, I guess, during that period of creativity, was stifling for him. He wanted to do some strange things that wouldn't have worked with Thin Lizzy. So that was a good experimental time, and I had two glorious years with him. Fond friend sadly missed."

In a career of peculiar guest slots, while in Sweden, Phil added one of his most obscure (and coolest), playing bass on the fist-pumpingly anthemic 'Free' by Swedish "NWOBHM" pioneers Heavy Load. The song would show up on the band's final album, Stronger Than Evil, as well as being issued as a single, both on the band's own Thunderload label.

There would be four more shows for Phil Lynott as part of the Thin Lizzy empire he had built. August 28th had the band playing the Reading festival in the UK. Headliner on the first night was The Stranglers, with the Ian Gillan-era Black Sabbath anchoring the second night a cut above Marillion. Thin Lizzy closed the third and final night, other bands on the day including Ten Years After, The Climax Blues Band, Little Steven, Steve Harley and neo-proggers The Enid and Twelfth Night. The show was captured by BBC Radio One and later issued as BBC Radio One Live In Concert.

The last gig was in Nuremburg, Germany, September 4, 1983, for a mainland version of Monsters Of Rock. Sadly representing a changing of the guard, Whitesnake received marquee billing — and let's not forget that John Sykes would shortly leave for fame and fortune within that act — with Thin Lizzy represented well up the pecking order along with Blue Öyster Cult, Ozzy Osbourne and Meat Loaf, followed by Saxon, Krokus, Survivor, Twisted Sister and Motörhead, now featuring nemesis Brian Robertson in the band!

"Well, that's an interesting question," muses Darren, asked whether he was aware that the band were playing their last gig. "Because there wasn't really any question in my mind that it wasn't the last tour. Truth be known, I think it was some decision that the management took, an announcement it was going to be basically... Scott and Phil needed some time off. They hadn't had any time off, so we all knew there was going to be a break, a substantial break, maybe six months to a year, where the guys could just go lie on the beach, get themselves sorted out for whatever problems, and that was really the idea. It seemed to snowball into a final split at some point after that. Phil got his solo thing together, and we all went off and started to do various little things. The momentum that we were going to get by it seemed to dwindle. I know Scott had spoken to Phil a little bit before he died. I mean Phil had gone... you know, the thing with Thin Lizzy, it was Phil's baby, and without having the band there to look after him, I think he probably deteriorated quite a lot in that period, after we finished."

"But yeah, the last concert we did was with Whitesnake, Monsters Of Rock, and it didn't feel like the last gig. Like I say, as far as I was concerned, we were to take a couple months off and give Scott and Phil time to recuperate and get their heads together. In the end, we just got to the airport at Heathrow and said goodbye, and there was no big farewell or anything like that. We just said goodbye at the airport. I don't think anybody really thought it was going to be the end. I basically went back to Manchester and just thought I'd try and write some songs. At that time I had been playing around with some ideas, and that's basically when I started to learn how to write songs, that period of the beginning of my band Dare."

"They had to have been," wonders Scott, on to what extent the guys were aware that it was all over. "Because it was a farewell tour that we were doing, although it was a farewell tour that never seemed to end. But yeah, sure, the tour was billed as a last hurrah tour."

On November 14th, 1983, long after the Lizzys had scattered, the double live album known as *Life/Live* would hit the streets. Like many a' follow-up live record in the '80s, it would be unfavourably compared with the authentic deal, namely the original live record when the boys were hungry and everything was a lark. In this diffused light, *Life/Live* was the band's Exit... Stage Left (Rush), Priest...Live!, Extraterrestrial Live (Blue Öyster Cult), Alive II (Kiss), and, God forbid, Nobody's Perfect (Deep Purple). Basically, the band sounds tired, going through the motions, the hall lifeless, performances and the electronic capturing thereof, muted.

"It was quite a trial, that particular album," notes Darren. "Everybody was a bit tired at that point. I remember I spent quite a lot of time in the studio with Phil, when he was able to get down there. It just seemed to be like a never-ending slog to get the album finished and out. It wasn't ideal, the way the album was put together, I must say. Phil was always involved and tried to put his sound into it. He obviously had a vision of what he wanted it to sound like, but I remember working with a couple of different guys in the studio, and it was one of those things. We didn't do too much on it. Personally I did think Phil and Scott and Brian just needed to take a good couple of months off and have a good rest. We just seemed to be slogging it constantly rather than just taking a step back. I don't think people could see the wood for the trees at that point."

The one fun kicker to the thing was that it was billed as a reunion of sorts, of all the Lizzy line-ups, everybody converging on the venerable Hammersmith to celebrate the big farewell. It went mostly to plan, explains Sören Lindberg.

"I could tell you loads about that because I was there for those shows," begins Lindberg. "Obviously it was the farewell tour, and they wanted to do something special. So they played Hammersmith Odeon in London, four nights in a row, and already, at the second night, rumours were starting to fly around about guitar players coming up. Eventually, on the last night it did happen. So we had a very interesting full day of rehearsals, actually. It started with Gary Moore; he came in and they had a bash at 'Black Rose', and it was very funny to see, actually, because Gary essentially stopped the band several times saying, 'Listen, guys, it doesn't go that way.' So he knew the parts better than the band, actually. So that was interesting, to see him standing there directing the whole thing. After that, they had Eric Bell in, for 'The Rocker', and 'Whisky In The Jar'; Eric was playing those songs anyway, and the rest of the band knows them, so that was cool."

"Robbo didn't make it for rehearsals though, because he was recording the Motörhead album at the time," continues Soren. "So he basically just walked in, straight on stage, he didn't even have time to take his jacket off. He just walked straight in and played the three numbers he did, on that night. Basically, I don't think a single note of that was used on the album, because he played really, really badly. So, I know that Lizzy flew him up to Glasgow, a week later, and he did those three numbers again. So I think that what you find on the live album was recorded up in Glasgow. Another funny anecdote about it: Snowy White was actually there with us in the audience, during the sound check, or rehearsal, so to speak, during the day. I mean, we were about ten, 15 people in there. He didn't go up on stage and say hello to the boys or anything. He just stood there and listened for about twenty minutes and then he left. I mean, he was never asked, but if they would have asked him, I think he would've done it."

So Snowy's presence on the album, to complete the round trip of guitarists, was a bit of a patch-up. "Yes, well, basically, the live album is a total mess. At the very most you have five tracks recorded on that day, at Hammersmith. The rest of the songs are taken from various gigs on the *Thunder And Lightning* tour, because basically they recorded more or less every night on that tour. The two tracks with Snowy White are just blended in there on side two on the LP, and basically, that's taken from two years earlier, when he was with the band. These are the entire performances. Also, one of the tracks there has quite a lot of overdubs done by Phil Lynott, when it comes to bass playing. If you hear the original live version, you wouldn't recognise that that one was taken from there, when it comes to the bass, but everything else is the same."

Says Sören as to the reason for his presence there, "At that time, I was part of the Swedish Thin Lizzy fan club, and we were three Swedes from the fan club, over there, so we obviously had all the backstage passes and whatnot. But, to a certain degree, you're young, you want to see your favourite band, we were more or less sneaking in any chance we could get. I saw all four shows."

Adds Sören on the differences between the four shows, "The only real difference is that they settle in at the venues. Every night was better than the night before, and of course the last night of the four was when all the guitarists came in, that was the grand finale. There are lots of funny stories. Obviously, we were in the dressing room with the boys afterwards as well. There were certain things happening, people turning up and whatnot, and it was all probably some of the best memories I have with Thin Lizzy. Some actors showed up, but you had Julian Lennon, you had Lemmy Kilmister's son. I remember one funny thing that's definitely going to stay with me forever. At the after-show of the last night, obviously they had a lot of drink and food and stuff in the backstage area, but Eric Bell's wife had made sandwiches for him, so he had something to eat. So he was walking around with a couple of sandwiches wrapped in cellophane, and he was like, 'Hey, Sören, do you want a sandwich?' It was nice to see, the difference from when he was in the band, which was very low-key, to this big machine that was going on at the time, in 1983."

"I also recall one little bit where I was sitting down, not on a chair, but on a table that was in front of a mirror. By accident, I knocked over a bottle of Coke, and the Coke ended up in an ashtray, where somebody's cigarette was sitting. Brian Downey, at that point, was trying to quit smoking, and so Brian said to me, 'Oh, that's an excellent idea!' So after that, you see Brian Downey running around in the dressing room, pouring Coca-Cola into people's ashtrays (laughs). Another thing that I remember, very vividly as well, was coming into the dressing room after the fourth night. You walk around and you say, 'Great gig' and stuff like that. I came up to Phil, and Phil was tearing the cap off a bottle of brandy with his teeth, and then in one swig, he drank half of it, in one blow. At that point I was 23, and I remember thinking, how can you? You don't drink half a bottle of brandy in one... that was very weird, and it obviously had to do with his drinking habit; I didn't understand that.

Another funny anecdote also, you know, crazy things backstage; at one point, I don't really know why, but Lemmy was feeding Darren Wharton with a sandwich, and Lemmy asked Darren to go down on all fours and bark like a dog as Lemmy was feeding him with a sandwich."

Got blank stares from Darren on this one. "There was always craziness when Lemmy was around, but it's a little hazy for me. I just remember it being good fun all around. Yeah, everybody came down, Gary Moore, Eric Bell, Robbo. Everybody showed up and just jammed, which was great. It was one of those great nights."

"I think more than anything, Phil Lynott was left on his own to do production," continues Lindberg on the album's trebly, clenched teeth sound. "The band members were all tired, and didn't really want to be involved. They didn't have an outside producer, so Phil was basically barking up the wrong tree. He was hitting his head into the wall with everything he did at that point, and he couldn't get anything right, production-wise, unfortunately. I remember Scott telling me years later, that every time he went in to listen to the mix, it sounded more and more horrible every time. In the end, he didn't even want to be involved with it. I also remember Phil saying that the whole idea with the production on that album — I don't know if this was an excuse — but the whole idea he had was that it should sound great in the car, on a mono system in the car. Because it doesn't really sound great when you play it on your hi-fi at home, does it?"

Scott indeed has said that he was in such bad shape during that period — using the terms "auto-pilot" and "mentally sick" — that he barely paid attention to the mix, asserting that to this day, he's only heard one side of the album. Brian Downey, for his part, seconds the claim that every time Phil, who had been working near around the clock on the thing, made any adjustments, the results were worse. Manager Chris Morrison laments not only the sonic disaster of the thing but the fact that it had cost an astronomical sum to mix, and that it missed a promising release window, essentially around Reading fest, when fans still half way cared, when they might have indeed rallied a fragile and impressionable Phil to keep some format of Thin Lizzy still together — after all, imagining himself with other guitarists had proven to be a proxy form of lifeblood in his ersatz twilight years.

And what condition did Phil think he was in? Well, October '84, he went on Good Morning Britain and confided, "I don't particularly think that I was an addict, as such. I messed around with it enough, and I know enough addicts. Second of all, I don't think the battle is over. The battle never actually ends, with the drug. But the frightening thing about heroin is that — and again, without trying to glamorise the drug at all — is that it is very enjoyable to take. It cuts off reality. If you've got a lot of problems, and you want to just... So it's very easy for me to just jump up on television and say, 'Hey, this is the pits; don't do it.' But the thing that's never put across on television very often is how enjoyable it can be. But after you go through that initial phase then you become dependent on the drug. Now I never got to the stage where I became so addicted that my body craved, physically for it. But mentally, that battle will continue for the rest of my life."

A year later and on death's door, Phil was asked if he planned to be involved in anti-drug campaigns in the future. "I try to, yeah," said a laconic Lynott. "I'm notorious for being busted, but I am anti-drugs for other people, yeah. Like he says, 'Have you ever been experienced?' I wouldn't advise people to do it.

As for John Sykes, Sören recalls "talking to him during those first four nights at Hammersmith in '83, and he was asking so much about Sweden, because obviously he'd never visited Sweden before at that point. So he was asking, 'Is it true that the girls are all blonde and gorgeous and very easy-going?' and stuff like that. I remember saying to him, 'Listen, with your looks and your long blond hair, you're going to have a field day in Sweden.' When they played Gothenburg, later on that same *Thunder And Lightning* tour, John was very, very ill. They basically kept him locked into the dressing room all the time; they wouldn't let anybody in. I had a very short conversation with Phil, and Phil said to me, 'It's all my fault,' which, at that time, I really didn't understand. So even when he was playing on stage, he was jumping up and down and playing his solos and whatnot, but he said, 'I had to go to puke behind the amps.' So that was pretty bad actually."

8

CAN'T GET AWAY

"Viva la bass!"

While Lizzy was busy wrapping things up, punctuating their end with a claustrophobic live album, two Lizzy alumni in particular — Gary and Robbo — found their careers humming right along.

First, Gary Moore had recorded what would become Dirty Fingers in early '81, followed by guest slots with Greg Lake and Cozy Powell. 'Nuclear Attack' proved that Moore could metal it up with the best of them, ushering in the man's considerable success as a heavy solo act, somewhat akin to Michael Schenker, even if Gary would later dismiss this phase of his career. Corridors Of Power would follow, as well as another round with Cozy Powell on his Octopuss album which was issued in May '83, same month as Moore's Rockin' Every Night — Live In Japan. The belated Dirty Fingers would be issued in '83 in Japan and '84 in Europe, Wild Horses' Jimmy Bain presiding on bass, Chris Tsangarides producing, followed by *Live At The Marquee* and then a well-received studio album into January of '84 called *Victims Of The Future*.

"The reason I've worked with Chris is that he's very good at recording a real band," Gary told me back in '07. "He gets a really organic sound. I've worked with Chris off and on for a long time and I just find he makes the band sound like it really sounds like. He has a great way of making it sound really natural and really warm like it's almost in the room with you. I really appreciate that about his work."

Moore would spend the rest of the '80s playing this conventional hard rock straddled into metal, releasing *Run For Cover* in '85, *Wild Frontier* in '87 and *After The War* in '89. Into the '90s, and Gary would find himself with a surprise hit record called *Still Got The Blues*, the album reaching gold in the states by 1995.

"I like Wild Frontier actually and I liked a couple of tracks on *After The War*, when I got more into the Irish thing," muses Gary, asked about the rock phase that very neatly took up all of the '80s. "I like the song on *After The War* called 'Blood Of Emeralds' which is my answer to 'Black Rose', I guess, if you look at it that way. With the Wild Frontiers stuff, I suppose it was a reflective time because it was just after Phil passed away and I shut myself in a room for a few months and started coming up with that stuff. He had a big influence on that one. What I would do if I had the choice, is that I would make a compilation of all of them and pick out the best parts. Because some of them as a body of work, I think, well, phoo. But if you put them all together, I think you could make a good one out of it, I reckon."

In North America, it seemed like *Victims Of The Future* had the biggest impact. "Really?" says Gary. "I think they liked 'Shapes Of Things' on the radio over there, yeah. But no way, no. Up until *Still Got The Blues*, the biggest one was Wild Frontier. No, *Victims Of The Future* was only like the second album and it was still building then. But eventually I realised it wasn't me. It was just... I'll tell you what it was. In the '80s, if you were a guitar player, you played heavy metal. It was that simple. If you wanted to have a career. So I convinced myself that I liked it, and I was doing my best to write in that idiom but I didn't really know what I was doing at the time. Bands like AC/DC were so great at all that stuff, and I'd seen them live. But I was just not one of those people and I never would be. It was that simple. When I met the people who played that music, I realised I wasn't one of those people and I realised I was in the wrong place. Eventually, at the end of the '80s, I found myself playing blues when I was alone in the dressing room. That's where 'Still Got The Blues' came from. I remember our bass player coming in and saying jokingly, 'You should make a blues album. It would probably be the biggest thing you ever did.' We just laughed our asses off, you know? Next thing you know I did *Still Got The Blues* and it was the biggest album."

"That record was just another one of those things — right place, right time, maybe. It was another album that was very easy to make and we were just really enjoy making that record, having fun. I was playing songs that I enjoyed playing when I was a kid; it was just me going back to my roots again and basically saying, I've had enough of this fucking heavy metal and I want to get out of this — and the record company amazingly backed me up. I thought they'd tell me to fuck off and instead they were really supportive. Maybe they thought I was only going to do it once and we'll indulge him, but there was no resistance. When they heard 'Still Got The Blues', that was it, as far as they were concerned, there wasn't going to be a problem."

"I remember when we did that track, it was recorded in one take also, with all the guitar and everything. I did all the vocals and everything and we were actually testing the studio out to see if it was a suitable place to record this album. We did 'Oh Pretty Woman' that day and we did 'Still Got The Blues'. 'Pretty Woman' was two takes, 'Still Got The Blues' was one, and we left it and said, we'll come back to it properly next time, and that was the track that ended up on the album. It was because of that song actually, that it crossed over to a lot of people. It wasn't really a blues song. You and I both know that it was a ballad but at the end of the day that's the song that got that record across to a huge audience. In the States it was a big breakthrough for me. I got my first gold album in the States because a lot of people liked that song and it is being played on the radio. It just crossed over big-time. But no one knew at the time. When we made it we thought, well, if this sells 100,000, it won't lose money, and we're going to do a club tour for three weeks. Six months later we were playing fucking parks to 100,000 people across Europe, and three million records later it's a different story. But you just never know. I was very happy, obviously."

Gary and I joked that in the '80s, he had become a cottage industry for gatefolds, remixes and 12 inch singles. "Well, that was the time for all that stuff, the '80s, wasn't it? (laughs). It used to drive me crazy. Because they would just come in and say, 'Whip us off a 12 inch.' And it ain't like that.

You've got to strip it all down. The record company was always under the impression, 'Oh yeah, a 12 inch, that won't take long, just go ahead and do it, half an hour, guys.' If you're going to do something and make a new version you've got to put the time into it. Otherwise, what's the point? You've already got the definitive version (laughs). I hate all that 12 inch shit. Nowadays it's like the dance remix. I mean, we actually did a rap version of 'Friday On My Mind' with Stock Aitken Waterman."

Way at the other end of rap and 'Friday On My Mind was Motörhead, and that's where Brian Robertson found himself, much to the surprise of fans of the band, most of which figured the axeman was too refined for the gig. Turns out that Brian Robertson still flew the independent streak that had him rankling Phil and the boys. Only this time he was up against a different breed of singing fat-stringer in Lemmy Kilmister.

"For me it was great," says Motörhead drummer Phil Taylor, "but for Lemmy, you see, Lemmy had the stupid attitude, just because of the way that Rob being a Scottish guy, like (in a Scottish accent), 'If Lemmy tells me not to do it, I'm going to fucking do it.' So the more that Lemmy... it was just ridiculous. Because Lemmy had nothing against Brian's playing. His playing speaks for itself; it was just the way he looked. When he joined the band, it was the tail end of the summer, and Robbo joined us in America and it was very hot and subsequently he wore shorts just like anybody else did. But unfortunately he didn't change from his shorts when we went on stage. But he didn't give a fuck. He's not that kind of guy. Admittedly, I said to him, 'Rob, you should at least put a pair of pants on.' 'Ar, ar all right.' Lemmy would go, 'Fuckin' hell Rob, you look like a fucking wanker!' Instead of being reasonable about it, well, of course, that got Robbo very pissed off, and it just got worse. He started wearing gay looking headbands and all this kind of thing, just to set Lemmy off, really. Rob was the sort of person… unfortunately, in a way I agreed with him; it's like, why should they give a fuck? Go listen to the music instead of looking at my fucking shorts. Which is fair enough, but on the other hand, I would say, 'Damn, well, Rob, it wouldn't hurt just to put a pair of pants on.' I mean, if that's what it takes to get the fans over, because after all, they… unfortunately, if you want to call them shallow or whatever, they are seeing the shorts, not the man, not the music."

"Which was too bad, because that line-up was good," continues Taylor. "I thought Another Perfect Day was the best album Motörhead ever made. So does Lemmy, as it happens. He just couldn't stand the image that Robbo projected. It's always down to… which was really stupid, because I used to have chats with Lemmy. I'd say, 'Lem, why can't you just like… when you speak to him about it, speak to him like a normal human being. Don't jump down his neck. Because you know he's just going to get worse.' 'Oh fucking, grr…' So anyway, he said he had to go — it's the shorts or you, so it was him."

"But apart from that, we got on really well, and musically it was really good, because Brian… Thin Lizzy has always been one of my favourite bands, and playing with Robbo was great; that whole album was virtually written by Robbo and me. I mean, not me from a musical point of view, but Lemmy was hardly ever at rehearsals. He came in and mostly did his bass parts in the studio. The arrangements were already done, and I think you can hear that just by listening to the album. There's not a great deal of Lemmy influence in there. Of course, Lemmy I think is one of the best lyricists of our time, for that genre. He could always write good lyrics. So yeah, that was the unfortunate time. But Motörhead with Brian Robertson… I regret that it couldn't have gone on longer, because it would have developed into a hell of a good band."

"I remember we played at a festival in London, that was run by the Hells Angels, and it was us and Motörhead," recalls Saxon's Biff Byford. "I think we just flew in from America, to do it, and Brian walked out on stage, in Motörhead, with a Hawaiian shirt on and a pair of blue shorts, and Lemmy was giving him absolute shit all night, because Lemmy wanted to be heavy and leather jackets. But the Hawaiian shirt and shorts was the killer. I don't know if he actually had flip-flops on, but it was something down there that it was... actually, he might've had cowboy boots on, which made it look even more like, 'Fuck you, Lemmy, I'm going to do what I want.' So I don't think he lasted much longer, after that."

"I hung out with Phil a few times, at Stringfellows, in London," continues Biff expanding on his Lizzy connections. "It's a lap-dancing club now, but it used to be like a disco downstairs, and food. That used to be the place where most people gravitated, nice girls there. He once introduced me to his wife, who actually turned out to be a waitress. He was like that, a real joker. Yeah, he was great. He came to a few gigs, to see us, and got on stage once and sang "747". Yeah, he was a lovely guy. Used to see them all the time. The last time I saw him was at Heathrow Airport with his kids. He was taking his kids on a holiday to Spain, and shortly after that he died. Brian, fantastic guitarist. Last time I saw him was at Sweden Rock four years ago. He was looking great. I don't know if he's fallen off the wagon again, I don't know. I was a huge fan of Thin Lizzy, first through 'Whisky In The Jar', with Bell and all that era with Gary Moore, it was great, really. We were huge Skid Row fans as well. Phil had played in that band, and then he played in his band, so it was a bit of a melting pot going on. They had an album called 34 Hours that was a big inspiration for us."

"If we did shows together, he always came around and we spoke," adds ex-Saxon bassist Steve Dawson. "If we went out and he was in a club or anything, he would come over, and he always said the same thing to me, Phil Lynott. Every time we met, in that classic Phil Lynott pose where he puts one arm up, he'd shout, 'Viva la bass!' The last time I saw him wasn't too long before he died. We were going to do a tour somewhere, and he was at the airport with his two little girls, going on holiday somewhere, and he said the same thing, 'Viva la bass.'"

"I really enjoyed it, from what I can remember," laughs Robbo, with regard to his one record cycle with Motörhead. "Because that was crazy. Because we were travelling in a bus. I'd never even done that before. Straight off the stage, into a bus, off to the next gig, blah blah blah. So it was a severe amount of Jack Daniels consumed, and other things. I enjoy the album thoroughly, but I did say to the boys when I joined the band, when they asked me, because I only went out to do the tour, just to help them out, because we were mates, right? Then they asked me to join, and I said if I do, and if we're going to do an album, you know it's not going to be like the old Motörhead, because it just won't be and they were like, 'No, that's cool'."

On the writing of Another Perfect Day, Robbo concedes that, "Lemmy came up with a few good riffs as well. But I spent a lot of time with Tony because he was actually engineer on the first studio session I ever did, with Lizzy, which was down in the south of England, and he was the house engineer. So we did our demos down there and then he did Back In Black as well. Tony and I were really good mates. We did all the overdubbing and I was always on the desk with Tony, and I guess that's why Philthy and Lemmy are going, 'Oh he's treating it like a solo album.' But that's not the case. That's the way I would do any album. Whatever was being recorded or put down, I would be there! You know, to give some input if I had anything worth saying. But they weren't used to working like that so they obviously thought I was a bit overbearing on that front (laughs); but it was just normal for me."

"It had run its course, basically, to be honest," laughs Robbo on why there wasn't a follow-up Motörhead record for him. "I didn't particularly want to carry on, and I don't think the boys wanted me to carry on with them either. It wasn't a personal thing either, because I started another band with Philthy after that, with Philthy and Chris Glen from Alex Harvey Band, so it wasn't a personal thing."

Great record though, Another Perfect Day is... "Well, it's funny, because, I remember reading one of the magazines where he was saying, 'It's the best album we'd ever done.' After I left or whatever, he'd started saying, 'It's shit.' So he's changed his mind again or whatever (laughs). But the proof is in the pudding, isn't it?"

Post-Motörhead, Robbo essentially dropped off the radar, way up until his 2011 solo album Diamonds And Dirt. Surely there must have been some high profile auditions through the '80s and '90s? "Well, a couple, but it's not really worth talking about, to be honest. I was busy working with Frankie Miller, actually, most of that period. On and off with Frank, and sessions for other people. But working with Frankie and Simon Kirke there, and Chrissie Stewart — that was just a great band. It was one of the highlights of my career, I think, although obviously not too many people know about it. But I do, anyway and that's the way I look at it. You're playing with one of the best drummers ever in rock, and probably the best singer I've worked with — it was a privilege."

As for Phil, well, Lord knows why, with a perfectly good band in his back pocket, he was off creating a new thing called Grand Slam. Listen to them live, and you'll hear Phil's solo songs, Lizzy songs, but new originals as well, which really don't amount to much, other than a slightly more commercial and keyboard version of the hard rock that was much better crafted and presented by his old band. If anything, Grand Slam was closely comparable with the very last version of Lizzy, Magnum's Mark Stanway a stand-in for Darren, the talented Laurence Archer, ex-Stampede, a stand-in for John Sykes.

"When I was playing in Wild Horses, Phil approached me then and made it clear he was interested in me as a player," explains Archer, who is referring to the version of the band after both Robbo and Clive Edwards had moved on, leaving just Jimmy as the anchor player. "He invited me down to the studio and we had a bit of a jam, had a bit of a play; he then played with Wild Horses on stage, and made it very aware that he was interested in wanting me to play in Thin Lizzy. But I made it plain that I was very determined to see the Wild Horses thing through. Although it was a second-generation band, it was a younger and more fiery band than Lizzy were at the time, and so I didn't turn it down as such. I wanted to do the Wild Horses thing, and agreed that we would work together at some point. Then at a later date, when Phil was doing solo stuff, Mark Stanway who is also a friend of mine, who had played keyboards on the Stampede album, called me and I said that Phil would like me to join the band. So we just met up and had a blow and it went from there. It was automatic. It was a very natural thing at the time. It didn't seem out of the ordinary, really."

Early days of Grand Slam, in fact two songs in, Phil framed the situation the following way. "These are songs I'd written that I thought I'd show the attitude of the band, because I wanted it to be as aggressive as Lizzy, and as melodic as the solo stuff. Everybody's working so hard, and like this is our day off, and we're in the studio putting down more of the new stuff, and every day we're nailing a new tune. It's really good fun for me. Whereas when I did the solo stuff, I was just doing something different, than being in Lizzy. But now this is like bread and butter to me, so it's far more dedicated; there's far more theory involved about the music."

In the same radio chat, Phil joked about how he'd better introduce the band properly before he gets ahead of himself. "Grand Slam consists of Mark Stanway on keyboards. He was with a heavy metal band called Magnum who I didn't particularly like, but he had a lot of class with his keyboards, and I met him when we did a solo tour in Sweden, and John Sykes introduced me to him. But he is a keyboard player with a lot of class, and he's very good with contemporary keyboards. As opposed to say Darren, who was very good technically, but Mark is much more a feel player. Robbie Brennan's on drums, and Robbie was... well, we met in Skid Row, like with Gary Moore, Brush and myself. Robbie is such a feel player; I'd done things with him with Auto Da Fe, and we've done solo tours. So we've always had a relationship going, because he was the most obvious guy to think of after Brian deciding he didn't want the gig. Doish Nagle, from the Bogey Boys... initially when Doish came to the band, he wanted a lead guitar gig, but I was adamant that this band not be based on dual guitars like Lizzy were. So I said, if you play rhythm concentrate on more guitar techniques like Andy Summers or The Fixx, for the rhythm parts. So it's an interesting job for him, and he's such a good singer and bass player as well. He has all that, and songwriter; so he fills in that slot. Laurence Archer is the one that the pressure's on, because he's the 21-year-old like whiz kid guitar player that has to take on the legend of the other guitar players that I've worked with in my time. Then of course there's the big bad wolf himself, myself. So it is a band, much more so than the solo me, Philip and his band. At the moment we're using my reputation to get some publicity and stuff, but I mean, when you come and see the band, I think it would become fairly obvious that they're all very talented people."

"I just thought, Lizzy, towards the end of the career, just became an imitation of itself to a certain extent," mused Phil. "It was almost as if we had to be heavy and there had to be dual lead guitars. I mean, I'm talking about, this is what Scott's saying to me when he's saying he wanted to leave, and I just thought everybody had to agree, we were becoming a parody of ourselves. So, with the solo stuff, I just had to do it as an alternative than going through this parody. But now I have a band that I can, okay, lead and be a member of."

Talk of Phil's relationship to the new wave led to the comment that that was a time when the bigger bands were leaving for America. "That's when Lizzy took the conscious decision to remain in Europe," asserts Phil. "In the end, we paid the toll for that, you know, because we never actually cracked America as big as we cracked Europe. Thin Lizzy could've done it if they'd concentrated — and sold their soul. The reason Def Leppard has done it, they've sold their soul. There are certain promotion people, and there are certain record labels, and there's percentages that you give away, to do in America. Now, what happened with Lizzy was, we were at a state in our career where we had so much money, that, why go to America to lose money, when you could tour Europe and make money? So if you're managing the band, what do you do? Whereas if you're a band like Def Leppard, just starting off, it's better that you do a deal where you're giving away a lot, initially, become famous, and then say, we're not paying any more."

Back on planet pub, keyboard player Stanway says the roots of Grand Slam included John Sykes. "Right, well, during the time rehearsing the band and everything, John Sykes got the call from Coverdale and made him an offer he couldn't refuse, really. So we replaced John Sykes with Laurence Archer, and continued, and did a good eight months of touring everywhere, with that. So that was a fun period in life. Lots of partying. But there were dark times. Phil was doing things that he shouldn't have been doing. This is during the latter part of Grand Slam, which is one reason we didn't get a major record deal. I think the record companies were a bit scared, or frightened of signing somebody that had got this association with heroin. It was nothing to do with the quality of the band. It was Phil's reputation, I'm afraid. Fortunately, I think it's a keyboard player trait, but this is going back to the days of cassette recorders, I would insist the sound engineer record the shows and so I could listen to it afterwards, and do that keyboard thing and analyse everything. I've got such good recordings that I actually had the master and I actually put some stuff out, about eight or nine, ten years ago. I just felt that it was good enough quality to put out and people should hear it. But I'm consolidating those now, and we're putting them all out again as one complete set. Of course obviously, the writing royalties will go, certainly from Phil's side, to his estate and the benefit will still be there for his family and everything. It's not a financial thing I'm doing it for. I just want to keep that part of my life alive. It's really the last things Phil did."

As to the mission of Grand Slam, Archer says that, "Grand Slam were trying to be more, for want of a word, a harder-edged, slightly heavier Lizzy, in a way. You can't get away from it. For a long time, the first generation of Grand Slam was just me — there wasn't a second guitar player. Then we got Doish Nagle in on second guitar, but we didn't really go down the guitar harmony road or anything like that. It was really about power and the edge and keeping it very Brit rock. So we had a harder edge than Thin Lizzy but it was still Phil doing a lot of writing. But whatever he does, it's going to have a Lizzy-esque character to it. But Phil didn't want to go on with Thin Lizzy. He wanted to move on, which is very much what we were trying to do. We didn't try to work a certain direction; we just tried to take a natural channel by selecting the players we had in it."

"I think there was a lot of internal politics going on," continues Laurence, on why Phil didn't want to carry on with Lizzy. "I think there was a falling out with Scott and the whole thing that happened with Brian. I would say generally, it was the end of an era. He realised that he wanted to move on, and being an artist, he had all these players that would allow him to widen his palette and have a fresh new start. Socially, Phil was very busy when we were in town, when we were in London. Before and after Grand Slam, he was obviously still quite active and social. I lived at Phil's house for quite some time, and quite a few people came and went, everybody from Fish from Marillion. There were just all sorts of people who would turn up. Whether we actually worked with them was a different matter. But certainly people were around. As I say, in the Wild Horses, he got up and played and I know that he did jam with Motörhead a couple of times, but, you know, he didn't really hang around the heavy metal scene particularly. The new wave of heavy metal scene — that was a community all to itself, really."

The band worked up quite a few originals, including 'Breakdown', 'Sisters Of Mercy', 'Crime Rate', 'Gay Boys', 'Can't Get Away', the contentious 'Military Man' and more contentious 'Dedication'.

Kerrang!'s Mark Putterford took note of the band's standout new tracks in a review of a gig he called best of the year. "'Newie Nineteen' scorched along on crude teenage energy featuring the digital brilliance of Laurence Archer, while 'Sisters Of Mercy' building into a princely reminder of 'Emerald'. 'Military Man' marched on brute raunchiness either side of its tear-jerking soft-centre and mushroomed into a mighty mountain-sized masterpiece, before Slam smooched into the realms of funk with the excellent 'Harlem'. Here Mark Stanway's silvery keyboard scatterings and the sweet twin-soloing of Archer and Doish Nagle iced Lynott and Brennan's funky foundations and showed us all that the band's songwriting aspirations don't lie solely in Riff Street. Next up, Lynott cast a nostalgic glance over his shoulder, steering Slam through the evergreen "Parisienne Blowjobs" and the sweltering 'Cold Sweat'. After that it was back to blistering newies in the shape of the cartwheeling 'Crazy' and the Lizzy- esque 'Dedication', as the boards burned and the sweat streamed and the sardines raved. Pausing only slightly for a well-earned gasp of breath, Lynott inevitably inquired if we were 'out there' then bounced into 'Dear Miss Lonely Hearts' to the accompaniment of our horse hollers and 'helping hands,' adding a few snatches of 'Some Guys Have All The Luck' and 'Every Breath You Take' before punching the air in triumph and withdrawing his troops."

"We would both bring ideas to the table," notes Archer, on the songwriting process within Grand Slam. "He had a studio in his back garden, basically, where we wrote most of the stuff. If he wasn't there, I would be in there myself banging ideas down, and then he would come in later and put stuff on top of it, or he would change it around and muck it about.

But a lot of the ideas came from things I did or that I had already had, or Phil had already had, in his head. Some of the stuff just evolved from things we had written on the spot. Like everybody does. The writing process is a strange one. Sometimes it's very productive, sometimes it's not. But Phil and I used to write quite a lot together, and sometimes I would bring the whole thing to the table and he would write the lyrics to it; he would accept the arrangement on the song and just write lyrics. A couple of the ideas, I had already recorded, while I was with Phil, but with a different singer when I was in the studio. I would play that for him."

'Dedication' is of course known as a posthumous Thin Lizzy song, a real corker in fact, that was highlighted to the point of being the title track to a later years hit pack. But it's not Lizzy, or even really Grand Slam, as Archer explains…

"That was one of those songs that I had already written. I had actually written it as a demo for Stampede, well before, and it was just an idea I had knocking around, and I put it down in the studio. I had the guitar parts worked out, and then I played it to Phil and he said he'd like to do it. We didn't record it for a long time. We rehearsed it up and played it live. Then did an EMI session where I eventually… Phil wasn't around, so myself and Robbie Brennan put backing tracks down, and I think I even played bass on it at the time, and then Phil came in and sang it. That was the only ever recording of it."

So you're saying it's the only recording? "Yes, what you hear on the record is… the only recording of Phil ever singing that song was that EMI session. What you hear on the Lizzy album is they've overdubbed on that session, and switched his vocal around, and probably put it through an auto-tuner or something. But essentially it's an edit, and an overdub on the same song, which obviously was never done with Scott or Brian or anybody in Thin Lizzy. But yeah, it was a song that I already had, registered to PRS, and unknowingly, they had overdubbed and re-recorded, and chopped Phil's voice onto the tracks, and they rearranged it slightly and released it as a Lizzy track. The first time I was aware of it was when actually a friend of mine called me and said, 'I just heard your song on the radio,' and I was like, 'Are you sure?' Anyway, I became aware that it was released as a Thin Lizzy single."

Did you write the lyrics as well? "Well, I wrote the chorus, yeah. The whole 'dedication' idea was mine, and that was part of the original song." 'Dedication' was issued as a single on the fifth anniversary of Phil's death, more or less, January 11th 1991. A full compilation album of the same name was issued a month later. The track blossomed in its final state as a thrilling Lizzy (?) classic, and indeed, Scott and Brian are playing on it, as is keyboard player, Leif Johansen, who would join Scott on the 21 Guns album the following year. The session had been conducted October 26th the previous year and despite reports, Gary Moore was not involved in the recording of this emotion-swirled anthem.

"Well I co-wrote about 80% of the Grand Slam stuff," says Stanway, somewhat counter to Archer's characterisation of the situation. "Phil was just so good with words. He could phrase; he was reminiscent of Hendrix, the way he could sing across a song, as opposed to write on the beat all the time. He could open the telephone book and sing it, he's so talented. Therefore he wasn't limited by style at all."

As mentioned 'Military Man' is the band's second contentious track, ownership of it really taken over by Gary Moore and Phil. According to

Stanway, "Yes, there's a bit of a thing on that, because Gary Moore was still playing that track up until his unfortunate death. I'm just lucky be a part of it all."

Answering to the contention that there seemed to be a growing social consciousness to Phil's lyrics, Mark figures, "Yes, very much so, on things like 'Military Man'. He's very influenced by his mother, which is obvious in so many of his songs. He knew he was doing wrong things, and I think a lot of guilt came out in his lyrics as well. He would pluck stuff out of the air. We would jam for hours on good songs, and then he would come back a few days later with lyrics. He would go away and write those privately. He would just take a cassette of the jamming that we would do and come back with some lyrics."

Another track embroiled in a bit of songwriting credit skullduggery is r 'n' b-ish ballad 'Harlem'. "Phil wrote that with Doish," says Lynott mentor and Skid Row bassist Brush Shiels, "But the lyrics are actually my song, from 1968. He never gave me any credit. He knew I would ring him up. We hadn't been talking for a good while. So the lyrics go, 'I have often wondered what it's like to be the friend, of someone who is black like you, and with that I'll pretend.' Well anyway, he died before that album came out, but that same song can be heard... somebody found these old tapes, and you can hear him singing that in 1968. But the impression I got was, he'd done that, he knew I'd ring him and maybe sort a few things out. Because honestly we hadn't been talking. Phil was not at his best, so there was no point in talking with him."

"I was working all the time," adds Brush, with a typically wry addition to the answer of why he didn't see the boys much through the '70s and '80s. "I never went to any gigs. Gary Moore never asked me to a gig and these are good friends of mine. They know better than to let me on (laughs). You know, even the last gig, it's called One Night In Dublin, Gary Moore, it was to do with Phil's statue, he's top of the bill, and I get a message sent down, if I was going on, if I was on the show, I wasn't to have a band, I was to play on my own just with a guitarist. But that's it. The boys love me, but they love me enough to not let me fuckin' anywhere close to second or the top with a band (laughs)."

With regard to the drum position in Grand Slam, the boys almost wound up with Motörhead's Phil Taylor clanging away back there. "Yeah, Philthy was always around. Basically, he was a good friend of Robbo. Phil really liked him; he liked his energy, and he liked him as a player, and he was a face back then that would've been quite interesting to have because originally Brian Downey was in the band. We played the initial gigs and did all the pre-production stuff and Brian was loving it. But then Phil had quite a few problems. He was suffering with drugs for a while, and Brian finally gave up the ghost and said I don't really want to be involved with this, if this was going to happen and then we had to look for another drummer. Philthy was certainly in the frame at that point, but then we got Robbie Brennan."

"Downey left because he didn't want to go back on the road again," said Phil, in conversation with Kerrang!'s Mark Putterford. "He'd had so much time off since Lizzy ended, he got used to being with his family an' that. He wasn't prepared to leave his home again for long periods of time." As Mark enquires as to the pact of sticking together through thick and thin, Phil quips, "Well, he made a bigger pact with his wife and kids, y' know! I think that one was a little more permanent than the one he made with me. But there's no bad blood between us at all and I wish him and Scott the best of luck in whatever they do in the future. I think he'll just do some session work in Ireland and he's hoping to set up a drum clinic as well. He'll just be taking things easy. He was the quiet one in Lizzy, I suppose — the one who always went to bed first! But it will be strange playing without him, all the same."

As for hooking up with Brennan... "During the break I'd been doing lots of silly things like production and basically just fiddling around in the studio trying to get away from it all. I'd worked with Junior, an Irish folk band and Auto-Da-Fe, who Robbie played for. He's a very good drummer and I've worked with him before, so when Downey left, he was an ideal choice."

As well, Phil reiterated his vision that Grand Slam not be a twin-lead band, despite the presence of two guitarists. "This time I'm featuring the one guitarist and I've got Doish there for that 'feel' I was talking about earlier. I found that it's easier to get a balance with the rhythm player because he knows his position and doesn't try to steal the spotlight from the other guitarist. Anyway, one of my aims for the band is to feature Laurence because I've worked with some of the best guitarists around and he's potentially as good as any of them."

A quarter century past the ill-fit band that almost was, Archer closes with a few reflections on Phil Lynott, the legend. "Phil was a gent; he was a complete gentleman, a lovely guy. I was only about 20 years old then, so he was an iconic figure. Lizzy was massive and I was a young guy, wanting to play guitar. He was a very caring and warm person, and unfortunately with drugs, they made him unpredictable towards the end. He did want to get off the drugs, but unfortunately it stopped him in his place. It's very tiring and hard to get somebody to stop when they're addicted, to get Philip to give it up. It wasn't just him; it was other people to blame, when you're in that situation. The management was trying to get him off drugs. We had a whole campaign to not have him surrounded by people. There were a lot of people hanging around who were of a certain type. But Phil was happy to... I didn't do drugs, I was really quite straight and I was in a straight relationship, so it was just really normal with me. We would have a few artistic rows now and again, as you do in any healthy writing relationship, but he was just a really nice gentleman. Because I was always quite straight, he used to get me to drive to his house to see his kids, and he'd have me about the house. The downside was really the drug side."

Late '84, with Gary Moore's profile riding high on a new hit called 'Empty Rooms', Gary issued his We Want Moore live album. Toward the end of the year, Phil recorded with Gary on 'Military Man' and 'Out In The Fields', and even showed up on stage with Gary in Belfast and in Dublin just before Christmas.

"Yeah, we didn't get on for a while, but I mean, that was three years ago, and to promote the single, everybody's jumped on that particular story," remarked Phil, talking about 'Out In The Fields' on Music Box. Asked about the instrument Gary plays on it, Phil explains that "It's a synthaxe. Yeah, you can play 'em like a keyboard. The strings are only there, because when you play it, they're only there just as a token gesture, just to show you the notes, so you don't have to relearn your instrument like a keyboard. They're really for guitar players to come to terms with synthesizers, so they can play things the way they do, a synthesizer really has the full spectrum of sound. I don't see why it just always has to be a keyboard, and I don't see why guitar players should have to relearn keyboards. I think the sound should be there for the musician."

Asked about the political tone of the song, Phil makes note first that it's Gary's song, adding that, "With him being from Belfast and me being from Dublin, Ireland is at the forefront, but it's just a general anti-war song. Obviously we leaned it more towards Ireland because it related more towards us, and you always talk about what you know. Due to the success of this one, and even if this one really hadn't been successful, it was successful as far as we were concerned, because we enjoyed doing it and we liked the end result. So he's gonna work on my solo album, and I'm going to do a couple of touches for him."

Into the New Year, Phil and Laurence Archer flew to the states to do some recording with Huey Lewis, most significantly 'One Wish' which was a re-do of 'Harlem'. Additionally, Phil played some bass for a track on Robin George's Dangerous Music, and got up on stage with The Pogues, who Frank Murray was now managing.

Grand Slam on the other hand had run its course. "Slightly unhappy, really," says Stanway. "Grand Slam weren't going anywhere, and Magnum had just picked up a really good deal with Polydor. So I went and saw Phil personally and I said, 'Look, this isn't going anywhere, and I've got an opportunity here to sign a record deal,' and he gave me his blessing on it. We realised Grand Slam wasn't going anywhere and realised the reason why. I think he just took the time off himself, although he'd always been messing in the studio with somebody. So you can't stop his creativity — that's what he did. So it was a bit sad, but certainly not a fallout or unhappy in that respect and of course it was only months later that he died. So it made me feel even worse. Not guilty, but just, what a shame."

"I mean, Grand Slam couldn't get a deal at all," said Phil, in his final TV interview, speaking with Dante Bonutto in December '85. "And then a couple of the lads got bored, and they left, so I was forced to go solo. The minute I went solo, people started offering me deals. I got a deal with Polydor, you know; Gary asked me to do some stuff with him. I was working with Paul Hardcastle, and writing some stuff with Rick Parfitt from Status Quo. All these things started happening to me, since I went solo. But I think, maybe Grand Slam suffered the backlash from the Thin Lizzy support. Because obviously, a band that potentially could be good compared to a band that had been around for twelve years with a string of hits, and playing major venues, and Grand Slam were doing smaller venues. I just don't think Grand Slam won in the comparison. All I'm saying is that Grand Slam couldn't get a deal. Maybe we were bad; maybe people just genuinely didn't like it. But I was giving it 100%, and when it fell through, things started to happen and I landed on my feet."

Stanway got a sense that putting Lizzy back together was never far from Phil's mind. "I'm sure he thought about it, because he yearned for the stage. If he had done that, it would've been at that point with John Sykes, and certainly Brian. I think the last single had just been released when we did the solo tour of Sweden, which was 'The Sun Goes Down', and I was fortunate to be there when they mixed that. That's when I met Phil. But as I say, Magnum picked up a deal and that was that."

"There was something in the paper, in the Daily Mirror yesterday, I think, saying that Thin Lizzy were gonna get back together again," Phil told Dante, somewhat tongue-in-cheek. "There's a quote from the management saying that we might get together to do a charity gig. We all keep in close communication, and I was working with Scott recently, and Brian Downey is gonna play. See, I'm going to get a band together for March, and tour with my album, I have another single coming out in January, and I'm doing another single with Gary Moore in January. So I'm going to get a band together, and Brian Downey has said he'll work in it."

But this was all about solo plans, with the idea that into 1986... "I may go for the two guitar thing, but I don't know. At the moment, I'm still in the process of working it out. I'm checking out guitar players and keyboard players. What I want to do is finish the album. When I get the album finished, then I'll know what I need in the band to promote the album. But as far as Lizzy's getting back together again, we haven't thought about getting back together again. I'd like to establish a solo career first before I start to live off past glories. The album is gonna be a Philip Lynott solo album, and once I get minor details like what it's going to be called, it doesn't matter to me. But it probably will be Philip Lynott and... it depends, really. When I'm in a band situation, regardless of who's upfront... I'd like there to be give-and-take from all the musicians in the band. I don't like a dogmatic structure where I go, 'You play this,' and, 'Play the same thing every night.' I like people to give input. Because the bass is part of the rhythm section, so it plays behind the voice or the lead guitar, so as a bass player, I like to play with the musicians, and obviously as a singer, front it, you know. So when I do get a band together, I'll be working on that basis. But it probably will be Philip Lynott and... and whoever — and Thin Lizzy, joke (laughs)."

When Dante asks about who the players might be on this proposed third solo album, Phil interestingly tacks toward producers and production. "With the album, the producers that I'm gonna use on the album, I'd like to go over the material with each individual producer. For example, they have Tom Dowd who does Phil Collins and Eric Clapton, and he did Molly Hatchet; he's been around ages. Now he likes certain songs that I've written, because it's two years since Lizzy broke up, I do have a lot of songs written. So I'll go with the songs he likes, if I like them, and get him to produce them. Then I've got Peter Collins to finish off the rest of the production. I'll go with that. But in general, it should be more balanced than my other solo albums, because when I had the other solo albums, I was in Thin Lizzy, and Thin Lizzy took all the heavy stuff. So my solo albums were much softer than I was, whereas this time, it should be a better balance. There should be more upfront hard stuff and a couple of ballads maybe thrown in."

In the summer of 1985, Gary Moore wound up getting married, with Phil in attendance to do a few numbers with the man. Less happy times... Phil was stung by not being invited to play Live Aid, which had been arranged by his old friend Bob Geldof. Phil nonetheless donated a bass, which went for the princely sum of £900. Fall of '85, Gary's flash and crafted Run For Cover album emerged, with Phil singing and playing on the aforementioned 'Military Man', 'Out In The Fields' and 'Nothing To Lose'. Phil, having beat a second drug charge and being free to go, found himself jumping on stage with Motörhead and more with Moore, highlight of his live cameos being his integral part on the anthemic 'Military Man', which, all told, is arguably the man's superlative creative moment post-Lizzy.

Most significant however was the release of a new solo track from Phil, 'Nineteen' being a tight taut rocker with equal parts metal, punk and Elvis. The song was one of the few compositions to be featured in Grand Slam sets that was not a co-write with Archer or Stanway. The single, which got biker-themed production video treatment, was issued with a dub mix of the song as a b-side, and then in double 7" and 12" versions adding live tracks. Phil's last appearance on TV would be a mimed performance of the song on the show Razzamatazz, guitarist for the dance being Robin George, drummer being Brian Downey.

Remarked Phil, "The point was, I got a solo deal, and I figured that, because this is the first single I've released on my own since Thin Lizzy broke up, I did think that I should establish that I was a rocker, rather than coming out with a ballad or something."

"One of the things about the heavy metal productions, I think they're becoming very bland," continued Phil, on his choice of Paul Hardcastle as techno-minded producer of the track. "I wanted to experiment with the production of it. With people like Van Halen working with Michael Jackson and ZZ Top doing dance mixes and stuff like that, I thought, when we were looking for a producer, obviously, because the title was the same (Hardcastle also was pushing a song called '19'), that's how Paul Hardcastle came about, and I knew that he was available to do productions. I thought it would be interesting if he put some scratch mixes out, dance mixes to a hard rock song. So that was my reasons for asking him, and he accepted because he wanted to show that he produced more than just dance records. He liked a lot of Thin Lizzy stuff, like 'Johnny The Fox Meets Jimmy The Weed'. So he was very keen to spread his wings, and do some other stuff. He ended up playing keyboards on it; he's a very good keyboard player. I got Robin George because he's the available guitar player. Gary was busy at the time, and some other friends of mine were busy at the time, and I played on Robin George's stuff, so we got Robin George down, because I wanted somebody I knew. I wanted to experiment with it. I think the problem is, like I do believe that heavy metal productions have become fairly bland, and there's not enough rock in the charts, and I think the same with the single Gary Moore and myself did together. We got a contemporary producer like Peter Collins who does Nick Kershaw, just to give it a dip and an atmosphere, rather than just the bland way you imagine heavy metal to sound. So I just thought it would be neat to experiment with the production, because there's so much new technology. So I thought why not experiment around it?"

The Hardcastle connection was also facilitated by the fact that Chris Morrison had recently struck a deal to co-manage Hardcastle, congruent, fortunately for him, with Hardcastle's own '19' zooming up the charts to No.1. Amusingly, Morrison's first meeting with Hardcastle was after the deal was done, at a Top Of The Pops filming, where Hardcastle, Dead Or Alive (another Morrison charge), and Phil, duetting on this occasion with Gary Moore, were all strutting their stuff for the cameras.

"The first time I met Phil, I auditioned for Thin Lizzy, and I didn't get the gig in the end," explains George, amusingly adding in other interviews that the lucky hire was a man by the name of John Snow! "But then I met him again years later. The next time, Mark Stanway, the keyboard player who was with Magnum, who I also worked with, and Grand Slam, brought Phil to the session that I was recording in DJM Studios in London, and Phil Lynott goes, 'I got my bass in the car. Should I go and get it?' I went, yeah, please! We sporadically stayed in touch after then. I used to see him more at gigs than in pubs, and of course clubs. The first amazing thing though was that, funnily enough, Phil did a Kerrang! interview and he was just really enthusiastic about my album, Dangerous Music. I just thought, wow, I'm gonna like this man and I did."

"Basically Phil and I were writing. We flew out to do a TV show, up in Newcastle, and he said to Brian and I, 'How would you like to reform Thin Lizzy?' Of course we both said yeah, so that was the plan. We'd been writing together for a period of time before that show, because this was leading up to Christmas, and of course the tragedy. What actually happened was that I was heading back to my home in the Midlands, from Phil's home in Kew, and he said, 'Oh, I'll get my driver to take you to the station. I'll come along, sit and have a chat on the way.' I had a tape of everything we'd done, and just as I was getting out of the car, Phil said, 'Oh, can I have that tape so I can work on it over Christmas? Because I think what we're doing is fab.' So I gave it to him. Of course, never saw or heard it since. One track called 'Crying Diamonds', Phil and I wrote the chorus — mostly the chorus is Phil's words, 'getting ready for a revolution' — sitting cross-legged with acoustic guitars in his bedroom, and it was wonderful, you know? But we wrote lots of stuff. He had a little studio in his garden, so we were recording and Thin Lizzy was on, basically."

As regards his work on 'Nineteen', Robin explains, "I was with him when he was finishing it, doing the rough bits at the end. I've heard people say that they think it's about Phil growing up being mixed race in Ireland, etc., but I didn't really get that vibe. I just thought it was a good rock 'n' roll motorbike-y song, which I like."

With respect to the session, Robin remembers Phil and Paul Hardcastle taking their time, hammering the track together. "Yes, I was in the studio with them for quite a while (laughs). This was in the

Roundhouse Studios in Camden, which was Bronze Records' studio. Which was very interesting. The sampling… you know, the motorbike on 'Nineteen', there was a motorbike shop in Camden, in London, and we got the owner to bring out the biggest Harley-Davidson he'd got, and Phil just revved it and revved it. People were coming out of their offices complaining, and he did not give a flying fuck, basically. Just revving it. That's the sound on the album. We had a fantastic photograph of it, but somebody nicked it, which is a shame. This was outdoors of course and it was hot, although it wasn't summer, I don't think. Anyway, the point being that Phil disturbed a lot of people and he enjoyed it immensely."

"Like David (ed. Byron — George had worked with the Heep great as well), Phil had a reputation as being really hard to work with and a complete bastard," noted Robin, in conversation with Kevin Julie. "I think I must be very lucky to slip under the radar with some people. But Phil was immensely talented. I loved working with him as well, but in a different way."

It is telling that word had got around about Phil being difficult, definitely an understatement at this point. Phil's heroin use had made him insulated from empathy toward his co-musicians, his fans, but most aggressively, his crew, who he saddled with unreasonable demand after unreasonable demand. Phil had become the ultimate prima donna rock star, materialistic as well, and without the reliability to back it up. Stories abound about short bursts of work and productivity followed by contempt and outright disappearance. All of this was exacerbated by Phil being smart enough to be sensitive to the fact that there were bands coming up capable of kicking him up the backside. Perhaps his response would have been to pull even further away from the hard rock that sent Lizzy to the top.

"I remember, the flight was early," notes Robin, recalling what would be Phil's last TV performance, a raucous live send-up of 'Nineteen'. "I went into Phil's bedroom where Brian Downey was already there, and they were already necking Jack Daniels, which was lovely. So I joined in of course (laughs). This is early, early in the morning. But yeah, that's rock 'n' roll.

Then we just flew up. I remember going around a few record shops with Phil and him getting mobbed (laughs). This is in Newcastle, up north in England; it was quite a good day. Then we did the show, but Phil was complaining about a backache. We'd done the video just before, and again, Phil was really complaining, which really wasn't his nature, to me. But I had no idea he was in such trouble. No idea whatsoever."

"I didn't see any of the really serious stuff with Phil," continues Robin. "Only really smoking. Not any of the serious stuff, heroin or anything.

I can't comment. If I wasn't there, I can't say. But no, there was no mood changes. I really liked Phil. We got on really, really well. I mean, there's loads of stuff that was just so great to be around. But then I remember, we were all booked, for example, to go out to a club, long before Christmas, and at last minute Phil said, 'Oh, I don't really feel like I can come.' That was the first time, apart from the backache thing, I thought, wow, this isn't really Phil. He's not coming to a party, and it's like a personally hosted thing, one of those major things. Yes, not good colour, for a man of Phil's original colour. We now know he was very, very unwell, but he still was a professional, right to the last second. When he asked me to join the band, and Brian, he was really excited and, 'Right, here we go,' and more or less, going to publicise it soon as Christmas is out of the way, 'Here we go; Thin Lizzy is back.' So he was up, man; he really was. I hope Brian has the same impression. But of course Brian knew Phil forever, whereas I knew him for only, unfortunately, a few months."

"He was looking forward to the future," reflects George. "He was having meetings with record companies around this time. I thought CBS was most likely, but I can't guarantee that. It might've been Polydor, but it was definitely a proper company. It was just looking so very, very positive. It was such a shock and I'll tell you this, because it may be of interest. I found out that Philip died by... I had a call from a live radio show, and they said, 'Can you comment on Phil Lynott's death?' The shock was immense. Because, as I say, we knew he wasn't well, but bloody 'ell, that's more than not well. So that's how I discovered that Philip had passed."

"There were just so many good occasions," recalls George, offering his closing thoughts. "All I can say is that working with Phil was magic to me — absolutely loved it. As I said, to be sitting cross-legged on his bedroom floor, looking at each other's eyes and writing songs, one specifically called 'Crying Diamonds', which, as I said, I wish Phil had sung — gosh, that was magical. So Phil lives in my mind a lot of the time. I like him a lot and man, I wish I had that tape. I've checked and checked. I've talked to many people, but no, they reckon somewhere there's a vault — with lots of stuff."

"It's to do with the aggression of the age of 19," remarked Phil, back to the man's last track, explaining to Bonutto the difference between his and Hardcastle's tune of the same name. "Also, there was a biker gang that, when I was in America, I was in a bar, and these Hells Angels walked into the bar, and this guy had 19... it must've been the 19th chapter or something, this guy came in, walked up to the bar, banged his fist on the counter, and went, I'm bad, give me a beer. From that I got the inspiration for the song as opposed to Paul Hardcastle's, which is, you know, the fact that the average age, mine was just about the aggression of feeling 19."

A biker-themed video was done for the track, out in LA, a part of the world not in the least associated with Phil or Lizzy... "The original bikers I'd seen was in Texas, but when it came time to do the video, I thought it would be good to have, instead of making a glamour video with lots of pretty girls and stuff, I thought I'd make a macho one without being chauvinistic. So I went for men and machines. Because there is bikes all over the record, I thought it would be good to go somewhere where they hadn't got the helmet laws, and try and get the Hells Angels gang to show up with their Harley-Davidsons. Some of them are, and some of them are extras. The guy I'm cruising around with at the end was... one of the guys that was an extra is the bass player from Twisted Sister. So he's on the bike there too. He's an extra in it, so, he's part of the Hells Angels gang, in this particular video."

For what would become Phil's last remarks on TV, Dante hits him up with a thoughtful comparison between what he's doing sonically on 'Nineteen', and Elvis Presley breaking down barriers in the '50s.

"Yeah, well, it's not so much that I'm trying to break down the barriers because I've always liked different types of music. I think one of the things that the music papers and the media, in general, do, to their detriment, is they make things separatist. Like Kerrang! only does heavy metal and NME does left-wing, off-the-wall, you know, musical stuff. So I've always been able to like, say, a dance record to a punk record to a rock song. My forte happens to be playing rock music, but I see no reason why... Every time there is a breakdown, like when Elvis did country and western, and black music, he's one artist that broke down barriers. When Hendrix messed around with fusions and stuff... I always think something new comes out of it. I always... I mean to continue to; it's a manner to which I've become accustomed."

One last gathering of friends and (broken) family over Christmas and Phil would be dead. Phil and Caroline were separated at this time, but they had vowed to spend Christmases together. This time, Caroline would not be coming, although Phil's mother Philomena had successfully collected the girls. Phil had wanted Big Charlie over as well, plus Jimmy Bain, who had just separated with his wife but had a daughter named Samantha that got along well with Phil's girls. "I was on tour with Dio, and I came back and saw him at Christmas, actually stayed at his house, and I had to leave on Boxing Day. I took his two kids over to see my daughter for Christmas Day and I never saw him again, because he was taken to hospital that day. I had to leave the day after Christmas and actually fly to Vancouver to pick up the tour again and I didn't get to go to his funeral. I was really destroyed by that. But these things happen and you never know when you're going to get taken. Pretty amazing. He's my daughter's godfather. We were really tight. I was born the same day as his eldest daughter, Sarah, and our wives were really tight, close together. We lived like, I don't know, three or four miles away from each other in London."

Phil's condition indeed continued to deteriorate through the days leading up to Christmas. One episode had him fully clothed in an overflowing bathtub telling his mother in panic that he couldn't get warm. After vomiting and being consigned to bed, two doctors were summoned that prescribed two different courses of action, neither which seemed to help, with Robbo having arrived suggesting the services of someone he called Doctor Diamond. Christmas day Phil had been rushed by Big Charlie and family friend Graham Cohen to a Clouds Clinic near Salisbury, where his condition worsened, prompting an upgrade to Salisbury General Infirmary. There Philip languished, Philomena deciding that too many visitors would be a strain, only Charlie, Caroline, Graham and herself attending to Phil, who only days later got to see his two girls, now five and eight years of age. On January 3rd, Graham and Big Charlie took Philomena back to Kew House, with Phil dying the next day, January 4th, Dr. Angela Scott announcing cause of death as a combination of heart, liver and kidney failure and blood poisoning.

"Lynott collapsed on Christmas Day at his house in Kew, London," reported Sounds, "and was initially rushed to a private clinic at East Knowle, Wiltshire, which specialises in treating drug and alcohol addiction. He was taken there by his estranged wife Caroline, daughter of The Price Is Right game show host Leslie Crowther, who had dashed from her Bath home on hearing news of his collapse. But later on Christmas Day he was transferred to Salisbury Infirmary where he was immediately put into intensive care suffering from septicaemia (blood poisoning) and kidney failure. Although his kidneys started to function again after spell on a dialysis machine, he then developed haemophilia and finally pneumonia which his heart was not strong enough to resist."

The NME added a few more details, alluding to the chaos that ensued as Phil's condition deteriorated. "Lynott, according to a witness, had spent the night of December 24/25 drinking heavily and taking an unspecified drug at his large home in Richmond, Surrey. However, he collapsed on Christmas Day from a mixture of blood poisoning and liver and kidney failure, and it's here that the oddities begin. Instead of being taken to a local hospital, Lynott remained in his home while his wife, contacted at her home in Bath, drove over 100 miles to pick him up. She then sped a further 70 miles to an alcohol and drug abuse centre at East Knoyle, Wiltshire.

Accounts of what happened then are sketchy but it seems that the stricken star was eventually turned away on the grounds that his condition was 'medical and not addiction related.' In desperation, Caroline Crowther drove Lynott a further 20 miles to Salisbury General, completing a journey of over 200 miles for her and over 100 for the apparently semiconscious Phil Lynott."

"Phil was a pretty amazing guy, really," said Scott, in a radio interview with Dave Fanning the night Phil passed. "He had a real complex personality. You couldn't really get to know the guy in one sitting. You had to really dive in there and get to know him. Like I say, pretty complex guy; he was the visionary of the band. He was the focal point and he was the driving force of Thin Lizzy. What else can I say? You know, he was one of my best friends and he's gone now. When we broke up, we were still the best of friends. It just broke up, I think, of us being overworked and just a little bit too tired of playing the same thing over and over again. People wanting to go on to newer things. It wasn't because we hated each other or anything like that. I kept up on what Phil was doing, and he kept up on what I was doing. The other guys that came and went through the band, we all pretty much kept in touch. It's not like the band quit and everybody just forgot about each other."

Asked whether in light of what happened, Phil would have been the first to warn people away from drugs, Scott quickly agrees. "I think Phil would be the first, and he has on other occasions said it. In fact, when I last spoke to him, he knew that that kind of lifestyle wasn't going to work anymore and he had actually knocked it on the head for quite a while. So that's why... he was in such a healthy state last time I saw him. That's why this whole thing has come as such a shock to everybody, because he was in such good spirits and he was in a good state of health. So nobody can figure out what happened."

In closing, Scott says of Phil's death, that "It's not only a tragedy for Irish rock 'n' roll, but for music in general, that a man with the talent and vision that Phil Lynott had, can be taken away so suddenly. One thing is for sure, I'll never forget, and I hope nobody else does. Another thing, he's left a lot of good songs behind him. As one of my best friends, this is a very sad day for me."

"I don't know how to express my feelings at the moment," added Brian Downey, reached in Ireland by Fanning cohort Leo Enright. "Completely shattered. I can't really believe what's happened. I was speaking to Phil a couple days before Christmas, and we were supposed to get together in the studio in London this month. He was booking two or three weeks in the studio to do some songs, and he wanted me to work on a new LP, and I said, 'Yes, of course.' He was fine before I left him. Seemed to be in great spirits, looking forward to Christmas, being with his family. He said to me again, 'I'll see you in the New Year. We'll have a good recording together.' But I can't believe this has happened. It's just unbelievable."

In a curious exchange on the subject of drugs, Brian commented that, "You know, when I was speaking to him he was fine. He had a few drinks. I mean, everybody does around Christmas time, but as I could see, he was off drugs. Phil, he didn't touch many drugs over the years. I think it maybe was an exaggeration, up to a point. With Thin Lizzy, he never really indulged, except a few drinks. But when Thin Lizzy broke up, I don't know what happened after that, which is around two or three years ago. We used to do a lot of tours together, and taking drugs in that situation just does not work. We could have never gone on stage and played, the way we used to play. We used to have a few drinks, okay fine, but I'd never seen Phil take many drugs."

Part patch-up of Phil's character at a crucial and raw moment? Perhaps, but in the telling, there's also the educated suspicion that things might have taken a turn for the worse at the fulcrum when and where Lizzy was no longer.

"I was destroyed when he died," remarks another close friend at the end, Jimmy Bain. "And I think about it even to this day. Every so often I would hear 'The Boys Are Back In Town' on the radio, and I would think, 'God, I hope you're having a good time up there, man.' Because I really miss the guy. You know, at the end too, he played me some stuff he had done in a small studio and he was really writing some good stuff. I don't know whatever happened to it, but he was back on a really positive musical avenue just before he died. It was so sad. A bit of this was Grand Slam, but it was just more himself in the studio again. He'd gone in and done some stuff. In fact he was asking me if I was into doing some stuff with him. Because we were always really close."

"He was lost in the shuffle for a little while," says Bain, intimating that Phil would have been feeling a bit passed-by after the silencing of Lizzy. "When I started with Dio, he was on top of the world and by the time I saw him after a year with us going at it hard, he had come down a peg or two and was trying to get his band Grand Slam started and couldn't get arrested. The songs weren't there, it wasn't Thin Lizzy, it didn't have the magic, and I was thinking he was really psychologically affected by the fact that his manager... he had introduced them to Ultravox and to that guy Steve Strange and Visage and stuff like that, and they ended up becoming the No.1 and No.2 band on Morrison O'Donnell's roster. I mean 'Vienna' was No.1 for what, a year or something like that? Like a thorn in his side because things like that took over a little bit at the time. So Thin Lizzy ended up down about No.4 or something like that, so he was hurt by all that shit. I felt he was a little bit beaten when I saw him. His spirits were down a little bit. It was during Christmas time, too. I got him back up and excited again and everything, but then I went off to pick up the Dio tour and I never saw him again because that was the year he got sick. Very sad; I was really saddened."

Clive Edwards, with Wild Horses part of the small Morrison O'Donnell stable, saw the drift of Lizzy from the inside, essentially from the management point of view. Like his band mate Jimmy, he also could see how Phil might have felt "lost in the shuffle."

"Chris Morrison, Chris O'Donnell... yeah, they were fine; they would tear their hair out at times," muses Clive. "When I was involved, and Wild Horses had come on, some of the good years had gone, and it was hard work then. Phil was misbehaving, Brian was misbehaving, and the bands weren't the same as in the early days. Everybody used to talk about the old days, like Scott would tell the story about, he used to have to share a room with Chris O'Donnell, and when he used to bring a girl back, he said he realised that Chris O'Donnell was sleeping with his glasses on. All these silly stories; and the same with Morrison. It was always about the old days, which would've been pre-*Live And Dangerous*, when they were coming up and they had to share rooms and it wasn't first class. They didn't have all the money in the world for all the girls and all the drugs. It was much more comrades in arms, and punch-ups on the Finnish border with Robbo and Lizzy fighting the Finnish security guards. All these stories. It would always come back as the good days..."

The constant line-up changes would have demoralised Phil as well. "Yeah, well, when I joined, obviously Robbo was out, Gary had joined, then Gary left, then they had to replace Gary, so they got a couple of guys in. Eventually they got Snowy in. I think we all agree that Snowy was not the right player for Lizzy. So there was a lot of people, and Phil would chuck his weight around. Ultravox had come on the scene, and I think Phil saw that as a bit of a diversion. Ultravox were probably easier to manage than Lizzy. Chris Morrison had heart problems, had to have a heart bypass, so you know, it was all getting much more stressful and much more about business."

"They were good guys; they did their best," says Clive about Chris and Chris. "But of course they would have liked to be able to control what was going on, but they couldn't. Phil was a law unto himself, effectively. Ultravox had 'Vienna', which was a huge hit. At that time, Lizzy had stopped having big, big hits. Their hits were prior to that. They were all 'Dancing In The Moonlight', 'The Boys Are Back In Town', so obviously Midge comes in, plays a little bit to help them out, and then they do their album, and 'Vienna' is like sliced bread. I mean, they never really followed it up, but at that particular time… The thing is, the company was founded on the money made by Lizzy, and then Chris Morrison and Chris O'Donnell quite likely, as businessmen, would then look to channel some of that money that they had earned with Lizzy into some other bands, to make more money and Ultravox was in there. Ultravox went bang; I don't think they hit No.1, but they were No.2 for ages. Lizzy hadn't had a No.2 or No.1 for a long time, and I do think that Midge and all the boys were that much more keen and far easier to manage."

"The other thing is, Phil had grown up with being a star. Phil was a star when the Morrisons weren't. He already had 'Whisky In The Jar', and so these guys had come in, and it wasn't like Phil looked up to Chris and Chris. It was like they were on equal terms. If anything, Phil was the man, and so they could never browbeat Phil into behaving himself. People knew Phil wasn't behaving himself, and when I'm saying that, I'm talking about the drugs. He would have people working for him who would have a vested interest that Phil didn't give up, because they were as bad as he was, and the management would fire them and stick a new guy in whose brief was, you keep him off the gear, you know, and you keep him straight. Of course Phil would just fire them and say fuck off and reinstate the guy who the management had been trying to get rid of; it's a vicious circle. That was the shit that was going on then."

"It definitely got worse toward the end," says Robbo, "I mean even at the end, I lived near to Phil, in Richmond. I was bringing up Ronnie Wood's son. I used to take him down to visit Phil all the time, and him and Phil would play train sets in the front room (laughs). So I was always fairly close. Never lost contact with Phil. I was there the night before they took him into the hospital, and his mum was there as well. In fact, I went upstairs to give him his Christmas present from me and Jesse James. I saw him in his bed, and I went back down to Phyllis downstairs and I said, 'Phyllis, this is not good. You've got to get him in the hospital.' Then Charlie said the same thing. So he was in the next day. But yeah, the drugs, they take over. I mean, even Scott would admit that. Honestly not from Downey's point of view. He was never really involved in that sort of stuff. It was more Phil and Scott, really. Some of us were partying harder than others obviously, and I think Phil got taken advantage of. Hangers on, you know, 'cause he was dependant on certain things and certain people supplied it, and they are the people you want to watch out for because they are not interested in you as a person. Just interested in selling their wares and that's it."

"Phil was an extremely caring man," is how engineer John Vasey remembers the rock legend. "He came to the hospital when my first child was born. His ambition was to create a working business for all the touring crew to be gainfully employed when Thin Lizzy was not touring. Thin Lizzy were ahead of their time as the current incarnation of Thin Lizzy still seems to entertain a whole new generation. It is Phil's songs that had a timeless empathy with the common man. His songs relate to the expectations of people around the world."

"What comes across is the honesty and the generosity of the man," muses Ricky Warwick, future singer for a renewed Thin Lizzy, offering a tale second-hand. "A good friend of mine, Jake Burns, played in Stiff Little Fingers. He went up to Phil's house one night to party, and it's quite near, right before Phil died, and he said there were a lot of hangers-on. You know, just lots of people that shouldn't be there that were just taking advantage and stuff like that. I think that's the guy that Phil was; like, he threw his home open to anybody, come on in, very generous, and Jake said he made a point of bringing a crate of beer — pretty much everybody else who came didn't bring anything. He said Phil was just blown away by this, and just couldn't thank him enough, and said right before he left... Phil was up in his bedroom, and Phil walked him to the gate and said, 'I'll see you soon, and thanks for coming.' I think that side of it, very honest and very nice guy, as well as being... he could be a hell-raiser and he could kick it up with the best of them, but I think he had this other side, talking to Scott and Brian, that he could be, just a good guy, just a good guy to have on your side."

"It just sounds like it was such a magical time and band to be in," continues Warwick. "I think Phil, just looking the way he did back then... Scott's told me Phil's always been a bit of a scrapper, but he didn't go looking for it. It always came to him because he was a good-looking guy, and he would go into bars and guys would feel threatened, thinking he's hitting on their girlfriend, and most the time he probably was. But I just think the great story that Scott tells me is they were in the studio in London, *Black Rose* era I think, and Cliff Richard is in the other studio doing his polished pop stuff. Phil was like, 'Wouldn't it be great if we could get Cliff in to hear the stuff?' (laughs). So they basically go in and harangued Cliff Richard into coming into their studio and blasting this stuff, and Cliff's there at the back tapping his foot. Meanwhile Scott and Phil are up to no good behind his back, tripping the light fantastic. I just think it's an interesting image of those guys out of their minds, and Thin Lizzy *Black Rose*, you've got squeaky-clean Cliff Richard going, 'Oh yeah, that's very nice'."

"I think the last time I saw him was about two years before he died," reflects Terry O'Neill, Thin Lizzy's first manager way back in '69. "It was just around the corner from where I live now, on the beach, in the borough. We had a house, and his daughters, maybe their fifth or sixth birthday party, and I went with my family then and my kids then, who are grown up now. I believe it was during the summer, because his daughter has a birthday in the summer. Basically everybody thought, including myself, that Philip was very, very together, very sussed street-wise, very sussed in every way, and I think we were surprised, and also to his own surprise, the drink and the drugs really got the better of him. But nobody would've seen that coming. You just think, 'Oh, Philip can handle it,' you know? Not like for example Shane McGowan, everybody saying, 'How come he hasn't died?' It's like he's a pathetic case. But Philip was always really together. He never gave the vibe that he was too wasted to do anything. He always looked smart, he always looked good, he was always able to engage with people and so on. He was never in the corner dribbling. I didn't even think that he was so far into it, what he was into. I thought he was a big coke fiend, but I didn't realise what he was doing, really. Like most people, I didn't really know that he had a problem."

"I remember one time, in London," continues Terry, offering one of few late career memories of being with Phil. "Called around to a flat that he had, that he owned, but Gary Moore was staying in it at the time, and we called around, and anyway, talking to Philip, to Gary. Gary was there with a couple of Swedish girls, around lunchtime, and there was some mail for Philip. I remember him opening an envelope and there's a PRS, you know, Performing Rights Society cheque, for I think about £35,000. But that's like the equivalent of about 500,000 now. It was a lot of money then. You know, you could probably buy a house for that. I remember him going, 'Look,' and showing me the cheque, and he crumpled it up and shoved it into his pocket. I said, 'You need to take care of that.' He says, 'No, don't worry, I get them every six months.' How shall I say, if there was anything wrong, Philip wouldn't really confide and tell you."

Enquiring of Eric Bell as to the last time he saw Phil, Bell wasn't all that equivocal — after all, you never really think it's going to be the last time. "Well, Philip, see, like now and again, they would phone me. The band management would phone me or they would get roadies to phone me, and I'd be playing somewhere with my own band. Like say, one night I was playing in Bristol, playing this little club, and the manager of the club come down, and he says, 'Right, phone call for you, Eric, upstairs.' I went up and took it, and it was one of the roadies for Thin Lizzy, and he said, 'Eric, we're playing Bristol town hall tonight (laughs), and Philip said, why don't you come over, we'll pick you up, and come up and do a few songs?' So the club I was in, at intermission, they would pick me up in his limo (laughs), and I just played to 300 people, and I go there, and it's 4,000. I go in, say hello, in the changing room, and talk about what songs we're going to play. I would play with them for about half an hour, 20 minutes, and then I would come back to the club and play the little tiny club. So things like that were going on now and again. So I would see Philip from time to time. But he was a changed guy. He wasn't the guy I used to know."

Last time his old mate Brush Shiels had seen Phil was, "probably about three months before he died. You know, basically when you overindulge like that, somebody else takes over your personality. I mean you're not dealing with reality at all, you're dealing with... honestly, it's a form of possession. If you watch The Exorcist or fuckin' Alfred Hitchcock, or one of these horror movies, you say yeah, yeah, that's it. Somebody just made that up, but when you meet the lads, and it was fuckin' taking over. You couldn't hold a conversation with him. You're not dealing... you're dealing with someone that is basically being possessed by fucking evil spirits. It was the worst."

"If Phil had not met his demise," muses Kit Woolven, closing on more of a career note, "and had Phil lived, Lizzy would've probably been one of the biggest comeback bands ever. Everybody, I mean, so many people cite them, right from Guns N' Roses through God knows. Even young bands now have been influenced by Lizzy."

Memorial services were held for Philip Parris Lynott on January 9th, 1986, Father Raymond Brennan presiding, the same minister who had conducted the marriage between Caroline and Phil. Two days later, there was a service at Church Of Assumption, Howth, Dublin, after which Philip was laid to rest in St. Fintans Cemetery, plot 13 in the St. Polans section.

With his death the world lost one of rock's most charismatic and thoughtful icons. Appreciated significantly at the time, Phil's legend would only grow as the decades wore on. Thin Lizzy is now widely regarded as one of the finest hard rock bands of all time, confirmed by the fact that despite only middling commercial success in America, they are often in the conversation for induction into the Rock and Roll Hall of Fame. Will justice prevail? Only time will tell. Hall of Fame or not, no one can take away from us the songs Philip Lynott left us, songs to celebrate life, to mourn, to address our struggles, to get us through the day, heads held high with pride, and at the same time, inspired by the man himself, with a knowing smirk and at least a little bit of style.

***

GIG LIST

The gig list was complied by Peter Nielsen. A more extensive version, with details of support and headlining acts, reviews, press ads etc can be found at his excellent website thinlizzyguide.com.
This list also includes all the gigs by The Greedies; The Three Musketeers; Phil Lynott's post Lizzy band, Grand Slam; his solo gigs plus various gigs involving guest appearances by one or more Thin Lizzy members. All of which are listed in italics.

1977

20th January	Civic Centre, Saginaw, Michigan, US
21st January	Louisville Gardens, Louisville, Kentucky, US
22nd January	Wings Stadium, Kalamazoo, Michigan, US
23rd January	Richfield Coliseum, Richfield, Ohio, US
25th January	Civic Center, Ottawa, Canada
26th January	Forum, Montreal, Canada
28th January	Chicago Stadium, Chicago, Illinois, US
29th January	Dayton Hara Arena, Dayton, Ohio, US *Cancelled*
30th January	Sports Arena, Toledo, Ohio, US
1st February	Maple Leaf Gardens, Toronto, Canada
3rd February	Springfield Civic Center, Springfield, Massachusetts, US
4th February	Cole Field House, University of Maryland, Madison, Maryland, US
5th February	Madison Square Garden, New York City, New York, US
6th February	Nassau Coliseum, Uniondale, Long Island, New York, US
8th February	War Memorial Auditorium, Syracuse, New York, US
9th February	Boston Garden, Boston, Massachusetts, US
10th February	Providence Civic Center, Providence, Rhode Island, US
11th February	Philadelphia Civic Centre, Philadelphia, Pennsylvania, US
19th February	Sportatorium, Hollywood, Florida, US
20th February	Civic Centre, Lakeland, Florida, US
21st February	The Omni, Atlanta, Georgia, US
22nd February	Boutwell Auditorium, Birmingham, Alabama, US
23rd February	Kiel Auditorium, St. Louis, Missouri, US
25th February	SMU Moody Coliseum, Dallas, Texas, US
26th February	Sam Houston Coliseum, Houston, Texas, US
27th February	The Novel Centre, Oklahoma, Oklahoma, US
1st March	Vets Memorial Coliseum, Phoenix, Arizona, US
2nd March	Forum, Inglewood, California, US
3rd March	Forum, Inglewood, California, US
5th March	Sports Arena, San Diego, California, US
6th March	Winterland, San Francisco, California, US
8th March	Memorial Auditorium, Sacramento, California, US*
9th March	Selland Arena, Fresno, California, US*
11th March	Pacific Coliseum, Vancouver, Canada
12th March	Paramount Theatre, Portland, Oregon, US
13th March	Arena, Seattle, Washington, US

16th March	Jubilee Auditorium, Calgary, Canada
16th March	Jubilee Auditorium, Calgary, Canada
18th March	Coliseum, Edmonton, Alberta, Canada
	All of these gigs were as support to Queen except * where Queen cancelled and Sammy Hagar performed instead.
6th August	Ruisrock, Turku, Finland
8th August	Chateau Neuf, Oslo, Norway
96th August	Liseberg, Gothenburg, Sweden
10th August	Gröna Lund Tivoli, Stockholm, Sweden
12th August	Tivolis Koncertsal, Copenhagen, Denmark
14th August	Bilzen Festival, Bilzen, Belgium
19th August	*Morans Hotel, Dublin Ireland Boomtown Rats gig with appearance by Lynott.*
20th August	Westwing Castle Townhouse, Celbridge, Ireland
21st August	Dalymount Park, Dublin, Ireland
27th August	Reading Festival, Reading, UK
3rd September	Zeppelinfeld, Nuernberg, Germany
4th September	Wildparkstadion, Karlsruhe, Germany
21st September	Fox Theatre, San Diego, California, US
23rd September	Paramount Northwest Theatre, Seattle, Washington, US
24th September	The Gardens, Vancouver, Canada *Cancelled*
25th September	Paramount Theatre, Portland, Oregon, US
27th September	Warner Theater, Fresno, California, US
28th September	Aladdin Hotel, Las Vegas, Nevada, US
29th September	Civic Auditorium, Santa Monica, California, US
30th September	Civic Auditorium, Santa Monica, California, US
1st October	Winterland, San Francisco, California, US
2nd October	Civic Auditorium, San Jose, California, US
4th October	Celebrity Theatre, Phoenix, Arizona, US
5th October	Celebrity Theatre, Phoenix, Arizona, US
6th October?	Regis Fieldhouse, Denver, Colorado, US
7th October	Music Hall, Oklahoma City, Oklahoma, US
8th October	Memorial Auditorium, Kansas City, Kansas, US
9th October	Kiel Opera House, St. Louis, Missouri, US
11th October	Municipal Auditorium, San Antonio, Texas, US
12th October	Convention Center Theater, Dallas, Texas, US
13th October	Music Hall, Houston, Texas, US
15th October	Taft Auditorium, Cincinnati, Ohio, US
15th October	Lizner Auditorium, Washington D.C, US *Cancelled*
16th October	Warner Theater, Washington D.C, US
18th October	Stanley Warner Theater, Pittsburgh, Pennsylvania, US
19th October	Stanley Warner Theater, Pittsburgh, Pennsylvania, US
20th October	Tower Theatre, Upper Darby, Philadelphia, Pennsylvania, US
21st October	Tower Theatre, Upper Darby, Philadelphia, Pennsylvania, US
22nd October	The Palladium, New York City, New York, US
23rd October	Orpheum, Boston, Massachusetts, US
26th October	Masonic Temple Auditorium, Detroit, Michigan, US
28th October	Seneca College Fieldhouse, Toronto, Canada
29th October	Music Hall, Cleveland, Ohio, US
31st October	Civic Center, St.Paul, Minneapolis, US
1st November	Riverside Theatre, Milwaukee, Wisconsin, US
2nd November	Dane County Memorial Coliseum, Madison, Wisconsin, US *Cancelled*
4th November	St. Paul Civic Center Theater, St. Paul, Minnesota, US
5th November	Uptown Theatre, Chicago, Illinois, US
11th November	City Hall, Newcastle, UK
12th November	The Apollo, Glasgow, UK
13th November	The Apollo, Glasgow, UK
14th November	Odeon Theatre, Edinburgh, UK
16th November	Empire, Liverpool, UK
17th November	Empire, Liverpool, UK
18th November	Spa Royal Hall, Bridlington, UK
19th November	New Theatre, Oxford, UK
21st November	Colston Hall, Bristol, UK
22nd November	Colston Hall, Bristol, UK

23rd November	City Hall, Sheffield, UK
24th November	St Georges Hall, Bradford, UK
25th November	Free Trade Hall, Manchester, UK
26th November	Free Trade Hall, Manchester, UK
28th November	Dome, Brighton, UK
29th November	The Guildhall, Portsmouth, UK
30th November	Winter Gardens, Bournemouth, UK
2nd December	Odeon Theatre, Birmingham, UK
3rd December	Odeon Theatre, Birmingham, UK
4th December	Civic Hall, Wolverhampton, UK
5th December	De Montfort Hall, Leicester, UK
7th December	Gaumont Theatre, Southampton, UK
8th December	Capitol Theatre, Cardiff, UK
10th December	Hammersmith Odeon, London, UK
11th December	Hammersmith Odeon, London, UK *Gary Moore joined Lizzy on stage.*
13th December	Odeon Theatre, Lewisham, UK
14th December	Odeon Theatre, Lewisham, UK
17th December	Kursaal Ballroom, Southend, UK

1978

16th February	Music Machine, London, UK *Cancelled. This was a Greedies gig.*
29th March	Rainbow Theatre, London, UK
15th April	*Roundhouse, London, UK Lynott guest at Elvis Costello and the Attractions gig.*
5th May	Audi Max, Hamburg, Germany *Cancelled*
7th May	Kongresshalle, Saarbrucken, Germany *Cancelled*
8th May	Stadthalle, Karlsruhe, Germany *Cancelled*
9th May	Stadthalle, Offenbach, Germany *Cancelled*
10th May	Nibelungenhalle, Nuremburg, Germany *Cancelled*
11th May	Circus Krone, Munchen, Germany *Cancelled*
12th May	Haldenberghalle, Göppingen, Germany *Cancelled*
13th May	Musikhalle, Hamburg, Germany *Cancelled*
15th May	Pinkpop Festival, Geleen, Holland
17th May	Ancienne Belgique, Brussels, Belgium
18th May	Stadium, Paris, France
25th May	*Baggot Inn, Dublin, Ireland Gig by Lynott, Downey & Brush Shiels.*
26th May	*Moran's, Dublin, Ireland Gig by Lynott, Downey, & Bell*
13th June	*Ulster Hall, Belfast, Northern Ireland*
	Lynott guests with Boomtown Rats on 'Route 66'.
14th June	Ulster Hall, Belfast, Northern Ireland
15th June	Ulster Hall, Belfast, Northern Ireland
17th June	The Apollo, Glasgow, UK
18th June	King's Hall, Belle Vue, Manchester, UK
20th June	City Hall, Newcastle, UK
22nd June	Wembley Empire Pool, London, UK
23rd June	Wembley Empire Pool, London, UK
6th July	Plaza De Toros, Ibiza
29th July	*The Electric Ballroom Camden, London, UK *Greedies gig.*
8th August	Coliseum, Jackson, Mississippi, US
9th August	Hirsch Memorial Coliseum, Shreveport, Louisiana, US
10th August	Mid-South Coliseum, Memphis, Tennessee, US
12th August	Myriad Convention Center, Oklahoma City, Oklahoma, US
13th August	Convention Center, Dallas, Texas, US
13th August	*Binary Club, Dallas, Texas, US*
	Thin Lizzy played with US. Kids drummer Mike Schwedler on his birthday.
14th August	Coliseum, El Paso, Texas, US
15th August	Veterans Memorial Coliseum, Phoenix, Arizona, US
16th August	The Forum, Inglewood, California, US
17th August	Roxy, Los Angeles, California, US
18th August	Cal Expo Grandstand, Sacramento, California, US
???? August	California State Fair, Sacramento, California, US
20th August	Cow Palace, Daly City, California, US
25th August	Palmer Auditorium, Davenport, Iowa, US
26th August	Alpine Valley Music Theatre, East Troy, Wisconsin, US

27th August	Alpine Valley Music Theatre, East Troy, Wisconsin, US
29th August	Lakeview Arena, Marquette, Michigan, US
30th August	Wings Stadium, Kalamazoo, Michigan, US
3rd September	Cape Cod Coliseum, South Yarmouth, Massachusetts, US
5th September	Paradise Theatre, Boston, Massachusetts, US
6th September	Paradise Theatre, Boston, Massachusetts, US
8th September	Tower Theater, Philadelphia, Pennsylvania, US
9th September	Stanley Theatre, Pittsburg, Pennsylvania, US
10th September	Fairgrounds Stadium, Louisville, Kentucky, US
11th September	I.M.A Auditorium, Flint, Michigan, US
13th September	Royal Oak Music Theatre, Royal Oak, Michigan, US
16th September	Palace Theatre, Cleveland, Ohio, US
22nd September	Aragon Ballroom, Chicago, Illinois, US
23rd September	Uptown Theatre, Kansas City, Missouri, US
24th September	Civic Auditorium Music Hall, Omaha, Nebraska, US
26th September	Wendler Arena, Saginaw Civic Center, Saginaw, Michigan, US
27th September	Ohio University Convocation Center, Athens, Ohio, US
28th September	Rochester Community War Memorial, Rochester, New York, US
29th September	The Palladium, New York City, New York, US
30th September	The Palladium, New York City, New York, US
1st October	The Palladium, New York City, New York, US
6th October	McNichols Sports Arena, Denver, Colorado, US
7th October	Salt Palace Arena, Salt Lake City, Utah, US
10th October	Seattle Center Coliseum, Seattle, Washington, US
11th October	Seattle Center Coliseum, Seattle, Washington, US
12th October	Pacific Coliseum, Vancouver, Canada
13th October	Coliseum, Spokane, Washington, US *Cancelled*
13th October	Music Hall, Houston, Texas, US
14th October	Tarrant County Convention Center Arena, Fort Worth, Texas, US
15th October	Civic Auditorium, Pasadena, California, US
20th October	Botanical Gardens, Brisbane, Australia
22nd October	International Sports Centre, Newcastle, Australia
27th October	Myer Music Bowl, Melbourne, Australia
28th October	Myer Music Bowl, Melbourne, Australia
29th October	Opera House, Sydney, Australia
1st November	Western Springs Stadium, Auckland, New Zealand *Cancelled*
16th December	*The Electric Ballroom, Camden, London, UK *Greedies gig.*
17th December	Hammersmith Odeon, London, UK
20th December	*The Stardust, Artane, Dublin, Ireland *Greedies gig.*
21st December	*The Stardust, Artane, Dublin, Ireland *Greedies gig.*
23rd December	*McGonagles, Dublin, Ireland *Greedies gig.*

1979

16th January	*London, UK * Greedies gig unconfirmed.*
2nd March	Mother Blues, Dallas, Texas, US *unconfirmed.*
3rd March	Convention Center Arena, Dallas, Texas, US
4th March	Municipal Auditorium, Shreveport, Louisiana, US
5th March	Memorial Coliseum, Corpus Christi, Texas, US
6th March	Civic Center, Beaumont, Texas, US
7th March	Sam Houston Coliseum, Houston, Texas, US
9th March	Orpheum Theatre, Memphis, Tennessee, US
10th March	Municipal Auditorium, Nashville, Tennessee, US
11th March	Kiel Auditorium, St. Louis, Missouri, US
12th March	Evansville Coliseum, Evansville, Indiana, US
13th March	Evansville Coliseum, Evansville, Indiana, US
14th March	Convention Centre, Indianapolis, Indiana, US
15th March	Hara Arena, Dayton, Ohio, US
16th March	Civic Centre, Charleston, West Virginia, US
17th March	Stanley Theatre, Pittsburg, Pennsylvania, US
18th March	Fairgrounds Coliseum, Columbus, Ohio, US
20th March	Dane County Memorial Coliseum, Madison, Wisconsin, US
21st March	McElroy Auditorium, Waterloo, Iowa, US
22nd March	Wings Stadium, Kalamazoo, Michigan, US

23rd March	Aragon Ballroom, Chicago, Illinois, US
24th March	Cobo Arena, Detroit, Michigan, US
25th March	Civic Centre, Saginaw, Michigan, US
29th March	The Brighton Centre, Brighton, UK
31st March	New Theatre, Oxford, UK
1st April	Odeon Theatre, Birmingham, UK
2nd April	Odeon Theatre, Birmingham, UK
3rd April	Trentham Gardens, Stoke, UK
4th April	Stamford Hall, Stamford, UK
5th April	De Montfort Hall, Leicester, UK
6th April	The Guildhall, Portsmouth, UK
7th April	Winter Gardens, Bournemouth, UK
8th April	Colston Hall, Bristol, UK
9th April	Colston Hall, Bristol, UK
10th April	Bingley Hall, Stafford, UK
11th April	City Hall, Newcastle, UK
12th April	City Hall, Newcastle, UK
14th April	Apollo, Glasgow, UK
15th April	Apollo, Glasgow, UK
16th April	Odeon Theatre, Edinburgh, UK
17th April	Guild Hall. Preston, UK
18th April	City Hall, Sheffield, UK
19th April	St George's Hall, Bradford, UK
20th April	Bridlington Spa Pavillion, Bridlington, UK
22nd April	Hammersmith Odeon, London, UK
23rd April	Hammersmith Odeon, London, UK
24th April	Gaumont, Ipswich, UK
25th April	Gaumont Theatre, Southampton, UK
27th April	Hammersmith Odeon, London, UK
28th April	Hammersmith Odeon, London, UK
1st May	Apollo, Manchester, UK
2nd May	Apollo, Manchester, UK
3rd May	Empire, Liverpool, UK
6th May	Konserthus, Gothenburg, Sweden
7th May	Chateau Neuf, Oslo, Norway
9th May	Olympen, Lund, Sweden
10th May	Falkonerteatret, Copenhagen, Denmark
11th May	Johanneshovs Isstadion, Stockholm, Sweden
14th May	Sartory Saal, Köln, Germany *Rory Gallagher jams on stage with Lizzy.*
15th May	Circus-Krone-Bau, Munchen, Germany
16th May	Volkshaus, Zurich, Switzerland
17th May	Rheingoldhalle, Mannheim, Germany
19th May	Hemmerleinhalle, Neunkirchen, Nuremburg, Germany
20th May	Kongresshalle, Saarbrucken, Germany
21st May	Stadthalle, Offenbach, Germany
22nd May	Musikhalle, Hamburg, Germany
24th May	Pop Meeting Lochem Festival, Lochem, Holland *Thin Lizzy cancelled*
25th May	Hall, Vosselaar, Belgium *Cancelled*
26th May	Salle Des Fetes, Liege-Droixhe, Belgium *Cancelled*
27th May	Jaap Edenhal, Amsterdam, Holland *Cancelled*
28th May	Ancienne Belgique, Brussels, Belgium *Cancelled*
29th May	Stadium, Paris, France *Cancelled*
30th May	Palais D'Hiver, Lyon, France *Cancelled*
29th June	Swing Auditorium, San Bernadino, California, US
30th June	Long Beach Arena, Los Angeles, California, US
1st July	Long Beach Arena, Los Angeles, California, US
2nd July	Selland Arena, Fresno, California, US
4th July	Oakland Stadium, Oakland, California, US
6th July	Coliseum, Reno, Nevada, US
12th July	Coliseum, Wichita, Kansas, US
13th July	Assembly Center, Tulsa, Oklahoma, US
14th July	Myriad, Oklahoma City, Oklahoma, US
15th July	T.H. Barton Coliseum, Little Rock, Arkansas, US

16th July	Civic Center, Huntsville, Alabama, US
18th July	The Warehouse, New Orleans, Louisiana, US
19th July	Hirsch Memorial Coliseum, Shreveport, Louisiana, US
21st July	Bayfront Center, Saint Petersburg, Florida, US
22nd July	Jai Alai, Miami, Florida, US
24th July	Fox Theatre, Atlanta, Georgia, US
25th July	Municipal Auditorium, Nashville, Tennessee, US
26th July	Mid-South Coliseum, Memphis, Tennessee, US
27th July	Louiseville Gardens, Louiseville, Kentucky, US
28th July	Lakefront Stadium, Cleveland, Ohio, US
29th July	Welsh Auditorium, Grand Rapids, Michigan, US
30th July	Wendler Arena, Saginaw Civic Centre, Saginaw, Michigan, US
1st August	Central Park, New York City, New York, US *Thin Lizzy cancelled*
3rd August	Convention Centre, Indianapolis, Indiana, US
4th August	Checkerdome, St Louis, Missouri, US
5th August	Comiskey Park, Chicago, Illinois, US
6th August	Kalamazoo, Michigan, US
7th August	Dane County Coliseum, Madison, Wisconsin, US
8th August	Alpine Valley Music Theater, East Troy, Wisconsin, US *Thin Lizzy cancelled*
10th August	Civic Center, Lansing, Michigan, US
11th August	Cobo Arena, Detroit, Michigan, US *Thin Lizzy cancelled*
12th August	Cobo Arena, Detroit, Michigan, US *Thin Lizzy cancelled*
12th August	O'Keefe Centre, Toronto, Ontario, Canada *unconfirmed*
13th August	Pinecrest Country Club, Shelton, Connecticut, US
14th August	Central Park, New York City, New York, US
25th August	Reading Festival, Reading, UK *Thin Lizzy cancelled*
24th September	Festival Hall, Osaka, Japan
25th September	Nakano Sun Plaza, Tokyo, Japan
26th September	Kookaido Hall, Nagoya, Japan
29th September	Korakuen Hall, Tokyo, Japan
30th September	Nakano Sun Plaza, Tokyo, Japan
31st September	*Electric Ballroom, Camden, London, UK*
	Lynott (two songs), Michael Schenker & Trevor Rabin jams with Wild Horses.
16th December	Apollo Theatre, Manchester, UK
17th December	Apollo Theatre, Manchester, UK
18th December	New Bingley Hall, Stafford, UK
20th December	*Rainbow Theatre, London, UK*
21st December	*Rainbow Theatre, London, UK*
	Lynott jams with Dire Straits on one of these shows, filmed by BBC2 "Arena"
25th December	Studio 21, London, UK
	All-Star jam charity show on behalf of London's orphans with members of Thin Lizzy, Sex Pistols, Generation X & The Banshees.

1980

2nd April	Leisureland Ballroom, Salthill, Galway, Ireland
3rd April	Astoria, Bundoran, Ireland Cancelled
4th April	Forum, Enniskillen, Northern Ireland
5th April	Forum, Antrim, Ireland
6th April	The Baymount Hotel, Strandhill, Sligo, Ireland
7th April	Downtown Ballroom, Dundalk, Ireland
8th April	Horizon Ballroom, Mullingar, Ireland
10th April	Carlton, Killkenny, Ireland
11th April	Oyster Ballroom, Dromkeen, Limerick, Ireland
12th April	St. John's (CYMS), Tralee, Ireland
13th April	City Hall, Cork, Ireland
22nd April	Chateau Neuf, Oslo, Norway
23rd April	Helsinki, Finland *unconfirmed*
24th April	Forum, Copenhagen, Denmark
25th April	Olympen, Lund, Sweden
26th April	Johanneshovs Isstadion, Stockholm, Sweden
27th April	Scandinavium, Gothenburg, Sweden
1st May	City Hall, Newcastle, UK *Brian Robertson on encore — 'Emerald' & 'Rosalie'*
2nd May	City Hall, Newcastle, UK

3rd May	Caird Hall, Dundee, UK
4th May	Odeon Theatre, Edinburgh, UK
5th May	Apollo Theatre, Glasgow, UK
6th May	Apollo Theatre, Glasgow, UK
	Lynott noticed that one of the bouncers was beating up a fan in the audience so he stopped the show.
7th May	Empire Theatre, Liverpool, UK
8th May	Empire Theatre, Liverpool, UK
10th May	Queens Hall, Leeds, UK
11th May	Guild Hall, Preston, UK
12th May	City Hall, Sheffield, UK
13th May	Bingley Hall, Stafford, UK
16th May	The Brighton Centre, Brighton, UK *Cancelled*
17th May	Coventry Theatre, Coventry, UK *Cancelled*
18th May	De Montfort Hall, Leicester, UK *Cancelled*
19th May	Sophia Gardens, Cardiff, UK *Cancelled*
20th May	Gaumont, Southampton, UK *Cancelled*
22nd May	Odeon Theatre, Birmingham, UK
23rd May	Odeon Theatre, Birmingham, UK
24th May	Colston Hall, Bristol, UK *Eric Bell on encore.*
25th May	Apollo Theatre, Manchester, UK
26th May	Apollo Theatre, Manchester, UK
28th May	Hammersmith Odeon, London, UK
29th May	Hammersmith Odeon, London, UK
30th May	Hammersmith Odeon, London, UK *Eric Bell on 'Whisky In The Jar'.*
31st May	Rainbow Theatre, London, UK
1st June	Rainbow Theatre, London, UK
3rd June	The Guildhall, Portsmouth, UK
4th June	New Theatre, Oxford, UK
5th June	New Theatre, Oxford, UK
7th June	Royal Dublin Society, Dublin, Ireland
8th June	Crofton Airport Hotel, Crofton, Ireland
9th June	King's Hall, Belfast, Northern Ireland *Eric Bell on 'Whisky In The Jar'.*
11th June	De Montfort Hall, Leicester, UK
12th June	Coventry Centre, Coventry, UK
13th June	Conference Centre, Brighton, UK
14th June	Gaumont, Southampton, UK
15th June	Sophia Gardens, Cardiff, UK
17th June	*Hurrah, New York, New York, US*
	Lynott on upright bass joined Iggy Pop, Johnny Thunders and a local rockabilly band The Rockats for a jam at this Manhattan club.
25th August	Theatre Royal, Nottingham, UK *Cancelled*
26th August	Theatre Royal, Nottingham, UK *Cancelled*
24th September	Nakano Sun Plaza Hall, Tokyo, Japan
25th September	Nakano Sun Plaza Hall, Tokyo, Japan
29th September	Nippon Seinenkan, Tokyo, Japan
30th September	Kokusai Hall, Kobe, Japan
1st October	Expo Hall, Osaka, Japan
2nd October	Nippon Seinenkan, Tokyo, Japan
3rd October	Kinro Hall, Nagoya, Japan
4th October	Nakano Sun Plaza Hall, Tokyo, Japan
9th October	Capitol Theatre, Sydney, Australia
10th October	Capitol Theatre, Sydney, Australia
11th October	The Playroom, Surfers Paradise, Australia
12th October	The Playroom, Surfers Paradise, Australia
13th October	Festival Hall, Brisbane, Australia
15th October	*The Old Lion Hotel, Adelaide, Australia*
	Thin Lizzy plays three songs as an unannounced follow-up to the Village People.
16th October	Apollo Stadium, Richmond, Australia
18th October	Entertainment Centre, Perth, Australia
20th October	Festival Hall, Melbourne, Australia
22nd October	Capitol Theatre, Sydney, Australia
25th October	Logan Campbell Centre, Auckland, New Zealand

15th November	Agora, Columbus, Ohio, US
16th November	Agora Ballroom, Cleveland, Ohio, US
17th November	Center Stage, Canton, Detroit, Michigan, US
18th November	Agora, Youngstown, Ohio, US
19th November	Park West, Chicago, Illinois, US
20th November	Uncle Sam's, Cheektowaga, New York, US
21st November	Triangle Theater, Rochester, New York, US
22nd November	JB Scott's, Albany, New York, US
26th November	Mr C's Rock Palace, Lowell, Massachusetts, US
29th November	Stage West, West Hartford, Connecticut, US
30th November	Mr. C's, Lowell, Massachusetts, US
1st December	Center Stage, Providence, Rhode Island, US
2nd December	The Paradise Theater, Boston, Massachusetts, US
4th December	Fountain Casino, Aberdeen, New Jersey,US
5th December	Ritz Theatre, New York, New York, US
6th December	Emerald City Ballroom, Cherry Hill, New Jersey, US
9th December	The Ontario Theater, Washington DC, Maryland, US
11th December	Agora Ballroom, Atlanta, Georgia, US
12th December	The Warehouse, New Orleans, Louisiana, US
13th December	The Agora Ballroom, Houston, Texas, US
14th December	Austin Opera House, Austin, Texas, US
15th December	McFarlin Auditorium, Dallas, Texas, US
16th December	Will Rogers Coliseum, Fort Worth, Texas, US
17th December	The Rainbow Music Hall, Denver, Colorado, US
19th December	Warfield Theatre, San Francisco, California, US
20th December	Santa Monica Civic, Los Angeles, California, US

1981

17th January	Foire Internationale, Lille, France
18th January	Pavillon Baltard, Paris, France
19th January	Tivoli, Strasbourg, France
21st January	Stadthalle, Offenbach, Germany
22nd January	Musensaal, Mannheim, Germany
23rd January	Kongresshalle, Saarbrucken, Germany
24th January	Messehalle, Sindelfingen, Germany
25th January	Lauda-Königshofen, Tauber-Franken-Halle, Würzburg, Germany
26th January	Hemmerleinhalle, Nuremburg, Germany
27th January	Neue Welt, Berlin, Germany
29th January	Niedersachsenhalle, Hannover, Germany
30th January	Stadshalle IV, Bremen, Germany
31st January	Westfalenhalle III, Dortmund, Germany
1st February	Musikhalle, Hamburg, Germany
3rd February	Vejlby-Risskovhallen, Aarhus, Denmark
5th February	Drammenshallen, Drammen, Norway
6th February	Scandinavium, Gothenburg, Sweden
7th February	Johanneshov Isstadion, Stockholm, Sweden
8th February	Olympen, Lund, Sweden
9th February	Forum, Copenhagen, Denmark
11th February	Hemmerleinhalle, Neunkirchen, Germany
13th February	De Vereeniging, Nijmegen, Holland
16th February	Oosterpoort, Groningen, Holland
17th February	Edenhal, Amsterdam, Holland
18th February	Messehalle, Stuttgart, Germany
20th February	Deutsches Museum, Munich, Germany
22nd February	Lyon, France
28th July	Gloucester Hall, Jersey, Channel Islands, UK
30th July	Beau Sejour Leisure Centre, Guernsey, Channel Islands, UK
2nd August	Cornwall Coliseum, St. Austell, UK
8th August	Milton Keynes Bowl, UK
10th August	Ice Rink, Kirkcaldy, UK
11th August	Fusion Ballroom, Aberdeen, UK
12th August	Ice Rink, Inverness, UK
13th August	Magnum Centre, Irvine, UK

16th August	Slane Castle Festival, Dublin, Ireland
29th August	Freilichtbuhne, St. Goarshausen, Loreley, Germany
27th October	City Hall, Newcastle, UK *Cancelled*
28th October	Playhouse, Edinburgh, UK *Cancelled*
29th October	Caird Hall, Dundee, UK *Cancelled*
30th October	Capitol Theatre, Aberdeen, UK *Cancelled*
31st October	Apollo Theatre, Glasgow, UK *Cancelled*
2nd November	Guild Hall, Preston, UK *Cancelled*
3rd November	City Hall, Sheffield, UK *Cancelled*
4th November	Empire Theatre, Liverpool, UK *Cancelled*
5th November	Leisure Centre, Gloucester, UK *Cancelled*
7th November	Gaumont Theatre, Southampton, UK *Cancelled*
9th November	Sophia Gardens, Cardiff, UK *Cancelled*
10th November	De Montfort Hall, Leicester, UK *Cancelled*
11th November	Cornwall Coliseum, St. Austell
12th November	Colston Hall, Bristol, UK
13th November	Arts Centre, Poole, UK
14th November	The Brighton Centre, Brighton, UK
16th November	Apollo Theatre, Manchester, UK
17th November	Apollo Theatre, Manchester, UK
19th November	Queens Hall, Leeds, UK
20th November	Odeon Theatre, Birmingham, UK
21st November	Odeon Theatre, Birmingham, UK
22nd November	Empire Theatre, Liverpool, UK
23rd November	Empire Theatre, Liverpool, UK
25th November	Hammersmith Odeon, London, UK
26th November	Hammersmith Odeon, London, UK
27th November	Hammersmith Odeon, London, UK
28th November	Hammersmith Odeon, London, UK
30th November	Gaumont Theatre, Southampton, UK
1st December	Sophia Gardens, Cardiff, UK
3rd December	Playhouse, Edinburgh, UK
4th December	Caird Hall, Dundee, UK
5th December	Capitol Theatre, Aberdeen, UK
6th December	Apollo Theatre, Glasgow, UK
8th December	Apollo Theatre, Coventry, UK
9th December	City Hall, Sheffield, UK
10th December	City Hall, Newcastle, UK
12th December	Guild Hall, Preston, UK
14th December	De Montfort Hall, Leicester, UK
15th December	Guildhall, Portsmouth, UK
16th December	Gaumont Theatre, Ipswich, UK
17th December	Assembly Rooms, Derby, UK

1982

20th January	*Savoy Theatre, New York City, US*
	UNICEF Benefit show. Lynott appears with Rick Derringer and Charlie Daniels.
4th February	Grugahalle, Essen, Germany
6th February	Holstebro-Hallen, Holstebro, Denmark
8th February	Vejlby-Risskov Hallen, Aarhus, Denmark
9th February	Olympen, Lund, Sweden
11th February	Drammenshallen, Drammen, Norway
12th February	Johanneshovs Isstadion, Stockholm, Sweden
13th February	Scandinavium, Gothenburg, Sweden
16th February	Whitla Hall, Belfast, Northern Ireland
17th February	Whitla Hall, Belfast, Northern Ireland
18th February	Whitla Hall, Belfast, Northern Ireland
20th February	R.D.S Simmonscourt Pavilion, Dublin, Ireland
23rd February	City Hall, Cork, Ireland
24th February	Leisureland, Galway, Ireland
25th February	Olympic, Newcastle West, Ireland
28th February	Pavillon Baltard, Nogent sur Marne, France
1st March	Maison des Sports, Clermont-Ferrand, France

2nd March	Palais d'hiver, Lyon, France
4th March	Velodromo De Anoeta, San Sebastian, Spain
6th March	Polideportivo Huerta Del Rey, Valladolid, Spain
7th March	Pavilhao Infante Sagres, Porto, Portugal
8th March	Pavilhao Alvalade, Lisbon, Portugal
9th March	Pabellon Del Real Madrid, Madrid, Spain
11th March	Pabellon Del Juventud De Badalona, Barcelona, Spain
14th March	Grobsporthalle, Crailsheim, Germany
15th March	Hemmerleinhalle, Nuremburg, Germany
16th March	Stadthalle, Offenbach, Germany
17th March	Eintracht, Frankfurt, Germany
18th March	Stadthalle, Freiburg, Germany
22nd March	City Hall, Sheffield, UK *Cancelled*
23rd March	Odeon Theatre, Birmingham, UK *Cancelled*
24th March	Apollo Theatre, Manchester, UK *Cancelled*
25th March	City Hall, Newcastle, UK *Cancelled*
26th March	Sports Arena, Los Angeles, California, US *Cancelled*
27th March	Dominion Theatre, London, UK *Cancelled*
28th March	Dominion Theatre, London, UK *Cancelled*
21st April	Apollo, Coventry, UK *Cancelled*
22nd April	Apollo Theatre, Oxford, UK
23rd April	Odeon Theatre, Birmingham, UK
24th April	Apollo Theatre, Manchester, UK
25th April	Apollo Theatre, Manchester, UK
26th April	City Hall, Sheffield, UK
27th April	City Hall, Newcastle, UK
29th April	De Montfort Hall, Leicester, UK
30th April	Dominion Theatre, London, UK
1st May	Dominion Theatre, London, UK
23rd May	The Ritz, New York City, New York, US *unconfirmed*

The rest of the year was taken up with gigs by Philip Lynott & The Soul Band:-

24th June	*Rialto Cinema, Londonderry, N. Ireland*
25th June	*The Emyvale Inn, Emyvale, Co. Monaghan, Ireland*
26th June	*Macroom Festival, Cork, Ireland*
27th June	*Mullingar Music Festival, Mullingar, Ireland*
29th June	*St.Francis Xavier's Hall, Dublin, Ireland*
30th June	*Rosnaree Hall, Drogheda, Ireland*
2nd July	*Baymount Hotel, Strandhill, Sligo, Ireland*
3rd July	*Pontoon, Co. Mayo, Ireland*
4th July	*Atlantic Hotel, Ballybunion, Ireland*
6th July	*St. Dominic's Hall, Glenties, Co Donegal, Ireland*
7th July	*The Lilac Ballrom, Carndonagh, Co Donegal, Ireland*
8th July	*Maysfield Leisure Centre, Belfast, Northern Ireland Cancelled*
9th July	*Castle Hotel, Knocknamoe, Omagh, Co Tyrone, Northern Ireland*
10th July	*Lisdoonvarna Festival, Lisdoonvarna, Ireland*
18th July	*Punchetown Festival, Punchetown, Naas, Ireland*
	This was a Lynott, Paul Brady & Rory Gallagher jam
1st August	*Castlebar Festival of Music, Castlebar, Ireland*
11th October	*Tivolis Koncertsal, Copenhagen, Denmark Cancelled*
12th October	*Vejlby-Risskov Hallen, Aarhus, Denmark Cancelled*
13th October	*Idraettens Hus, Vejle, Denmark Cancelled*
15th October	*Nöjesparken, Varberg, Sweden*
	Lemmy Kilmister & Brian Robertson joined for
	'Are You Ready' and 'Baby Drives Me Crazy'.
16th October	*Lobo (Folkets hus), Gothenburg, Sweden*
18th October	*Nidaröhallen, Trondheim, Norway*
19th October	*Folketshus, Östersund, Sweden*
20th October	*Ritz, Stockholm, Sweden*
22nd October	*Holstebro-Hallen, Holstebro, Denmark*
23rd October	*Fyns Forum, Odense, Denmark*
24th October	*Åkademiska Föreningen, Lund, Sweden*

25th October	*Tivolis Koncertsal, Copenhagen, Denmark*
27th October	*Idraettens Hus, Vejle, Denmark*
28th October	*Stakladen, Aarhus, Denmark*
29th October	*Markthalle, Hamburg, Germany*
31st October	*Paradisio Club, Amsterdam, Holland*
2nd November	*Le Palace, Paris, France*
27th December	*The Milestone Inn, Balbriggan, Ireland*
28th December	*Savoy Entertainment Centre, Waterford, Ireland*
29th December	*Greenhills Hotel, Limerick, Ireland*
31st December	*TV Club, Dublin, Ireland*

1983

1st January	Town Hall, Kiltimagh, Ireland *Philip Lynott & The Soul Band.
2nd January	Community Centre, Ashbourne, Ireland *Philip Lynott & The Soul Band.
26th January	Regal Theatre, Hitchin, UK *Philip Lynott & The Soul Band.
28th January	The Tube, Newcastle, UK *Philip Lynott & The Soul Band.
9th February	Futurist Theatre, Scarborough, UK
10th February	Queens Hall, Leeds, UK
12th February	Apollo Theatre, Manchester, UK
13th February	Royal Court Theatre, Liverpool, UK
14th February	City Hall, Sheffield, UK
15th February	City Hall, Sheffield, UK
17th February	De Montfort Hall, Leicester, UK
18th February	Assembly Rooms, Derby, UK
19th February	Apollo Theatre, Coventry, UK
21st February	Odeon Theatre, Birmingham, UK
22nd February	Odeon Theatre, Birmingham, UK
24th February	Gaumont Theatre, Ipswich, UK
25th February	The Brighton Centre, Brighton, UK
26th February	The Guildhall, Portsmouth, UK
27th February	Apollo Theatre, Oxford, UK
28th February	Apollo Theatre, Oxford, UK
1st March	St. Georges Hall, Bradford, UK
2nd March	Gaumont Theatre, Southampton, UK
3rd March	Colston Hall, Bristol, UK
4th March	Leisure Centre, Gloucester, UK *Cancelled*
6th March	Arts Centre, Poole, UK
9th March	Hammersmith Odeon, London, UK
10th March	Hammersmith Odeon, London, UK
11th March	Hammersmith Odeon, London, UK
12th March	Hammersmith Odeon, London, UK *Robertson, Moore & Bell guested.*
14th March	Guild Hall, Preston, UK
15th March	Market Hall, Carlisle, UK
17th March	Playhouse Theatre, Edinburgh, UK
18th March	The Capitol, Aberdeen, UK
19th March	Apollo Theatre, Glasgow, UK *Brian Robertson guested.*
20th March	City Hall, Newcastle, UK
21st March	City Hall, Newcastle, UK
23rd March	St. Georges Hall, Bradford, UK
24th March	Royal Centre Concert Hall, Nottingham, UK
25th March	Victoria Hall, Hanley, UK
27th March	St. David's Hall, Cardiff, UK
28th March	Odeon Theatre, Birmingham, UK
29th March	Apollo Theatre, Manchester, UK
31st March	Cornwall Coliseum, St Austell, UK
5th April	City Hall, Cork, Ireland
6th April	Leisureland, Galway, Ireland
8th April	King's Hall, Belfast, Northern Ireland
9th April	Royal Dublin Society, Dublin, Ireland
10th April	Royal Dublin Society, Dublin, Ireland
23rd April	Hammerleinhalle, Nuremburg, Germany *Cancelled*
24th April	Lowenbraukeller, Munich, Germany *Cancelled*
25th April	Eizer Hof, Mainz, Germany *Cancelled*

26th April	Philipshalle, Dusseldorf, Germany *Cancelled*
27th April	Vejlby-Risskov Hallen, Aarhus, Denmark
28th April	Falkoner Teatret, Copenhagen, Denmark
29th April	Scandinavium, Gothenburg, Sweden
30th April	Johanneshovs Isstadion, Stockholm, Sweden
3rd May	Gaumont Theatre, Ipswich, UK
4th May	Leisure Centre, Gloucester, UK
17th May	The Sun Plaza, Tokyo, Japan
19th May	Shibuya Kohkaidoh Hall, Tokyo, Japan
20th May	Aichi Kosei Nenkin Kaikan, Nagoya, Japan
21st May	Banpaku Kinen Hall, Osaka, Japan
23rd May	Shinjuku Kosei Nenkin Kaikan, Tokyo, Japan
22nd July	*Folkparken, Gävle, Sweden *Three Musketeers gig.*
23rd July	*Masten, Kristianopel, Sweden *Three Musketeers gig.*
26th July	*Folkets Park, Västerås, Sweden *Three Musketeers gig.*
27th July	*Bökensveds idrottsplats, Västervik, Sweden *Three Musketeers gig.*
28th July	*Folkets Park, Hunnebostrand, Sweden *Three Musketeers gig.*
29th July	*Lobo (Folkets hus), Gothenburg, Sweden *Three Musketeers gig.*
30th July	*Alingsåsparken, Alingsås, Sweden *Three Musketeers gig.*
1st August	*Garage, Stockholm, Sweden *Three Musketeers gig.*
2nd August	*Folkborgen, Norrköping, Sweden *Three Musketeers gig.*
3rd August	*Folkets Park, Karlskoga, Sweden *Three Musketeers gig.*
4th August	*Folkets Park, Södertälje, Sweden *Three Musketeers gig.*
5th August	*Brunnsparken, Örebro, Sweden *Three Musketeers gig.*
6th August	*Folkets Park, Avesta, Sweden *Three Musketeers gig.*
8th August	*Gröna Lund, Stockholm, Sweden *Three Musketeers gig.*
28th August	Reading Festival, Reading, UK
2nd September	Monster of Rock 83, Westfalenhalle, Dortmund, Germany
3rd September	Monster of Rock 83, VFR Fussballstadion, Kaiserslautern, Germany
4th September	Monster of Rock 83, Zeppelinfeld, Nuremburg, Germany
23rd September	*Sherwood Rooms, Nottingham, UK Lynott & Sykes jam with Mama's Boys.*
23rd December	*Savoy Entertainment Centre, Waterford, Ireland Lynott solo gig with Sykes.*

1984

With Lizzy disbanded, Lynott toured in 1984 with his new band Grand Slam.
Except where notified, all 1984 gigs are by them.

20th February	*Marquee Club, London, UK Lynott jams with Magnum for 20 minutes.*
26th April	*The Bridge, Waterford, Ireland*
27th April	*The Castle, Salthill, Galway, Ireland*
28th April	*Travellers Friend Hotel, Castlebar, Ireland*
29th April	*The Pink Paradiso Inter County Hotel, Lifford, Ireland*
1st May	*Kelly's, Portrush, Ireland*
3rd May	*Rialto, Derry, Ireland*
4th May	*Queens University, Belfast, Northern Ireland*
5th May	*The Baymount Hotel, Strandhill, Sligo, Ireland*
6th May	*The Rose Hill, Kilkenny, Ireland*
8th May	*Parkway, Limerick, Ireland*
9th May	*Sir Henry's, Cork, Ireland*
10th May	*S.FX Centre, Dublin, Ireland*
11th May	*White Horse Hotel, Drogheda, Ireland*
24th May	*Mayfair, Newcastle, UK unconfirmed*
25th May	*Victoria Hall, Hanley, UK unconfirmed*
26th May	*Apollo Theatre, Oxford, UK*
28th May	*Derngate Theatre, Northampton, UK*
30th May	*The Marquee, London, UK Cancelled*
31st May	*The Marquee, London, UK Cancelled*
14th June	*Polytechnic, Sheffield, UK*
15th June	*Whitehouse, Whitehaven, UK*
18th June	*Marquee Club, London, UK*
19th June	*Marquee Club, London, UK*
28th June	*Crystal Palace, London, UK*
10th July	*Assembly Hall, Worthing, UK*

11th July	Town Hall, Middlesbrough, UK
12th July	Palais, Nottingham, UK
14th July	Selhurst Park (Crystal Palace Garden Party), London, UK
24th August	Royal Standard, Walthamstow, UK
26th August	Lilford Rock Festival, Northamptonshire, UK Cancelled
27th August	Nostell Priory Music Festival, Wakefield, UK
4th September	Rock at the Bell, London, UK
5th October	University, Dundee, UK
6th October	University, Glasgow, UK
11th October	Leas Cliff Hall, Folkestone, UK
12th October	Ladbrokes Seashore Centre, Great Yarmouth, UK
13th October	University Great Hall, Bradford, UK
16th October	Keisa's Club, Leicester, UK
17th October	Polytechnics Ents Hall, Portsmouth, UK
19th October	University, Bath, UK
20th October	Civic Hall, Wolverhampton, UK
21st October	Queensway Hall, Dunstable, UK
22nd October	The Marquee, London, UK
24th October	University, Hull, UK
26th October	Pavilion, Ayr, UK
27th October	The Heathery, Wisham, UK
28th October	Fusion Ballroom, Aberdeen, UK
29th October	Tamdhu Club, Bannockburn, UK
30th October	The Mayfair, Glasgow, UK
31st October	The Oasis, Dumfries, UK Cancelled
2nd November	Summerlands Leisure Centre, Isle of Man
7th November	Paris Theatre, London, UK
21st November	Goldiggers, Chippenham, UK
22nd November	University, Loughborough, UK
23rd November	Middlesex Polytechnic, London, UK
24th November	School of Economics London, UK
26th November	Rock City, Nottingham, UK
2th November	Polytechnic, Huddersfield, UK
28th November	Clouds, Preston, UK
29th November	Polytechnic, Hatfield, UK
30th November	Polytechnic, North Staffordshire, UK
1st December	Verulam Arms, Watford, UK
2nd December	Winter Garden, Eastbourne, UK
4th December	Marquee Club, London, UK
5th December	King Charles Ballroom, Gillingham, UK
6th December	Rock House, Derby, UK
7th December	Royal Standard, Walthamstow, UK Grand Slam last gig.
17th December	Ulster Hall, Belfast, Northern Ireland Lynott guests with Gary Moore Band.
18th December	Ulster Hall, Belfast, Northern Ireland Lynott guests with Gary Moore Band.

1985

21st January	Marquee Club, London, UK *Grand Slam gig Cancelled
22nd January	Marquee Club, London, UK *Grand Slam gig Cancelled
17th March	Hammersmith Clarendon, London, UK Lynott guests at Pogues gig.
8th April	Cliff Castle Hotel, Dalkey, County Dublin, Ireland Clann Eadair gig. Lynott got up in the second half of the gig and played "A tribute to Sandy Denny" and 'Sisters Of Mercy'. He then played a number of traditional Irish jigs and reels.
28th June	Hammersmith Odeon, London, UK Lynott guests with Motörhead.
6th August	Discoteca Marbella, Spain Lynott solo gig at a friend's club.
23rd September	Apollo Theatre, Manchester, UK Lynott guests with Gary Moore Band.
27th September	Hammersmith Odeon, London, UK Lynott guests with Gary Moore Band.
28th September	Hammersmith Odeon, London, UK Lynott guests with Gary Moore Band.

***

BIBLIOGRAPHY

Although I pride myself on not having directly quoted from any of these fine books, they nonetheless proved to be useful research and corroboration tools. Good folks, all!

The Ballad Of The Thin Man:
The Authorised Biography Of Phil Lynott & Thin Lizzy
(Bailie, Stuart. Boxtree, 1997)
My Boy: The Philip Lynott Story (Lynott, Philomena. Hot Press Books, 1995)
The Rocker (Putterford, Mark. Castle Communications, 1994)

Additional Citations

Circus. 'Bad Reputation' Is Best Bet For Thin Lizzy's Future by Andy Edelstein. Issue No.165. September 29, 1977.
Circus. Lizzy's Loose by Mark Mehler and Rosie Horide. September 28, 1978.
Good Morning Britian. Interview with Phil Lynott. October 13, 1984.
High Roller. Phil Lynott… Thin Lizzy's Man Of Dubious Reputation by Toby Goldstein.
September 11, 1977.
Hit Parader. Thin Lizzy: Phil Lynott's Piece Of The Rock by Liz Derringer. 1980.
Hit Parader. Thin Lizzy Step By Step: All Systems Go For Heady Metal Band by Toby Goldstein. July 1982.
Hot Press. Saga Of An Ageing Orphan by Niall Stokes. September 2, 1977.
Hot Press. Searchlight On The Future by Niall Stokes. July 20, 1978.
Hot Press. Chinatown review by Dermot Stokes. November 21, 1980.
Hot Press. Ballad Of A Thin Man by Liam Mackey. February 28, 1981.
Kerrang!. Can this man get Lizzy Syke-d up? by Howard Johnson. 1982.
Kerrang!. Lizzy: Back In The Fight by Pete Makowski. 1983.
Kerrang! Grand Slam concert review by Mark Putterford. 1984.
Kerrang! Grand Master Flash by Mark Putterford. 1984.
Klein, Robert. TV Interview with Phil Lynott.
Late, Late Show, The. Interview with Phil Lynott by Gay Byrne. April 18, 1981.
Lynott, Phil. Solo In Soho record label biography. 1980.
Lynott, Phil. Radio interview. 1984.
Melody Maker. Ireland's own by Harry Doherty. January 8, 1977.
Melody Maker. Battle Of The Bands by Harry Doherty. 1977.

Melody Maker. Cutting it Thin by Harry Doherty. July 16, 1977.

Melody Maker. Terry Bozzio quote. 1978.

Melody Maker. Deutschland liebtLizzy by Harry Dohery. June 16, 1979.

NME. 'Me And The Boys Were Wondering How You And The Girls Are Getting Home From Here Tonight' by Roy Carr. April 9, 1977.

NME. Bad Reputation review by Charles Shaar Murray. September 10, 1977.

NME. The Boys Are Back On Vinyl by Nick Kent. March 31, 1979.

NME. Gary goes with a grouse by Chris Salewicz. July 28, 1979.

NME. Romeo, Romeo, wherefore art thou at, Romeo? by Paul Du Noyer. July 5, 1980.

NME. The Last Dance by Danny Kelly. January 11, 1986.

Record Mirror. Saint Among Sinners by Rosalind Russell. February 5, 1977.

Record Mirror. Moore or Less Lizzy by Ronnie Gurr. February 17, 1979.

REG. Reg #29: An Interview with Snowy White by Michael Simone. 2000.

Rock Special. Thin Lizzy: These Boys Are Back – For Good! by Andy Secher. Summer 1980.

Rolling Stone. Bad Reputation review by Stephen Demorest. Issue #250. October 20, 1977.

Rolling Stone. Live And Dangerous review by John Milward. Issue #274. September 28, 1978.

Rolling Stone. Renegade review by David Fricke. Issue #367. April 15, 1982.

RTE Radio 2. Interviews with Scott Gorham and Brian Downey by Dave Fanning and Leo Enright. January 4, 1986.

Sounds. Lizzy Rule At Reading OK? by Pete Makowski. August 27, 1977.

Sounds. Mind Over Matador by Robbi Millar. March 27, 1982.

Sounds. Farewell, Phil. January 11, 1986.

Trax. The Old Cock Lynott by Max Blake. April 1st-7th, 1981.

Trouser Press. Phil Lynott talks… and talks… Catching up with Thin Lizzy's big bass man by Peggy Wolfe and Dave Schulps. No. 19. April/May 1977.

Universal Wheels. Interview with Robin George by Kevin Julie.

Worth, Liz. Treat Me Like Dirt: An Oral History Of Punk In Toronto And Beyond 1977 – 1981 (Bongo Beat Books, 2009).

Interviews With The Author

Airey, Don. July, 2007.

Airey, Don. November 5, 2008.

Appice, Carmine. 2011.

Archer, Laurence. 2011.

Bain, Jimmy. August 10, 1999.

Bain, Jimmy. April 15, 2003.

Bain, Jimmy. 2011.

Bell, Eric. June 29, 2011.

Bushell, Gary. 2011.

Byford, Biff. October 11, 2011.

Carter, Neil. December 10, 2004.

Collen, Phil. July 28, 2011.

Cook, Paul. July 5, 2011.
Dawson, Steve. January 6, 2012.
Downey, Brian. February 26, 2009.
Downey, Brian. February 11, 2011.
Downey, Brian. March 30, 2011.
Edwards, Clive. June 14, 2011.
Fitzpatrick, Jim. June 21, 2011.
Flett, Dave. June 24, 2011.
George, Robin. June 26, 2012.
Gorham, Scott. February 24, 2004.
Gorham, Scott. February 11, 2009.
Gorham, Scott. March 4, 2011.
Gorham, Scott. December 14, 2011.
Grainge, Nigel. July 4, 2011.
Ingham, John. 2011.
Lindberg, Soren. September 15, 2011.
Moore, Gary. December 4, 2002.
Moore, Gary. July 2, 2007.
Murray, Frank. September 7, 2011.
O'Neill, Terry. July 1, 2011.
O'Neill, Terry. September 1, 2011.
Robertson, Brian. February 17, 2009.
Robertson, Brian. January, 2011.
Robertson, Brian. March, 2011.
Robertson, Brian. September 8, 2011.
Robinson, Paul. June 2007.
Ross The Boss. December 16, 2001.
Scabies, Rat. 2011
Shiels, Brendan "Brush." August 30, 2011.
Slamer, Mike. June 22, 2007.
Squire, Chris. August 6, 2011.
Stanway, Mark. April 11, 2011.
Taylor, Phil. December 10, 2009.
Tsangarides, Chris. February 17, 2006.
Tsangarides, Chris. February, 2011.
Vasey, John. February 21, 2012.
Warwick, Ricky. December 15, 2011.
Weir, Robb. 2011.
Wharton, Darren. March 11, 2011.
Wharton, Darren. December 14, 2011.
White, Allan. August 6, 2011.
Woolven, Kit. February, 2011.
Wright, Raymond. September 20, 2011.
Young, James. January 13, 2012.

ABOUT THE AUTHOR

At approximately 7900 (with over 7000 appearing in his books), Martin has unofficially written more record reviews than anybody in the history of music writing across all genres. Additionally, Martin has penned approximately 75 books on hard rock, heavy metal, classic rock and record collecting. He was Editor In Chief of the now retired Brave Words & Bloody Knuckles, Canada's foremost metal publication for 14 years, and has also contributed to Revolver, Guitar World, Goldmine, Record Collector, bravewords.com, lollipop.com and hardradio.com, with many record label band bios and liner notes to his credit as well.

Additionally, Martin has been a regular contractor to Banger Films, having worked for two years as researcher on the award-wining documentary Rush: Beyond the Lighted Stage, on the writing and research team for the 11-episode Metal Evolution and on the ten-episode Rock Icons, both for VH1 Classic.

Martin is the writer of the original metal genre chart used in Metal: A Headbanger's Journey and throughout the Metal Evolution episodes. Martin currently resides in Toronto and can be reached through martinp@inforamp.net or www.martinpopoff.com.ns and ordering information for the books of his that are currently in print.

Martin Popoff - A Complete Bibliography

The Sun Goes Down: Thin Lizzy 1977-83 (2018)
The Clash: All the Albums, All the Songs (2018)
Led Zeppelin: All the Albums, All the Songs (2017)
AC/DC: Album by Album (2017)
Tornado of Souls: Thrash's Titanic Clash (2017)
Caught in a Mosh: The Golden Era of Thrash (2017)
Rush: Album by Album (2017)
Beer Drinkers and Hell Raisers: The Rise of Motörhead (2017)
Metal Collector: Gathered Tales from Headbangers (2017)
Hit the Lights: The Birth of Thrash (2017)
Popoff Archive – 4: Classic Rock (2017)
Popoff Archive – 3: Hair Metal (2017)
Popoff Archive – 2: Progressive Rock (2016)
Popoff Archive – 1: Doom Metal (2016)
From Dublin to Jailbreak: Thin Lizzy 1969-76 (2016)
Rock the Nation: Montrose, Gamma and Ronnie Redefined (2016)
Punk Tees: The Punk Revolution in 125 T-Shirts (2016)
Metal Heart: Aiming High with Accept (2016)
Ramones at 40 (2016)
Time and a Word: The Yes Story (2016)
Kickstart My Heart: A Mötley Crüe Day-by-Day (2015)
This Means War: The Sunset Years of the NWOBHM (2015)
Wheels of Steel: The Explosive Early Years of the NWOBHM (2015)
Swords And Tequila: Riot's Classic First Decade (2015)
Who Invented Heavy Metal? (2015)
Sail Away: Whitesnake's Fantastic Voyage (2015)
Live Magnetic Air: The Unlikely Saga of the Superlative Max Webster (2014)
Steal Away the Night: An Ozzy Osbourne Day-by-Day (2014)
The Big Book of Hair Metal (2014)
Sweating Bullets: The Deth and Rebirth of Megadeth (2014)
Smokin' Valves: A Headbanger's Guide to 900 NWOBHM Records (2014)
The Art of Metal (co-edit with Malcolm Dome; 2013)
2 Minutes to Midnight: An Iron Maiden Day-By-Day (2013)
Metallica: The Complete Illustrated History (2013); update and reissue (2016)
Rush: The Illustrated History (2013); update and reissue (2016)
Ye Olde Metal: 1979 (2013)
Scorpions: Top of the Bill (2013);
Updated and republished as Wind of Change: The Scorpions Story (2016)
Epic Ted Nugent (2012);
Updated and republished in the UK as Motor City Madhouse (2017)
Fade To Black: Hard Rock Cover Art of the Vinyl Age (2012)
It's Getting Dangerous: Thin Lizzy 81-12 (2012)
We Will Be Strong: Thin Lizzy 76-81 (2012)
Fighting My Way Back: Thin Lizzy 69-76 (2011)
The Deep Purple Royal Family: Chain of Events Through '79 (2011);

republished as The Deep Purple Family Year by Year Vol 1 (to 1979) (2016)
The Deep Purple Royal Family: Chain of Events '80 – '11 (2011);
republished as The Deep Purple Family Year by Year Vol 2 (1980 - 2011) (2018)
Black Sabbath FAQ (2011)
The Collector's Guide to Heavy Metal: Volume 4: The '00s
(2011; co-authored with David Perri)
Goldmine Standard Catalog of American Records 1948 – 1991,
7th Edition (2010)
Goldmine Record Album Price Guide, 6th Edition (2009)
Goldmine 45 RPM Price Guide, 7th Edition (2009)
A Castle Full of Rascals: Deep Purple '83 – '09 (2009)
Worlds Away: Voivod and the Art of Michel Langevin (2009)
Ye Olde Metal: 1978 (2009)
Gettin' Tighter: Deep Purple '68 – '76 (2008)
All Access: The Art of the Backstage Pass (2008)
Ye Olde Metal: 1977 (2008)
Ye Olde Metal: 1976 (2008)
Judas Priest: Heavy Metal Painkillers (2007)
Ye Olde Metal: 1973 to 1975 (2007)
The Collector's Guide to Heavy Metal: Volume 3: The Nineties (2007)
Ye Olde Metal: 1968 to 1972 (2007)
Run For Cover: The Art of Derek Riggs (2006)
Black Sabbath: Doom Let Loose (2006)
Dio: Light Beyond the Black (2006)
The Collector's Guide to Heavy Metal: Volume 2: The Eighties (2005)
Rainbow: English Castle Magic (2005)
UFO: Shoot Out the Lights (2005);
updated and republished in the UK as
Lights Out: Surviving The 70s with UFO (2017)
The New Wave of British Heavy Metal Singles (2005)
Blue Öyster Cult: Secrets Revealed! (2004); update and reissue (2009);
updated and republished in the UK as
Agents of Fortune: The Blue Oyster Cult Story (2016)
Contents Under Pressure: 30 Years of Rush at Home & Away (2004)
The Top 500 Heavy Metal Albums of All Time (2004)
The Collector's Guide to Heavy Metal: Volume 1: The Seventies (2003)
The Top 500 Heavy Metal Songs of All Time (2003)
Southern Rock Review (2001)
Heavy Metal: 20th Century Rock and Roll (2000)
The Goldmine Price Guide to Heavy Metal Records (2000)
The Collector's Guide to Heavy Metal (1997)
Riff Kills Man! 25 Years of Recorded Hard Rock & Heavy Metal (1993)

See martinpopoff.com for complete details and ordering information.